Is This Any Way to Run a Democratic Election?

Stephen J. Wayne
Georgetown University

CQ PRESS

A Division of Congressional Quarterly Inc., Washington, D.C.

CQ Press
1255 22nd Street, NW, Suite 400
Washington, DC 20037

Phone: 202-729-1900; toll-free, 1-866-4CQ-PRESS (1-866-427-7737)

Web: www.cqpress.com

Cover design: McGaughy Design

⊗ The paper used in this publication exceeds the requirements of the American National Standard for Information Sciences—Permanence of Paper for Printed Library Materials, ANSI Z39.48-1992.

Printed and bound in the United States of America

11 10 09 08 07   1 2 3 4 5

Library of Congress Cataloging-in-Publication Data

Wayne, Stephen J.
  Is this any way to run a democratic election? / Stephen J. Wayne. — 3rd ed.
    p. cm.
  Previously published: Boston: Houghton Mifflin, 2003.
  Includes index.
  ISBN-13: 978-0-87289-405-1 (alk. paper)
  ISBN-10: 0-87289-405-3 (alk. paper)
  1. Elections—United States. 2. Political campaigns—United States. I. Title.

JK1967.W38 2007
324.973—dc22

                                                                    2006038180

To my son, 2nd Lt. Jared Wayne, USA

*Defending democracy is a noble cause;
imposing it on others is not.*

*May you and your generation
keep the flame of American democracy
burning brightly in the United States.*

CONTENTS

W e are a nation of critics, self-critics. As we laud our democratic system, we also complain about it. The election process in particular has been the source of much lament and critical commentary, especially in the aftermath of the controversial presidential election of 2000.

WHAT'S WRONG WITH AMERICAN ELECTORAL POLITICS?

A lot, say its critics. Their complaints are legion. The election cycle is too long, too complex, and too costly. The system is controlled by and for the few, the special interests, not the public's interest. Election laws are biased in favor of those who enacted them—the major parties and their candidates—and sometimes they have been implemented in a discriminatory manner. Money drives the process, and wealthy contributors exercise disproportionate influence over the candidates, parties, and campaigns, and on what follows from this election activity—public policy making. The news media are more interested in a good scandal than in discussing substantive policy issues and their consequences for society. Politicians are not to be trusted; they will say and do almost anything to get elected, and once elected, they are beholden to their large contributors and the special interest groups that aided their campaign. Moreover, incumbents have stacked the deck in favor of their own reelection, thereby undercutting two of the basic goals of a democratic electoral process—to keep public officials responsive to the people and to hold them accountable for their public policy decisions and actions.

And as if these allegations are not enough, there is the charge that election returns today do not result in winners who are compatible with one another, who are willing to compromise on policy issues, and who put the public's interest ahead of their own private interests. Nor does the outcome of the vote easily translate into a governing agenda and a majority coalition for achieving it. All of these charges have produced negative perceptions of the electoral process today and undoubtedly have contributed to public cynicism, apathy, and mistrust of politicians and the politics in which they engage. Something is very wrong with American electoral politics, or so its critics allege.

Are these charges correct? Is the current way the best way to run a democratic election? Have we drifted from the ideals and goals of the American political tradition? If so, how and when did we do so, and what, if anything, can be done about it? If not, why are there so many persistent complaints, and why do so many people not vote? These are some of the questions that concerned citizens should be asking about our electoral system and that public officials, party leaders, political scientists, and others should be answering.

This book is intended to help its readers address these questions and thereby participate in the debate on American electoral politics. Its aim is to explore critical and controversial issues that confront our political system today, and to do so in a reader-friendly way. *Is This Any Way to Run a Democratic Election?* looks at American democracy in theory and practice, notes where and why practices deviate from theory, and then proposes reforms to close the gap.

THE ORGANIZATION AND FEATURES OF THE BOOK

The book's first chapter discusses democratic theory in general and the democratic electoral process in particular. The next five chapters (chapters 2–6) examine key aspects of electoral politics: suffrage and turnout, representation, money, media, and political parties. Each of these factors shapes a political contest, affects its outcome, and has consequences for governing. From the environment in which elections occur, the last three chapters (chapters 7–9) turn to the electoral process itself: the nomination and general election, and their impact on governing.

Each chapter of the book includes useful features intended to pique a reader's interest in electoral issues and foster critical thinking and participation. The chapters each begin with "Did You Know That . . . ," an opening feature that presents interesting and sometimes disturbing facts about democratic election practices, processes, and outcomes that may not be widely known. After a discussion of the electoral dilemmas and ways to overcome them, each chapter concludes with a short summary, followed by a critical thinking section, "Now It's Your Turn." Included in this section are Discussion Questions, Topics for Debate, research-oriented exercises that encourage use of the Internet, and a listing of Internet Resources and Selected Readings.

NEW TO THE THIRD EDITION

This third edition has been thoroughly updated to consider the many controversies that have resulted from the elections in the early twenty-first century, including

- voter turnout problems;
- the persistence of representational bias, fraud, and voting irregularities;
- the Electoral College–popular vote discrepancy;
- disproportionate contributions and expenditures for incumbents and challengers;
- new legislation designed to reform the campaign finance system and the consequences of that legislation;
- the reemergence of partisanship;

- the lack of competitiveness in congressional elections;
- the computer-based technology of modern campaigns;
- the use of the Internet by candidates and the general public;
- the continuing front-loading of the nomination process;
- misinformation of political advertising and the "spin" of the news media; and
- the more ideological character of the governing parties.

A lot has happened to electoral politics, yet many of the same problems remain.

President George W. Bush has made democratization a fundamental goal of his administration. He has promoted democratic elections abroad. But do Americans have them at home? Are U.S. elections really democratic? Should they be? Let's find out.

ACKNOWLEDGMENTS

I would like to thank the people who worked on this edition at the CQ Press: Brenda Carter, Charisse Kiino, Dwain Smith, Steve Pazdan, Paul Pressau, and Margot Ziperman. A special thanks goes to Lorna Notsch for her skillful copy editing, paging layout, and other production-related work, her diligence in correcting my errors, and her patience in attending to my persistent concerns.

Finally, I would like to thank the reviewers of my manuscript, Stephen R. Routh, California State University, Stanislaus, and Fred Monardi, Community College of Southern Nevada, for their thoughtful and helpful comments.

—*Stephen J. Wayne*
January 2007

chapter 1

Democratic Elections

What's the Problem?

Did you know that. . .

- a majority of the voting-age population does not vote in most elections in the United States?
- Bill Clinton and George W. Bush, when first elected president, each received the votes of only about one quarter of those eligible to vote?
- most members of Congress have no effective opposition in running for renomination, and that some have no opponents in the general election?
- more than 95 percent of House members and 85 percent of senators have gotten reelected in the period from 1960 through 2006?
- third-party presidential candidate H. Ross Perot received 19 percent of the popular vote in 1992 and 8.5 percent in 1996 but no electoral votes in either election?
- there were more ballots discarded or undercounted in New York City and Chicago in the 2000 election than there were disputed ballots in the controversial Florida presidential vote election?
- about $4 billion was spent on federal elections in 2004, including $24 million donated or spent by financier George Soros and $22.5 million by insurance executive Peter Lewis?
- the average length of time that presidential candidates appeared on the evening news shows of the major broadcast networks in the last two elections was about seven seconds, and that the anchors and correspondents on those same shows were on the air six times as much as the candidates?
- more than 50 percent of candidate advertising in recent federal elections contained some negative reference to an opponent's character or policy positions?
- There was a 235 percent increase in political advertising in the 2004 presidential election compared to the 2000 election?
- only about one third of the people can name the member of Congress who represents them during nonelectoral periods?

Is this any way to run a democratic election?

These facts suggest that something is terribly wrong with our electoral process. They raise serious questions about how democratic the American political system really is. They also point to the major problems within that system: low voter turnout; fraudulent, error-prone, and discriminatory voting practices; high costs and unequal resources for those running for office; short, compartmentalized, and negative media coverage; and contradictory, often inconclusive results. Let's take a look at some examples of these problems.

CONTEMPORARY ELECTION ISSUES

Low Voter Turnout

People fight for the right to vote when they don't have it. Americans certainly did. In 1776, British colonists, protesting taxation without representation in Parliament, declared their independence with a rhetorical flourish that underscored the people's right to alter or abolish a government that wasn't fulfilling the purpose for which it was established.

Now, more than 230 years later, in a country that prides itself on its long and successful political tradition and on its fundamental democratic values, a majority of the electorate does not vote on a regular basis. What's wrong? Why do so few people vote? Does it have to do with the candidates running for office, the ways they conduct their campaigns, a lack of confidence in the major parties and the candidates they nominate, or a basic mistrust of politicians and elected officials?

Congress considers low turnout to be a problem, a sign that the democracy is not as vigorous as it could or should be. During the last several decades, it has enacted legislation to encourage more people to vote. At the end of the 1970s, an amendment to the Federal Election Campaign Act (FECA) was passed to permit parties to raise and spend unlimited amounts of money on building their grassroots base and getting out the vote. Yet turnout continued to decline.

During the 1980s, amendments were added to the act to broaden its applicability and facilitate minority participation in the electoral process. Yet the turnout of most population groups continued to decline.

In 1993 a "motor voter" bill, designed to make it easier for people in all fifty states to register to vote, was enacted into law. Since that law went into effect, millions of people have been added to the voter registration rolls, yet the percentage of the adult population reporting that they have registered has declined.

In 2002, Congress enacted the Help America Vote Act, which provided money to states to computerize their voter registration lists, buy more accurate voting machines, and allow for provisional voting for people who claim that they registered but whose names did not appear on the lists in the precinct in which they voted. An additional twelve million new voters registered between 2000 and 2004, although the growth in newly registered voters has not kept up with the growth of the voting-age population.[1] Turnout increased in 2004 but about four out of ten eligible voters still did not vote. In 2006, that figure was six out of ten.[2]

The issue of nonvoting raises serious questions about the vibrancy of America's civic culture and the health of democratic political institutions in the United States. With so many people not voting, do elections reflect the judgment of all the people or of a small and unrepresentative proportion of them? Similarly, to whom are elected officials responsive—the entire population or those who elected them? Do elections with low participation rates still provide an agenda for government and legitimacy for its actions? If they do not, then what does?

A related but equally important issue is who participates and what impact they have over the election outcome. If a relatively small group of people, distinguished by their education, wealth, and professional status, the intensity of their beliefs, and the time they have to devote to political activities, exercise the greatest influence on the election, won't these same individuals benefit more from the decisions of the officials they elect?

Fraudulent, Error-Prone, and Discriminatory Voting Practices

The Florida voting controversy in the 2000 election highlighted many of the voting problems that have plagued the U.S. electoral system since its creation. For most of the nation's first one hundred years, parties ran American elections. They designed the ballots, rallied their supporters, got them to the polls, and made sure they voted "correctly" by distributing color-coded ballots on which only the names of their candidates appeared. Allegations of fraudulent practices, including voting by noncitizens and the deceased, casting multiple ballots in the same election, and under- and over-counting of the votes, were rampant. The adoption of the secret ballot, the administration of elections by state officials, the expansion of suffrage, and eventually, the development of machines to tabulate the vote were responses to these unfair, underhanded, and undemocratic election practices. But problems persisted.

In most states, legislatures designed election laws and legislative districts to benefit those in power. Registration and residence requirements limited the size of the electorate. Geographic representation in one of the two legislative bodies gave rural areas disproportionate advantage and, in some cases, the ability to negate policies that addressed urban and suburban concerns. Moreover, in some states, the laws were administered in a discriminatory fashion, making it more difficult for racial and other minorities to vote.

Not until the 1960s did the Supreme Court and Congress address some of these issues.[3] The Court ruled that population and population alone had to be the criterion by which representation was determined: one person–one vote.

The Voting Rights Act of 1965 was intended to end discriminatory practices and effectively extend the vote to all eligible citizens. Registration requirements also were eased, voting hours were extended, absentee voting was facilitated, and for a time, money for party-building and get-out-the-vote activities was exempted from federal contribution limits.

These laws and judicial decisions went a long way toward extending the franchise, encouraging turnout, and ending the fraudulent and discriminatory practices that undercut the democratic character of U.S. elections. But they did not eliminate these problems. After the 2000 election controversy in Florida, the U.S. Commission on Civil Rights issued a report that concluded that African Americans in that state were much more likely than white voters to be turned away from the polls.[4] Researchers at the Massachusetts Institute of Technology (MIT) and the California Institute of Technology (CalTech) deduced that between four million and six million votes for president in the 2000 election were not counted, some because of registration foul-ups, some because of voter confusion and error, and some because of faulty equipment.[5] In close elections, such as the presidential election in 2000, these undercounted voters could have made a difference, even changed the final outcome.

Can an election be considered democratic if eligible voters are prevented from voting? Can the results be regarded as legitimate if the votes of a sizable proportion of a state's population, enough to have changed the outcome of the election, are not correctly counted? Can the election be said to represent the will of the people if the ballots are confusing to many voters and if some of the votes were not properly cast or included in the total? Can the winner claim to be legitimate if the true outcome of the election remains in doubt? Six months after the Supreme Court's decision that effectively determined George W. Bush's victory in Florida and thus in the Electoral College, 26 percent of the American people indicated that they still did not regard him as the legitimate president.[6]

High Costs and Unequal Resources

Despite problems of turnout and eligibility, campaign finance is the number one electoral issue and has been for the last three decades. The federal election campaign finance system has broken down. From 1992 through 2002, both major parties used a loophole in FECA to solicit large contributions from wealthy donors and spend hundreds of millions of dollars on behalf of their candidates for federal office.

The Bipartisan Campaign Reform Act (BCRA), enacted in 2002, was designed to end this practice, but it has not done so. Although the act prohibits national parties from accepting contributions that exceed federal limits, it has not stopped their supporters from creating nonparty groups that solicit and spend contributions not subject to the federal limits. In 2004, these groups raised a total of $426 million and used this money to fund surrogate campaigns on behalf of their respective parties and candidates.[7]

To make matters worse, each party used its access to and the facilities of its officeholders as inducements and rewards for obtaining larger donations, the maximum allowed by law. Private telephone numbers of cabinet secretaries and congressional committee heads were regularly made available to top contributors. As president, Clinton held numerous coffee hours in the White House to facilitate the solicitation of money for the Democratic Party. He rewarded those who gave the most money with trips on Air Force One, trade missions with the commerce secretary, and sleepovers in the Lincoln bedroom. Not to be outdone by his Democratic predecessors, Vice President Dick Cheney lavishly entertained the most generous GOP contributors at a gala at his official residence in April 2001.

Even without the illegal solicitations and legal circumvention of the campaign finance legislation, the amount of money required to mount an effective campaign for federal office has become a major issue. Expenditures for mass media advertising have gone sky high, with no end in sight. Moreover, the advertising itself has distorted rather than enhanced political debate.

Is too much money being raised for and spent on election campaigns? Do those who contribute represent a cross section of Americans or do they overrepresent the most prosperous individuals and groups in society? And what do they get for their money? Do their contributions enhance their access and influence? Are they directly or indirectly "buying" public policy that will benefit themselves at the expense of others? And even if they are not, does the public perception that the rich have more influence undercut the democratic character of the electoral system?

Compartmentalized and Negative Media Coverage

Closely related to the issue of money is that of news coverage. For better or worse, the mass media have become the principal vehicle through which candidates for national office communicate to voters. Political parties have become much less effective intermediaries between their candidates and the electorate. Dependence on the news media would not be so bad if the goals of the press were similar to those of the parties and the candidates, but they aren't.

The mass media are not oblivious to the need to energize and educate the public, thereby providing the information necessary for an informed vote. But as a business, they also are interested in making money, and the more, the better. They get money through advertising that is priced according to the size of the audience. To enhance audience size, the news media present the news that is most interesting to the most people most of the time. In campaigns, the most newsworthy items are the dramatic ones—the horserace, with all its color and drama; the unexpected occurrences, the "screw-up's," and the confrontations, as well as the human dimensions of a candidate's personal character and family. These subjects engage readers, viewers, and listeners but don't necessarily educate, energize, or motivate them to participate in the campaign and to vote. In fact, press compartmentalism, negativism, and interpretive "spin" often are blamed for low turnout and for the public's cynical attitude toward candidates, parties, and the political system.[8]

How to square the interests of largely private media with the needs of an informed and involved electorate is no easy task, nor one that Congress wishes to tackle. Not only must First Amendment protections for the press be considered, but the desires of the public for the news it wants, not necessarily the news it needs, also must be weighed in the balance.

Contradictory, Often Inconclusive Results

Another problem, less obvious but equally dangerous for a democratic political system, is that elections may not contribute to governing, but actually make governing more difficult. Candidates make promises, parties present platforms, and groups promote their issues. But in a heterogeneous society, policy priorities and positions are likely to be diverse and even inconsistent with one another. Elections in the United States reflect this diversity far better than they mirror a popular consensus. They regularly produce mixed and incompatible results with unclear meanings and undefined mandates. Parties share power, thereby making the institutional divisions that much greater and more difficult to overcome. In an age of political polarization, these divisions have become more pronounced, political rhetoric has become more strident, civility among elected officials has declined, and compromises on major policy issues have suffered as a result.

Each of these problems has become a contemporary political issue. Each points to shortcomings in the democratic electoral process in the United States, to gaps between theory and practice. One goal of this book is to examine those gaps; another is to discuss ways they could be narrowed or, perhaps, eliminated. Finally, the book aims to stimulate thinking about democracy in general and democratic elections in particular.

To answer the central question, "Is this any way to run a democratic election?" This chapter first examines the nature of democracy and some of the ways in which such a political system may be structured. The discussion then turns to the role of elections in a democracy and the criteria that these elections must meet to be considered democratic. Finally, the chapter concludes with a look at the inevitable tensions within a democratic electoral system between political liberty and equality, between majority rule and minority rights, and between a free press and an informed electorate.

THE NATURE OF DEMOCRACY

A **democracy** is, simply put, a government of the people. Initially used in ancient Greece, where such a system was first practiced, the term itself comes from the Greek words *demos,* meaning "people," and *kratos,* meaning "rule." In a democracy, the people rule.[9]

But which people? Everyone? Everyone who is a citizen? Every citizen older than eighteen years of age? Every eighteen-year-old citizen who is literate and mentally competent? Every eighteen-year-old, literate, and mentally competent citizen who has knowledge of the issues and can apply that knowledge to make an intelligent judgment? The list of qualifications could go on and on. Naturally, an informed electorate is desirable, but the more people excluded because they lack certain characteristics, the less likely the electorate will reflect the general population.

And how do the people rule? By themselves? By selecting others and holding them accountable? By agreeing to a set of rules and procedures by which some are selected to perform certain public tasks, such as teaching school, maintaining law and order, or protecting against foreign attack?

There is no single right answer to these questions. There are many types of democracies, distinguished by *who* and *how*: by who makes the decisions and by how power is distributed.[10]

TYPES OF DEMOCRACIES

Who Makes Public Policy Decisions?

When the people themselves make public policy decisions, the democracy is said to be a **direct democracy**. A New England town meeting in which all residents participate on matters of local interest, such as where to build a new town hall or whether to recycle disposable waste, is an example of direct democracy at work. A state ballot initiative on which voters indicate their preferences on a range of issues, such as legalized gambling, same-sex marriage, or public benefits for illegal immigrants or new residents, is another example of direct democracy. When George W. Bush, as a managing partner of the Texas Rangers, helped convince voters of Arlington, Texas, to support a special tax to pay for two thirds of the cost of a new baseball stadium, he was engaging in direct democracy.

In a direct democracy there is true collective decision making. Obviously, in a country as large and diverse as the United States, such a system would be impractical and undesirable for the nation as a whole. There would be too many people with limited information and understanding of the issues participating in too many decisions. As a consequence, most democracies are by necessity **representative democracies**, in which people choose others to represent them in government, to formulate and implement public policy, and sometimes even to adjudicate it.[11]

A basic goal of representative government is to be responsive to the needs and interests of the people who elected that government. How can these needs and interests be identified? One way is through elections. Although elections aren't the only way that public views find expression and can influence public policy, they are the most decisive and popular means for doing so. That's why they are such a critical component of a democratic political system. Elections are a mechanism through which the citizenry expresses its desires and by which it can evaluate the performance of those in office. Elections link government to the governed.

How Is Power Distributed?

Another way to categorize democracies is according to how they distribute power. In a **popular**, or **plebiscitary**, **democracy**, the people exercise considerable influence over the selection of government officials and the policies they pursue. Such a system provides opportunities for the populace to initiate policy issues and vote on them directly as well as to elect candidates and, if necessary, to remove them from office. Ballot access is easy, there are few impediments to voting, and the people have the last word.

In a **pluralistic democracy**, a wide variety of groups—from political parties to groups with economic interests (such as business, labor, and the professions) to those motivated by social and political (ideological and issue-oriented) beliefs—compete for influence. They do so in line with their own interests and beliefs, using their own resources to gain and maintain public support. James Madison argued in *The Federalist*, No. 10, that such factions in society were inevitable and that one of the merits of the Constitution that was being debated for ratification was that it prevented any one of them from dominating the government.[12]

A third model is an **elitist democracy**, in which power is concentrated in fewer hands than in a pluralistic system. There is more hierarchy, and more discretion is exercised by those in power. However, because it is a democracy, there is still competition between elites to gain election to government and to exercise influence within it.

In all three systems, government officials remain accountable to those who elected them. Whatever the form of democratic government, it rests directly or indirectly on popular consent. Elections anchor that government to its popular base. Without elections, a democratic political system cannot exist.

ELECTIONS AND DEMOCRACY

Elections tie citizens to their government. They provide a mechanism by which the people can choose those government officials—legislators, top executives, and, in some cases, judges—the people that make, implement, and adjudicate public policy. Elections are also a means by which the public can hold these officials accountable for their actions and keep them responsive to the people's needs, interests, and desires.

In order to make decisions on who should be selected to lead the government and make judgments on the performance of those in government, voters need information. A free press is a conduit for that information. Without a free press reporting the election news, the electorate would be either dependent on gathering and analyzing its own information or dependent on those with a vested interest in doing so, such as the candidates, parties, and interest groups.

Naturally, those with an interest in the election might be inclined to release only information that puts them in the best possible light. The public needs alternative sources that are credible and objective, hence a free and unbiased media.

In choosing the people who will run the government, elections directly or indirectly provide direction to that government. They establish the agenda— the promises and policy positions of the winners— that guides public officials, and they help build coalitions that facilitate governing.

Elections also confer legitimacy on government and what it does. By giving citizens an opportunity to select public officials and influence their policy agendas, elections contribute to the ongoing support for the policy decisions and administrative actions of government as well as for those who make or execute them. Whether people agree with a particular policy or not, they are more likely to accept it as valid and lawful if those who made it were selected in a fair and honest way and make their decisions according to an established set of rules and procedures. They also will be more likely to accept the policy if they know that they will have other opportunities down the road to express their opinions, participate in a political campaign, or vote for the candidates of their choice. Similarly, people will respect and abide by the decisions of elected officials, even approving their performance in office when they do not like them personally, as long as they consider their election to be legitimate. Take President Clinton, for example. His job approval exceeded his personal favorability throughout his second term and especially after his affair with White House intern Monica Lewinsky became public.[13]

Criteria for Democratic Elections

For elections to be consistent with the basic tenets of a democratic political system, they must be "free, fair, and frequent." [14] Adult citizens must be able to vote; they must be able to exercise this right without fear or coercion. The votes must be counted equally in determining the winner. The results of the election must be accepted as official and binding for a limited period of time, after which another election must occur. Without the guarantee of a future election, it would be difficult to hold those in office accountable for their actions.

Let's explore these essential criteria: political equality, universal suffrage, meaningful choice, and the free flow of information about the candidates, issues, and their parties.[15] **Political equality** is essential. It is a basic building block for a democracy. There can be no classes or ranks, no individuals or groups whose positions elevate them to a higher status. As Thomas Jefferson put it in the Declaration of Independence, "All men are created equal."

If everyone is equal, then all should have the opportunity to exercise an equal voice in the running of the political system. At the very least, this means that the principle of one person–one vote must apply to all elections unless otherwise specified by the Constitution. It also means that all votes count equally, that no individual, group, region, or jurisdiction should gain extra representation or exercise extra influence. Translated into election terminology, equality requires **universal suffrage**, the right of all adult citizens to be able to vote.

Unless all adult citizens have an opportunity to participate in the electoral process, the election results cannot be said to reflect the views of the entire country. The exclusion of any group of citizens because of any characteristic other than those directly related to their capacity to exercise an informed and intelligent vote (such as being literate and having the mental capacity to make an intelligent voting decision) naturally weakens the representative nature of the system. The more people excluded for whatever reason, the less the government can be said to reflect the consent of the governed.

Not only must adult citizens be given the opportunity to vote, but the voting decision must be made freely. And that decision has to represent a **meaningful choice**. If there were only one candidate for an office or if all the candidates had equal qualifications and voiced essentially the same views, then there would be grounds for claiming that the voters did not have a meaningful choice.

To choose is to select from among diverse alternatives. But how diverse should they be? A choice among candidates who differ widely in their beliefs, particularly if the views of some of them are extreme, may amount to no real choice at all for most Americans. If the major parties were to agree on the same candidate and the only other candidate was unknown to most voters, the choice for most voters would not be meaningful. In other words, the choices should lie within the broad parameters of public acceptability yet be distinctive enough for voters to distinguish between them and weigh them on the basis of their own values, attitudes, and opinions.

Related to making a meaningful choice is the **free flow of information and ideas**. At the very least, there should be alternative sources of information, not just the candidates, the parties, the government, or a dominant group that controls the news media. Unless there is ample information and discussion within the public arena, people will have difficulty understanding the issues—much less determining which candidates are most qualified and merit their support.

A free press is essential. Few, if any, subjects, issues, or questions should be off limits. Few, if any, arguments should be precluded, no matter how unpopular they may be. That is why the allegation of being unpatriotic if opposition to government policy is expressed undercuts the very fabric of a democratic electoral process. The objective must be the creation of an environment in which voters can make informed judgments based on an enlightened understanding of the issues.[16] That objective can only be accomplished in a society in which free and broad expression is encouraged and protected.

Democratic Electoral Systems

The number of people elected, the way winners are determined, and the size and shape of electoral districts may vary within the country as well as among countries. In the United States, the United Kingdom, and some other democratic nations, public officials are elected on the basis of **plurality rule in single-member districts**. Simply put, this means that the candidate who receives the most votes for a particular office within an electoral district wins. Unless rules specify otherwise, the winner need not receive a majority of the vote; a simple plurality is usually sufficient. If there is a majority requirement, however, and no candidate receives more than half the votes in the initial balloting, there is a runoff election between the top two vote getters in the first round of voting.[17]

The U.S. Supreme Court has ruled that all legislative districts must be equal in population to ensure that the one person–one vote principle prevails. This is true except, of course, for the Senate, in which each state, regardless of its population, has two senators and for the Electoral College, in which each state is entitled to electors equal in number to its congressional delegation.[18]

The main advantage of a plurality voting system is that it is simple and direct. The winner is easily and usually quickly determined, and the elected representative is accountable to the entire district. Responsibility, in other words, can be pinpointed.

The principal disadvantage of such a voting system is that those in the minority are less likely to be represented by a candidate of their choice. Their views and interests may not be adequately considered when public policy decisions are made. Moreover, plurality voting tends to enlarge the advantage of the majority if that majority is equally dispersed across the entire electoral area.[19] What happens is that those in the majority tend to vote for candidates who have similar demographic and attitudinal characteristics. Overcoming this voting behavior requires that minorities be a large proportion of the voters within an electoral district.

To improve minority representation in Congress, the U.S. Department of Justice, citing the 1982 Voting Rights Act and several Supreme Court decisions, pushed states to create legislative districts in which minority groups, such as African Americans or Latinos, constituted the voting majority. However, the Supreme Court subsequently declared that race could not be the primary factor for determining the boundaries of these districts, once again putting minorities at a disadvantage in the U.S. system of plurality voting in single-member districts.

There is another way, however, to achieve broader representation: by instituting a system of **proportional voting**, in which the winners are determined in proportion to the vote that they or their party receives. In some democratic countries, such as Canada and Israel, parties run slates of candidates in districts. Similarly, in the presidential nomination process in the United States, there may be proportional voting. Democratic Party rules require, and Republican Party rules permit states to prescribe, the election of delegates pledged to their party's national convention in proportion to the vote they receive.

The principal advantage of proportional voting is that it provides a fairer and more accurate representation of minorities in the government. A principal disadvantage is that majoritarian sentiment is more difficult to discern. Such sentiment, often referred to as political, or policy, consensus, must be constructed after the election by those who have been elected rather than by the electorate in the votes they have cast.

Proportional voting also increases the likelihood of a splintered government in which coalitions among competing parties may be necessary to achieve a working majority. Such coalitions in turn are likely to be more fragile and less able to agree on public policy than would a government composed of a single party. Moreover, it will be more difficult to assign credit or blame for what the government does in the case of a multiparty coalition than with a single party.

In a plurality system, coalition building occurs primarily within the major parties, not between them. Each of these parties tries to reach a broad cross section of the electorate. In doing so, they have to balance diverse and often conflicting interests. Thus the major parties in a plurality system are more heterogeneous and, conversely, are more homogeneous in a proportional voting system.

As the plurality-proportional voting dichotomy suggests, election procedures and rules are not neutral. They benefit some at the expense of others. These clashes of interests create ongoing tensions within the democratic electoral system. They are what politics is all about, temporarily resolving tension on an issue-by-issue basis.

TENSIONS WITHIN A DEMOCRATIC ELECTORAL SYSTEM

The problem of obtaining a fair election outcome underlies the natural tensions in a democratic political system between political liberty and equality, between majority rule and minority rights, and between a free press and an informed electorate.

Liberty versus Equality

If a democracy is based on the consent of the governed, then the ability to give that consent and, if need be, to take it away is essential. That's why political liberty is so important. It is the freedom to decide for oneself and act on the basis of that decision. Take that freedom away, and a democratic government cannot exist.

In the electoral process, liberty is the right to vote as one chooses, not to vote if one chooses, and in either case, to make the voting decision freely and without duress. It is the right to exercise personal choice within the framework of the political system. Accessible voting places, secret ballots, and privacy in casting votes help protect the exercising of this right.

Personal freedom to support the candidate of one's choice, however, can undermine the equity principle. A conflict is created because certain people have more resources at their disposal than others to use in campaigns. Should individuals and groups be free to spend as much money as they want to promote their ideas and beliefs, or should their spending be limited to allow a citizen more opportunity to affect the outcome of the vote?

Proponents of unlimited expenditures cite the constitutional protection of free speech and the right of people to spend their money as they see fit. Opponents argue that elected officials are more likely to be responsive to large donors than to the average citizen who does not contribute or gives only a small amount. Moreover, they claim that the advantage of the wealthy extends past the election to governing and to the public policy that government makes.[20]

A related issue is that of actual participation, of personally getting involved. For a variety of reasons, those with a higher income participate at a higher rate than do those at the lower end of the socioeconomic scale.[21] This higher rate of participation magnifies their influence on the election results.

There are many forms of participation, from the simple act of voting, to working for a candidate (ringing doorbells, handing out literature, sending e-mail, coordinating events, and the like), to contributing money to a candidate's campaign, to spending money to promote one's own views, which may or may not coincide with those of a particular candidate. Placing no restrictions on these activities allows those with the interest, time, resources, and will to do more and, as a result, to potentially exercise more influence. At what point should a line be drawn between voluntary actions by citizens in the electoral process, which should be encouraged, and actions that give an unfair advantage to those with superior resources at their disposal?

Majority Rule versus Minority Rights

Plurality voting decisions seem to be a pretty straightforward criterion for a democratic society. If every vote is equal, those with the most votes should win. The problem, as we have already mentioned, is that plurality voting systems overrepresent the majority; proportional systems give more representation to minorities than they would otherwise have in a plurality system of voting. Proportional voting also tends to inhibit the building and maintenance of a governing majority.

Many factors affect the majority-minority relationship: the ways the boundaries of electoral districts are drawn and the number of people elected within them, how the ballot is organized, whether candidates are listed by office or by party, and even where, when, and for how long voting occurs. If voting places are few and inaccessible, the hours for voting are too short, and the ballot is complicated and confusing, then turnout will be lower, those in power will more likely remain in power, and those who benefit under the current arrangement will continue to do so.

Representation of groups within the society also can be affected by ballot access. In 1992 and 1996, Ross Perot's Reform Party spent millions of dollars and used hundreds of volunteers and paid workers to obtain the necessary signatures for its candidates to appear on all fifty state ballots. The Reform and Green Parties did this as well, albeit less successfully, in 2000 and 2004. But for the Republican and Democratic candidates, ballot access is automatic. They have a built-in advantage. Is that fair?

The majority-minority issue extends to government as well. Should majority rule be restricted so that minorities are better protected when public policy decisions are made? James Madison thought so. Fearing that the "tyranny of the majority" could deny the minority its basic rights, he argued successfully for a divided government that separates institutions representing differing constituencies so that no single group can easily dominate. But in the process, Madison and his colleagues at the Constitutional Convention created a system that has enabled powerful minorities to exercise a tyranny of their own, preventing change and thereby thwarting the desires of the majority or plurality in violation of a basic precept of democratic theory.

A Free Press versus an Informed Electorate

The framers of the Bill of Rights believed that a free press is essential. In a government based on the consent of the governed, those in office must be held accountable for their actions. Similarly, the qualifications, promises, and positions of candidates for elective office must be evaluated.

The public cannot assess candidates running for office or the performance of those in office unless they have the necessary information to do so. The problem is that most providers of such information—the candidates, their parties, interest groups, policy-oriented think tanks, even government officials—have a stake in the outcome which affects the information they present and how they present it. Although this information is still valuable, it must be evaluated with the interests of the source in mind.

Here's where a free press comes in. For some of the same reasons that we select others to represent us in government, we also depend on others to inform us about politics and government, to help us sort out what's going on and make informed judgments about it. That's the role of the news media—to be a watchdog, to provide the information they believe we need to know or would be interested in knowing. Anticipating that the press will perform this role is itself an incentive for those running for and holding office to stay attuned to public opinion and not to behave in a manner that would draw unfavorable attention and admonishment.

A free press is unfettered but not necessarily neutral. News reporters describe the campaign as they see it. Naturally, their perceptions are influenced by their own political beliefs, their journalistic needs, and their personal feelings about the candidates and issues. To the extent that many in the news media share similar political and professional orientations, their reporting of the campaign reflects a pack mentality, a collective reading and interpretation of events.[22] This journalistic outlook colors the public's understanding and evaluation. The electorate gets a jaundiced view that highlights the dramatic and human elements of the campaign, usually at the expense of a detailed debate over substantive issues.

What can be done about the media's orientation and their perceived bias? Restricting press coverage is not only impractical but also violates the First

Amendment's protection of freedom of the press. Relying on the candidates to monitor the coverage they receive seems equally impractical given their vested interest in favorable coverage. Nor can the government take on a supervisory role over political communication in a campaign, especially in light of the number of incumbents who seek reelection. How, then, can citizens obtain the information they need, particularly as it relates to policy issues and their impact on society—information that many consider essential for voters to make an informed judgment based on an enlightened understanding of the issues?

SUMMARY: DEMOCRATIC ELECTION DILEMMAS IN A NUTSHELL

In theory, a representative democracy is a government of the people, by some of the people, and for all of the people. It is connected to the people through elections. One democratic dilemma is how to provide citizens with equal opportunities to affect the electoral and governmental processes without reducing their freedom to pursue their own interests and utilize their own resources as they see fit. Another dilemma is how to provide electoral mechanisms that are efficient and representative, effective and accountable, dynamic and deliberative—a tall order, to be sure!

To meet these criteria, citizens must be accorded universal suffrage and equal voting power. They must be free to vote and have a meaningful choice when doing so, and be able to obtain timely information about the parties, candidates, and issues that is sufficient to make informed, enlightened judgments on election day.

In practice, contemporary elections fall short of each of these criteria. There is universal suffrage in theory, but large-scale nonvoting in practice. There are many choices of candidates and some of policy initiatives as well, but a lot of people still complain that their choices are unsatisfactory because they are too narrow, too broad, or all distasteful.

All votes count equally, but all groups do not benefit equally from current electoral procedures and practices. Ethnic and racial minorities in particular seem to be disproportionately disadvantaged by plurality voting in single-member districts. Wealthy people have the advantage that superior resources provide. Finally, the United States has a free press but, in the view of much of the electorate, neither an objective nor a responsible one. Complaints that the media are too powerful, too judgmental, and too negative are regularly reported in survey and anecdotal research.[23] That much of the electorate is underinformed and underinvolved has been attributed in large part to the press's penchant for reporting entertaining news, as well as to inefficient and ineffective grassroots operations by party and nonparty groups and personal attacks by the candidates against each other. But from the perspective of the mass media, driven by audience size, a very competitive news environment, and conventions of contemporary journalism, interesting and exciting news is what the public wants, so they provide it.

The disjunctions between democratic theory and practice arise from many sources: the manner in which the electorate can and does participate in elections; the ways in which elections are structured and representatives chosen; the structure of the party system and the candidate orientation of electoral politics; the laws governing financial contributions and expenditures; press coverage, particularly its emphasis on the contest, its orientation toward personal character issues, and its general negativity; the parties' methods for selecting their nominees; the ways campaigns are conducted, appeals communicated, and images created; and finally, incompatible outcomes, unclear meanings, and vacuous mandates.

Now It's Your Turn

Discussion Questions

1. How nearly universal must suffrage be for the popular will to be heard?
2. Can elections be structured to reflect both majority sentiment and minority views at the same time?
3. What current electoral issues pit individual liberty against political equality?
4. To what extent is the democratic goal of an informed electorate that makes enlightened judgments on election day realistic, and to what extent is it necessary?
5. Can the news media serve the informational needs of the electorate and the profit motives of media owners simultaneously?
6. What are the most serious electoral problems today that threaten the democratic character of the political system?

Topics for Debate

Challenge or defend the following statements:

1. It is possible to have political freedom and equality simultaneously.
2. If the majority always rules, then the rights and interests of the minority are always going to be threatened.
3. A press that is both free and fair is a contradiction in terms.
4. To make sure that voters can make informed judgments, they should be required to know the principal candidates and their major issue positions before they are allowed to vote.
5. A democratic government cannot exist without a democratic electoral process.

Exercises

1. How democratic is the constitutionally prescribed electoral process?
   a. Answer this question by first examining what the Constitution requires and allows for national elections, noting its democratic and nondemocratic features.
   b. To the best of your knowledge, have the nondemocratic features been changed by amendment, law, or practice? If so, how and why; if not, why not?
   c. Is the electoral system becoming more or less democratic today, and are the changes that have occurred in the electoral process good or bad for the country as a whole?
   d. What aspects of the last presidential election reflect negatively on the democratic character of the U.S. election system? Do you anticipate that the same aspects will be apparent in the next election?

2. Advocates of democracy have urged that the electoral system be made as democratic as possible to achieve the ideal of a government of, by, and for the people. Others are reluctant to change a system that has worked so well for so long and has become so large a part of America's political tradition. What do you think? Would more democracy be better, or would it actually impede the functioning of the electoral and governing systems? Might too much democracy be a bad thing? If you had to choose between liberty and equality or between majority rule and minority rights, how would you choose and why?

INTERNET RESOURCES

The Internet is a rich and immediately available source of information on campaigns and elections. Here are some of the best generic sources for all kinds of information. Most of them contain links to the news media, public interest groups, ongoing political campaigns, polling organizations, and appropriate government agencies. In addition, you may access the Congressional Quarterly's Web site, www.cq.com, for links to other sites of interest to students of American government.

Generic Sites on Campaigns

- C-SPAN: www.cspan.org
  Contains up-to-date information on elections, including candidate speeches and critical commentary.
- Democracy in Action: www.P2008.org
  Contains information on the process and product of electoral politics: candidates, issues, news sources, polls on the 2008 presidential election.

- Patrick Ruffini: www.patrickruffini.com/2008wire
  Information from blog sites and media sources on the 2008 election.
- Politics1: www.politics1.com/p2008
  General information and links on the 2008 election.

Government Sites on the Electoral System

- Census Bureau: www.census.gov/prod/2005pubs/06statab/election.pdf
  Publishes the yearly *Statistical Abstract,* which contains information on
  registration, turnout, and voting results in recent federal elections.
- Election Assistance Commission: www.eac.gov
  Established by the Help America Vote Act, the commission provides
  information on how to register and vote, state and federal election laws,
  and surveys of who registers and who votes.
- Federal Election Commission: www.fec.gov
  Provides easily accessible data on campaign finance activities filed by
  candidates and compiled in tabular form by analysts at the FEC.
  Bookmark this site!
- Library of Congress: http://thomas.loc.gov
  You can use this site to access Congress, its committees, members, leg-
  islative process, rules, and schedules, as well as reports on campaigns
  and elections.
- National Archives and Records Administration, Office of the Federal
  Register: www.nara.gov/fedreg
  Contains official statistics about past presidential elections, the
  Electoral College, election laws, and presidential documents.
- White House: www.whitehouse.gov
  Contains not only information on presidential and vice presidential
  activities, speeches, press releases, and official business, but also links to
  all other parts of the government.

SELECTED READINGS

American Political Science Association Task Force on Inequality and
American Democracy. "American Democracy in an Age of Rising
Inequality," *Perspectives on Politics* 2 (December 2004): 651–666.

Barber, Benjamin R. *A Passion for Democracy.* Princeton: Princeton University
Press, 1998.

Dahl, Robert A. *Democracy and Its Critics.* New Haven, Conn.: Yale University
Press, 1989.

——. *How Democratic Is the American Constitution?* New Haven, Conn.:
Yale University Press, 2001.

——. *A Preface to Democratic Theory.* Chicago: University of Chicago
Press, 1956.

Downs, Anthony. *An Economic Theory of Democracy.* New York: Harper and Row, 1957.

Dryzek, John. *Discursive Democracy.* Cambridge: Cambridge University Press, 1990.

Graham, Keith. *The Battle of Democracy: Conflict, Consensus, and the Individual.* Brighton, Sussex, UK: Wheatsheaf Books, 1986.

Held, David. *Models of Democracy.* Cambridge: Polity Press, 1996.

Hirst, Paul. *Representative Democracy and Its Limits.* Cambridge: Polity Press, 1990.

Stout, Jeffrey. *Democracy and Tradition.* Princeton: Princeton University Press, 2004.

Tocqueville, Alexis de. *Democracy in America.* New York: HarperCollins, 1988.

Warren, Mark, ed. *Democracy and Trust.* New York: Cambridge University Press, 1999.

Young, Iris Marion. *Inclusion and Democracy.* New York: Oxford University Press, 2000.

NOTES

1. Election Assistance Commission, "The Impact of the National Voter Registration Act, 2003–2004," 13.
2. Michael McDonald, "Voter Turnout: The Numbers Prove that 2004 May Signal More Voter Interest," *Milwaukee Journal Sentinel,* November 27, 2004, www.brookings.edu/views/op-ed/Mcdonald200431127.htm.
3. In the past the Court had stayed out of controversies over legislative districting by contending that they involved political and therefore nonjusticiable issues. In other words, they were not subject to judicial review.
4. U.S. Commission on Civil Rights, "Voting Irregularities in Florida During the 2000 Presidential Election," June 2001, www.usccr.gov/vote2000. Florida state officials and Republican members of the commission criticized the conclusions of the report, asserting that there was no evidence that the disproportionate disfranchisement of African American voters resulted from discriminatory behavior of state and county election officials.
5. Massachusetts Institute of Technology and California Institute of Technology, "Voting: What Is and What Could Be," report issued July 17, 2001.
6. Gallup Poll, "Seven out of 10 Americans Accept Bush as Legitimate President," July 17, 2001, www.gallup.com/poll/releases/pr010717.asp.
7. Campaign Finance Institute, "CFI Releases Latest Financial Data on Federal 527 Political Organizations," April 4, 2006, www.CampaignFinanceInstitute.org.
8. For example, see Stephen Ansolabehere and Shanto Iyengar, *Going Negative: How Political Advertisements Shrink and Polarize the Electorate* (New York: Free Press, 1995), and Thomas E. Patterson, *Out of Order* (New York: Knopf, 1993).
9. For a good basic discussion of democracy, see Robert A. Dahl, *On Democracy* (New Haven, Conn.: Yale University Press, 1998). Dahl has written extensively on this subject. Two of his

other well-known works on democratic theory are *A Preface to Democratic Theory* (Chicago: University of Chicago Press, 1956) and *Democracy and Its Critics* (New Haven, Conn.: Yale University Press, 1989).

10. An excellent discussion of types of democratic systems appears in David Held, *Models of Democracy* (Cambridge: Polity Press, 1996).

11. In many of the southern states, judges are elected in partisan or nonpartisan elections. In other states, they are appointed by the governor, legislature, or special commission, in some cases later subject to an up or down vote by the electorate. At the federal level, judges are nominated by the president and appointed with the advice and consent of the Senate. Federal judges serve during good behavior for life.

12. James Madison, *The Federalist*, No. 10.

13. Gallup Poll, "Presidential Approval Trends, 1997–2000," www.gallup.com/poll/trends/pt.jobapp_BC.asp.

14. Robert Dahl, "What Political Institutions Does Large-Scale Democracy Require?" *Political Science Quarterly* 120 (Summer 2005): 188.

15. For a classic discussion of the fundamental principles of democracy, see James W. Prothro and Charles M. Grigg, "Fundamental Principles of Democracy," *Journal of Politics* 22 (May 1960): 276–294.

16. Dahl, "What Political Institutions," 196.

17. Several southern states, such as Louisiana and Georgia, require runoffs if the winning candidate does not receive more than half the total vote.

18. The exception is the District of Columbia, which has no voting representation in Congress but does have three electors. That number was determined on the basis of what representation it would have if it were a state on the basis of census data at the time (1961).

19. Dahl, *On Democracy*, 132–134.

20. Sidney Verba, Kay Lehman Schlozman, and Henry E. Brady, *Voice and Equality: Civic Voluntarism in American Politics* (Cambridge, Mass.: Harvard University Press, 1995), 512.

21. Ibid., 511–533.

22. S. Robert Lichter, Stanley Rothman, and Linda S. Lichter claim in their book *The Media Elite* (Bethesda, Md.: Adler and Adler, 1986) that most national correspondents are liberal in ideology and Democratic in political allegiance.

23. *Striking the Balance: Audience Interests, Business Pressures, and Journalists' Values* (Washington, D.C.: Pew Research Center for the People and the Press, 1999); and Pew Research Center for the People and the Press, "Big Doubts about News Media's Values: Public Votes for Continuity and Change in 2000," February 25, 1999.

chapter 2

Popular Base of American Electoral Politics

Suffrage and Turnout

Did you know that. . .

- less than one fifth of adults living in the United States were eligible to vote in the first election held under the Constitution?
- by 1800, about one third of those eligible actually voted—practically all of them adult white males?
- Congress almost refused to allow Wyoming to enter the Union in 1890 because its state constitution allowed women the right to vote?
- about 1.4 million African Americans, mostly males, are temporarily or permanently disfranchised because they are incarcerated or have been convicted of a felony?
- at the beginning of the twentieth century, three out of four eligible voters cast ballots in the presidential election; at the end of the century, only two out of four did so; only one out of three regularly votes in the midterm elections?
- Hispanics, the fastest growing group in the population, turn out at lower rates than do most other minority groups?
- of all the countries with a long democratic tradition, the United States has one of the lowest rates of turnout of its voting-age population?
- less than 50 percent of those eligible voted in the presidential elections of 1920 and 1924?
- the people who do vote are disproportionately better educated and have higher incomes than those who don't?
- election day is not and never has been a U.S. national holiday?
- nonvoters are less informed, less partisan, and less trustful of government than are voters?

Is this any way to run a democratic election?

T o be democratic, an electoral system must allow all citizens to vote and to have their votes count equally.[1] Such a system also should encourage people to vote. To what extent do U.S. elections meet these democratic goals? To what extent do they achieve participatory democracy in theory and in practice?

This chapter will answer these two questions, questions that underlie the popular foundation of American democracy. It begins with a historic overview of suffrage and turnout and then turns to the reasons why people do not vote, the factors that influence those who do, and the difference turnout makes for a democratic political process. Proposals for increasing voter turnout are then assessed in light of contemporary trends in the American electoral system.

SUFFRAGE IN AMERICAN ELECTIONS

A participatory democracy was not what the framers had in mind when they drafted the Constitution. Most delegates who attended the Philadelphia convention neither desired nor encouraged large-scale public involvement in politics. The relatively low level of public education at the time, poor communications within and between the newly independent states, and the distrust that pervaded relations among the people of the thirteen states led the delegates at the convention to design a government that would be responsive to various segments of the society but not necessarily to the popular mood of the moment.

Who should vote was a contentious issue in 1787. Not wanting to derail the Constitution's ratification by imposing conditions of suffrage to which some states might object, the framers decided not to decide who should be allowed to vote. They left the matter to the individual states, subject to any restrictions Congress might later establish.

Expanding the Right to Vote

Initially, most state constitutions limited suffrage to white male citizens twenty-one years of age and older who owned property and were Christians. Gradually, these restrictions were eliminated. By the 1830s, most states had removed religion and property ownership as conditions for voting, thereby enfranchising about 80 percent of adult white males.[2]

In some northern states, African American males also were allowed to vote. The vast concentration of African Americans, however, was in the South, and not until after the Civil War were they granted suffrage. The Fifteenth Amendment, ratified in 1870, removed race and color as qualifications for voting. In theory, it enfranchised all African American males who were citizens. In practice, only those who lived in the North and border states could easily vote. A series of institutional devices, such as poll taxes, literacy tests, and restrictive primaries in which only Caucasians could participate (so-called white primaries), effectively combined with social pressure to prevent African Americans in the South from voting for another hundred years.[3]

Women, too, were denied the right to vote. Wyoming was the first territory to grant women equal voting rights with men in 1869, and the first state to do so after being admitted to the Union in 1890. Congress actually tried to compel Wyoming to rescind women's suffrage as a condition for entering the Union, but the Wyoming legislature refused, declaring, "We will remain out of the Union 100 years rather than come in without the women." [4] Congress relented. Only a few other states, primarily in the West, followed Wyoming's lead. By 1904, only four states permitted women to vote.[5]

The almost exclusive authority that states exercised to determine eligibility began to break down after the Civil War. Over the next hundred years, Congress essentially nationalized the right to vote. A series of constitutional amendments and statutes limited the states' power to restrict suffrage. First, the Fifteenth Amendment (1871) prevented states from discriminating against otherwise eligible voters on the basis of race, color, or previous condition of servitude. The Seventeenth Amendment (1913) required all states to elect their senators by popular vote. The Nineteenth Amendment (1920) prohibited gender from being use as a qualification for voting, and the Twenty-fourth Amendment (1964) precluded states from denying the vote for federal officials to residents who failed to pay a poll tax or any other tax.[6] The last constitutional restriction on the states, the Twenty-sixth Amendment (1971), forbade them from setting an age older than eighteen years as a condition for voting.

These constitutional strictures have been supplemented by legislation that also has limited state discretion on suffrage. The 1964 Civil Rights Act prevented a literacy test from being required for any citizen with a sixth-grade education from an accredited school in the United States or its territories. The 1965 Voting Rights Act authorized the federal government to send examiners to register voters in any legislative district in which 50 percent or more of the eligible adult population was not registered to vote. Amendments to this law further precluded states from imposing a residence requirement of more than thirty days for voting in any presidential election. The 1993 "motor-voter" bill requires states to make registration material available at their motor vehicle and social services offices, as well as at military recruitment centers, thereby enabling residents to register at these offices or by mail when they apply for or renew their driver's license, receive state health or welfare benefits, or enlist in the armed services.

Together, these constitutional amendments and statutes have established nearly universal suffrage, a policy that most Americans support. Prior to the enactment of the Twenty-sixth Amendment, 70 percent of the population favored lowering the voting age to eighteen.[7] Since 1944, a majority of American have favored eliminating the Electoral College and using a direct popular vote to select the president.[8]

Legal and Practical Limitations on Voting

The only state restrictions that remain in place are those that prevent otherwise qualified citizens from voting because they are or have been in jail or a mental institution. Fourteen states temporarily or permanently disfranchise felons and those who have been dishonorably discharged from the military.

The jail and felony restrictions disfranchise between 4.5 and 5 million Americans.[9] Of this number about 1.4 million are African American males, approximately 13 percent of all African American men. In states that permanently disenfranchise felons, that percentage rises to about 25 percent.[10] To help rectify this problem, the National Commission on Federal Election Reform has recommended that voting rights be restored to convicted felons who have served their time in jail.[11] States that prohibit felons and ex-felons from voting have been slow to make this change, however.

Since the 2000 election, there also have been allegations that minority voters, especially those who live in low-income areas, are much more likely than other voters to be prevented from voting or of having their votes voided for not completing the ballot properly. A report by the U.S. Commission on Civil Rights after the controversial 2000 Florida election condemned officials of that state for their unequal treatment of African American voters. The commission noted that 54 percent of the disqualified ballots were cast by African Americans, a group that constituted only 11 percent of Florida's electorate at the time.[12]

Another study, this one prepared for Democrats on the House Governmental Reform Committee, found that in the country as a whole, 4 percent of all ballots cast in low-income districts were not counted, compared with 1.2 percent in higher-income districts.[13] Whether the differential in disqualified votes is a consequence of discriminatory behavior by state election officials, better voting machines in more affluent districts, or simply more errors made by less educated voters remains a subject of considerable controversy. Voting irregularities and fraudulent voting practices also were alleged in 2004.[14]

Even though universal suffrage has been established in the United States, the costs of voting are not uniform among the population. They may be higher for single parents, higher for parents with young children, higher for the elderly and infirm, and higher for low-wage earners who work two or more jobs to make ends meet. They also may be higher for those who have to travel considerable distances to vote. Generally speaking, people who fall into the "high-cost" category tend to be those with lower incomes. This fact introduces an economic bias into the voting population.

Some people may lack the skills to read the ballot and comprehend the differences among candidates and their parties; they may not be able to cope with the registration requirements, understand ballot initiatives, or know how to cast their ballots properly. Punching out the chad in Florida was a problem in 2000 that led to many untabulated vote cards. People with physical disabilities may have difficulty getting to the polls, especially if the elections are held in facilities inaccessible to the handicapped. Obtaining absentee ballots also may be a problem, particularly in states that require proof of out-of-state business or disabled status before such a ballot is issued.

THE UPS AND DOWNS OF VOTER TURNOUT

Although suffrage has been extended to most citizens, many do not exercise their right much of the time. In the 1996 presidential election, a majority of the adult population (51 percent) did *not* vote; in 2000, a bare majority did. The turnout in 2004 was higher, 57.7 percent of the voting-age population (VAP), or 60.3 percent of the voting-eligible population (VEP), which excludes noncitizens, incarcerated individuals, ex-felons, and others precluded by state law from voting.

In nonpresidential elections, the proportion of the population voting is even lower, usually in the range of 30 to 40 percent. In 2002 and 2006, about 60 percent of eligible voters failed to vote.[15]

Turnout in primaries is less than the general election. (See Figure 2.1.) In 2004 and 2006, turnout in the primaries averaged 15 percent of the voting-age population, although it was higher in the more competitive states that held their contests early, before the nominees had been effectively determined.[16]

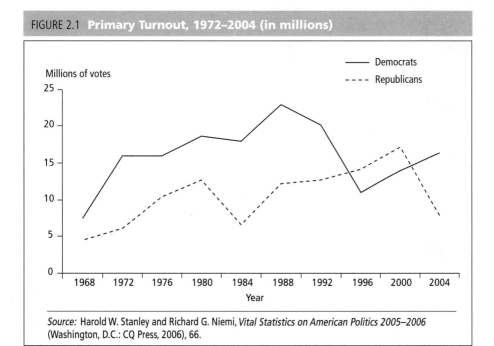

FIGURE 2.1 **Primary Turnout, 1972–2004 (in millions)**

Source: Harold W. Stanley and Richard G. Niemi, *Vital Statistics on American Politics 2005–2006* (Washington, D.C.: CQ Press, 2006), 66.

TABLE 2.1 Voter Turnout in the United States, 1789–2006 (percentages)

Presidential Election Years		Midterm Elections	
1789	11.6	1790	21.6
1792	6.3	1794	25.0
1796	20.1	1798	36.0
1800	32.2	1802	42.0
1804	23.8	1806	45.8
1808	36.8	1810	49.8
1812	40.4	1814	52.8
1816	16.9	1818	41.1
1820	10.7	1822	44.7
1824	26.9	1826	50.1
1828	57.3	1830	55.7
1832	57.0	1834	63.0
1836	56.5	1838	70.8
1840	80.3	1842	61.8
1844	79.2	1846	60.3
1848	72.8	1850	60.5
1852	69.5	1854	66.1
1856	79.4	1858	69.1
1860	81.8	1862	65.1
1864	76.3	1866	71.4
1868	80.9	1870	67.0
1872	72.1	1874	65.0
1876	82.6	1878	65.2
1880	80.5	1882	65.7
1884	78.2	1886	63.9
1888	80.5	1890	64.6
1892	75.8	1894	67.4
1896	79.6	1898	60.1

TABLE 2.1 **Voter Turnout in the United States, 1789–2006** *(continued)*

Presidential Election Years		Midterm Elections	
1900	73.7	1902	55.6
1904	65.5	1906	51.3
1908	65.7	1910	52.0
1912	59.0	1914	50.4
1916	61.8	1918	39.9
1920	49.2	1922	35.7
1924	48.9	1926	32.9
1928	56.9	1930	36.7
1932	56.9	1934	44.5
1936	61.0	1938	46.6
1940	62.4	1942	33.9
1944	55.9	1946	38.8
1948	52.2	1950	43.6
1952	62.3	1954	43.5
1956	60.2	1958	45.0
1960	63.8	1962	47.7
1964	62.8	1966	48.7
1968	62.5	1970	47.3
1972	56.2	1974	39.1
1976	54.8	1978	39.0
1980	54.2	1982	42.0
1984	55.2	1986	38.1
1988	52.8	1990	38.4
1992	58.1	1994	41.1
1996	51.7	1998	38.1
2000	54.2	2002	39.5
2004	60.3	2006	40.4

Source: Harold W. Stanley and Richard G. Niemi, *Vital Statistics on American Politics 2005–2006* (Washington, D.C.: CQ Press, 2006), 12–13. Updated by author.

Turnout in the Nineteenth Century

After 1800, the development of the party system provided the incentive and organizational mechanism to expand the proportion of the population who voted. Turnout rose, ranging from 25 to 50 percent of those eligible between 1800 and 1828, with the higher rates in elections in which the parties were most competitive. But the competition didn't last long. One of the parties, the Federalists, ran its last presidential candidate in 1816 and effectively disintegrated after that. With the advent of one-party dominance, turnout began to decline (see Table 2.1).

By the mid-1820s, however, factions within the Democratic-Republican Party led to a more competitive political environment and, ultimately, to the reemergence of a two-party system. As that system evolved, the parties tried to get more people involved and out to vote, and they were successful, by popularizing election campaigns.[17] Beginning in the 1840s, rallies, oratory, and parades were bringing out the faithful and the curious alike, thereby contributing to higher turnout.[18]

The new party activism continued in nonelectoral periods as well. Patronage jobs, political influence, and even a little monetary aid were given to loyal supporters, who were expected to return the favor on election day. This expectation was reinforced by the parties' oversight of the voting process. Precinct captains got out the voters, and the parties printed their own color-coded ballots, which contained only the names of their candidates. Poll watchers recorded who voted and how.[19]

As a consequence, turnout soared, some elections involved more than 80 percent of the eligible electorate in the second half of the nineteenth century (see Table 2.1). But corruption and fraudulent voting practices also increased. Allegations of multiple voting, ballot stuffing, vote tampering, and irregularities in tallying the vote led states to print their own ballots and monitor activities more closely in and around the areas where people voted. Additionally, registration procedures were instituted to ensure that only the eligible voted.

Although these reforms were designed to protect the integrity of the electoral process, they also made the act of voting more difficult. People had to register first, sometimes well in advance of the election, and do so at places and times designated by the states. Some states also enacted poll taxes to pay for the cost of the election. These taxes were particularly onerous for low-income voters.

That wasn't the worst of it, however. The taxes and literacy tests were implemented in a discriminatory manner by election officials in the South. They became barriers to prevent African Americans, as well as many poor whites, from voting.

Decreasing competition between the political parties in the South following the Civil War also contributed to lower turnout. The South became a one-party region, dominated by the Democrats. Because the winner of that party's nomination was a prohibitive favorite to win the general election, there was less incentive for southerners to vote. The Republicans also gained sufficient strength to dominate in the Northeast with much the same effect on turnout.

On top of all this, both parties seemed determined to establish as many safe congressional seats as possible for their candidates. The adoption of the seniority rule in selecting the chairs of standing committees in Congress provided added incentive for state parties to protect their congressional incumbents who had risen to positions of power by "creative" districting that effectively secured their seats.

Contemporary Trends in Voter Participation

Although a reform movement at the end of the nineteenth century gave more power to rank-and-file voters through the introduction of presidential primaries in many of the states, it did not increase the rate of turnout. And by the end of World War I, this reform movement had all but dissipated. States reverted to nomination procedures that facilitated control by party leaders. With the exception of the 1928 presidential election, turnout throughout the 1920s was less than 50 percent of those eligible to vote.

The realignment of political parties in the 1930s, and especially the appeal of Franklin Roosevelt's Democratic Party to those on the lower rungs of the socioeconomic ladder (blue-collar workers, poor farmers, and racial and ethnic minorities), reenergized the electorate, contributing to a larger proportion of the population voting, especially in presidential elections, for the next thirty years. Turnout, however, did not return to the levels it reached in the second half of the nineteenth century.

By the end of the 1960s, it was again on the decline. The civil rights movement and the Vietnam War created divisions within the majority party, the Democrats, marking the beginning of a trend of less intense partisan allegiances among supporters of that party. Technological advances in communication, particularly the advent of television campaigning, increased the candidate-centeredness of elections, weakened party organizations, and led to a decline in partisan loyalties. Television proved to be a less effective way to mobilize voters than personal contact by party workers and volunteers.

In recent years, partisan parity has resulted in closer elections; partisan voting patterns have increased, and the parties have placed greater emphasis on grassroots organizing and turnout campaigns. Each of these factors has contributed to the increases in the proportion of the electorate voting in presidential elections in the twenty-first century.

INFLUENCES ON VOTING

Why People Do Not Vote: Excuses Real and Concocted

More people claim they vote than actually do. In 2004, the National Election Study reported that 77 percent of the people surveyed after the election said that they had voted, compared to the actual percentages of 57.7 for the voting-aged public and 60.3 percent for the eligible adults of voting age.[20] Why do people not tell the truth?

Most people consider voting a civic responsibility. According to national surveys conducted by the Pew Research Center for the People and the Press, almost 90 percent of those surveyed agreed with the statement "I feel it is my duty as a citizen to always vote."[21] More than 60 percent also said that they feel guilty when they do not do so.[22] So most people say they do, as indicated in Table 2.2.

Despite the widespread belief that voting is an important responsibility of citizenship, many people do not vote. They lack the motivation to do so. Why? Some people subscribe to the proposition that "most elected officials do not really care about what people like me think."[23] They don't see what difference it makes to them who wins the election. Nor do they see their vote mattering all that much, although in Florida in the 2000 presidential election, in the 2004 governor's election in the state of Washington, and in several of the congressional midterm elections of 2006, a small number of additional votes could have changed the official results.

People are cynical. They distrust politicians. When a national survey prior to the 1996 election asked voters what changes would improve the system the most, they most often cited candidate honesty and truthfulness, followed by more pertinent information and less negative campaigning.[24]

When negativity is examined within the context of other factors, however, such as the level of mistrust people bring to the election, it seems to be a less important influence on voting.[25] Much depends on how campaign news and ads are viewed and by whom. For example, if the negativity seems appropriate, such as opposition to a popular issue, it actually may increase turnout. But if it seems excessive or inappropriate, such as mudslinging or harsh and vindictive ads, it can adversely affect turnout and even boomerang against the candidate who resorts to such tactics.[26]

There are a myriad of other reasons or excuses people give. Some say that they are too busy trying to earn a living, raise a family, or meet other day-to-day responsibilities. And perhaps they are. Some people may be conflicted, unable to decide among competing candidates, parties, and policy alternatives. Their decision not to vote may be a considered choice. The candidates may not seem appealing, qualified, or sufficiently different from one another. They make take positions with which people strongly disagree. The issues may not seem relevant. People may want to protest by not voting.

Another reason for not voting has to do with election rules and procedures, particularly registration. Despite enactment of the "motor-voter" law, some people still find registration difficult or inconvenient and either fail to register or fail to do so on time. Others are prevented from voting because their registrations are not properly recorded or they come to the wrong precinct to vote. A study conducted by researchers at MIT and CalTech estimated that three million people were not able to cast valid ballots in 2000 because of reg-

| TABLE 2.2 **Percentage of People Who Claim They Vote, 1987–2003** | | | | | | | |

Question: "How often would you say you vote?"

	Always	Nearly Always	Part of the Time	Seldom	Nearly Never	Never	Other	
May 1987	34	37	11	6	9	2	1	=100
January 1988	39	33	12	8	6	1	1	=100
February 1989	45	30	10	8	6	1	*	=100
May 1990	33	35	12	10	8	1	1	=100
November 1991	38	37	13	9	3	0	*	=100
May 1992	41	32	13	11	3	*	*	=100
July 1994	40	30	14	11	5	*	*	=100
October 1995	41	32	12	11	3	*	1	=100
June 1996	41	30	12	12	4	1	*	=100
June 1997	42	25	12	13	6	1	1	=100
June 1998	40	29	15	12	—	4	*	=100
August 1999	41	27	14	10	7	1	*	=100
June 2000	46	24	11	11	7	1	*	=100
August 2002	42	29	12	12	4	1	*	=100
June 2003	36	29	14	11	8	1	1	=100

*Indicates less than 1 percent.

Source: Pew Research Center for the People and The Press, "The 2004 Political Landscape: Evenly Divided and Increasingly Polarized," November 5, 2003, www.people-press.org/reports/print.php3?PageID=761.

istration mishaps of one type or another. This is in addition to the four to six million individuals whose votes were not counted.[27]

To help rectify this problem, Congress enacted the Help America Vote Act in 2002 to provide for provisional voting when registration disputes occur. A person claiming to be registered but whose name does not appear on the precinct voting list may cast a provisional vote that will be counted if the registration issue is resolved in the voter's favor.

Rules and procedures, designed to maintain the integrity of a democratic voting system, place burdens on potential voters. As previously mentioned, finding the time, physically getting to the polls, understanding the intricacies of the ballot, and even knowing how to vote—which lever to push, hole to punch, or box to check—all are factors that discourage some people from voting or disqualify votes that were cast improperly.

The controversy over the "butterfly" ballot in Palm Beach County, Florida in the 2000 election is a case in point. Under Florida's election law at that time, individual counties were responsible for the design of the ballots, the monitoring of elections, and the tabulation of votes within their areas of jurisdiction. In Palm Beach County, Democratic election officials designed an easy-to-read ballot on which the names of all the candidates appeared on a single punch card. To fit everything on one side of the card, the ballot contained two columns of names but only one column of "chads," the perforated holes that voters were supposed to punch out (see Figure 2.2). Some voters were confused and punched the chads for the wrong candidates; other voters punched two chads, thereby automatically voiding their ballots. Additionally some voters did not punch out the chads completely, leaving them dimpled or hanging. The voting machines undercounted ballots with chads that were not completely removed.

Finally, the competitiveness of the election and the campaigns of the candidates also affect turnout, with more competitive elections contributing to a larger vote. The more competitive the election is, the more likely the major party candidates will be well funded and conduct a more vigorous campaign, which should turn out more voters. In the 2000 and 2004 presidential elections, the battleground states that both presidential campaigns targeted had higher turnout levels than did states that did not receive as much candidate attention (see Table 2.3).[28]

Are elections in the United States becoming less competitive? Some people believe so, citing increasing costs, incumbency advantages, and more sophisticated polling and targeting of voters as principal reasons.

Why People Do Vote?

Political Attitudes. Identification with a political party is a primary motivation for voting. The stronger a person's partisan affiliation is, the more likely that person will vote. Thus, the weakening of partisan identities from the mid-1960s to the early 1980s and the increase in self-declared independents during this period resulted in lower turnout.

But other attitudinal factors contributed as well. People have become more apathetic and less trusting. Many feel that the government is insensitive to their needs, that it is run by and for special interests, that politicians will say and do practically anything to get elected, that public officials are more interested in serving their own needs than those of their constituents, and that it just doesn't matter all that much who wins.[29] Confidence in politicians and government has declined.

In addition to political attitudes, there are other attitudinal distinctions between voters and nonvoters. Those who vote more regularly have more well-defined issue positions, ideological perspectives, interest in the election, and concern about the outcome; they have a greater sense of their own political

FIGURE 2.2 **2000 Presidential Election Ballot Used in Palm Beach County, Florida**

OFFICIAL BALLOT, GENERAL ELECTION
PALM BEACH COUNTY, FLORIDA
NOVEMBER 7, 2000

**ELECTORS
FOR PRESIDENT
AND
VICE PRESIDENT**

(A vote for the candidates will
actually be a vote for their electors.)

(Vote for Group)

(REPUBLICAN)
GEORGE W. BUSH – PRESIDENT
DICK CHENEY – VICE PRESIDENT

(DEMOCRATIC)
AL GORE – PRESIDENT
JOE LIEBERMAN – VICE PRESIDENT

(LIBERTARIAN)
HARRY BROWNE – PRESIDENT
ART OLIVIER – VICE PRESIDENT

(GREEN)
RALPH NADER – PRESIDENT
WINONA LaDUKE – VICE PRESIDENT

(SOCIALIST WORKERS)
JAMES HARRIS – PRESIDENT
MARGARET TROWE – VICE PRESIDENT

(NATURAL LAW)
JOHN HAGELIN – PRESIDENT
NAT GOLDHABER – VICE PRESIDENT

OFFICIAL BALLOT, GENERAL ELECTION
PALM BEACH COUNTY, FLORIDA
NOVEMBER 7, 2000

(REFORM)
PAT BUCHANAN – PRESIDENT
EZOLA FOSTER – VICE PRESIDENT

(SOCIALIST)
DAVID McREYNOLDS – PRESIDENT
MARY CAL HOLLIS – VICE PRESIDENT

(CONSTITUTION)
HOWARD PHILLIPS – PRESIDENT
J. CURTIS FRAZIER – VICE PRESIDENT

(WORKERS WORLD)
MONICA MOOREHEAD – PRESIDENT
GLORIA LaRIVA – VICE PRESIDENT

WRITE-IN CANDIDATE
To vote for a write-in candidate, follow the
directions on the long stub of your ballot card.

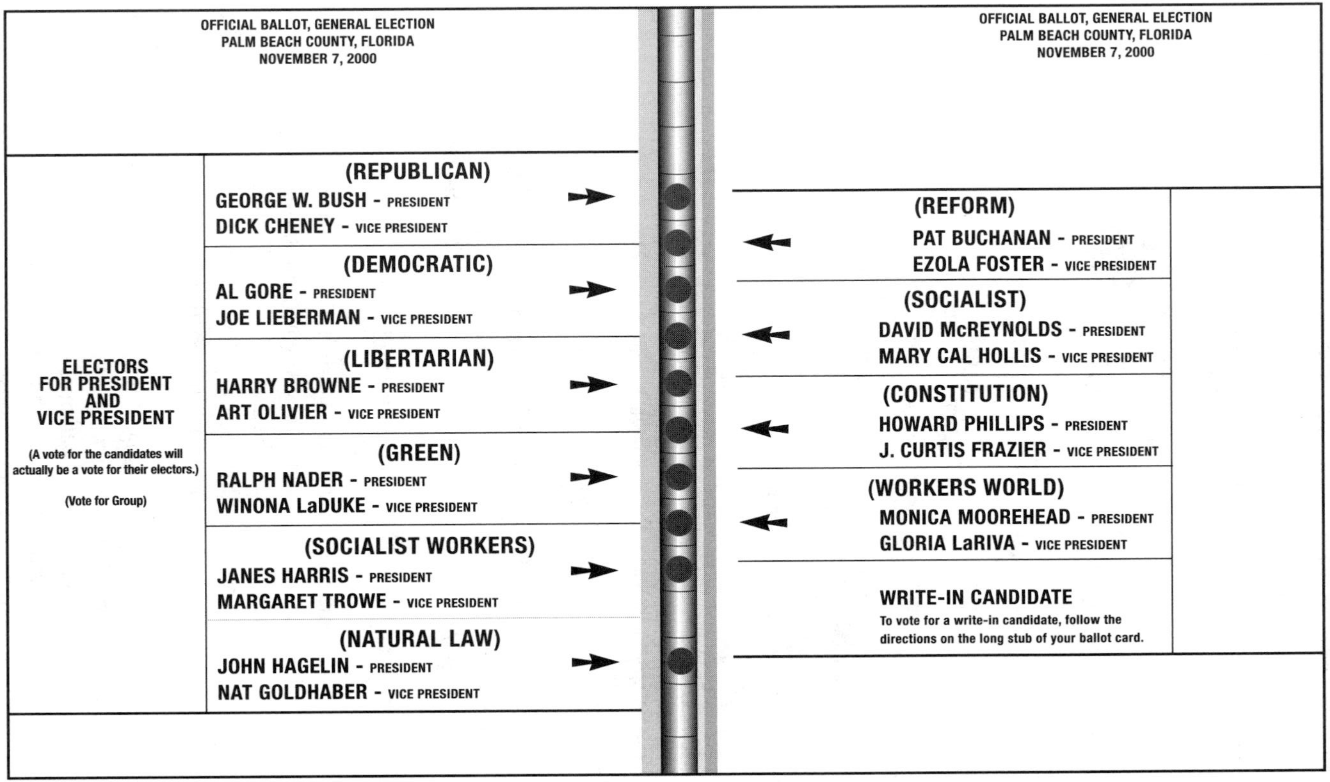

Source: The *Washington Post*, October 23, 2001, www.thewashingtonpost.com.

TABLE 2.3 Citizen Voting Turnout in Battleground States, 2000–2004*

State	Percentage	
	2000	2004
Florida	50.6	63.3
Iowa	60.7	68.4
Michigan	57.5	66.2
Missouri	57.5	64.9
Minnesota	68.8	76.1
Ohio	55.8	67.2
Oregon	60.6	71.4
Pennsylvania	53.7	62.6
Washington	56.9	65.4
Wisconsin	66.1	74.1

*Figures based on voting-age population.

Source: Election Assistance Commission, "Voter Registration and Turnout-2000," www.eac.gov/election_resources/00to.htm, and Election Assistance Commission, "A Summary of the 2004 Election Day Survey," September 2005, www.eac.gov/election_survey_2004/intro.htm.

efficacy—the belief that their vote can make a difference.[30] In contrast, non-voters are more cynical and less "socially connected." [31] They belong to fewer politically oriented groups and associate with like-minded people who are also nonpolitical. Nonvoters are more likely to be single, younger, with lower incomes and less of a stake in the community than those who vote.[32]

Demographic Distinctions. Motivation and beliefs are but two of the many variables that distinguish those who vote from those who do not.

Education is another. The greater a person's education, the more likely that person will vote.[33] Higher learning develops the cognitive skills necessary to process information and make informed judgments. It provides the skills to maneuver through the intricacies of the electoral process: meeting the registration requirements, obtaining absentee ballots, and understanding the ballot and how to mark it correctly.

Education also affects personal success. It increases a person's stake in the system, interest in an election, and concern over the outcome. Because the lesson that voting is a civic responsibility is usually learned in the classroom, schooling can contribute to a more highly developed perception of civic responsibility.

Education, income levels, and occupational status tend to correlate with one another. College-educated people have better connections, more skills, and greater knowledge; as a consequence, they have more opportunities to earn more money than those who lack these resources. Individuals with higher incomes and more professional jobs also have higher rates of voter turnout. According to the National Election Study, only about half of those in the lowest income bracket reported that they voted in the 2004 presidential election, compared to almost 90 percent in the top income bracket.[34] In midterm elections the differential is even greater.

Income differentials are even more evident in other forms of electoral activity, such as volunteering to help a campaign and, especially, contributing money. Naturally, the large donors are the most affluent citizens.

Age is another factor that contributes to voting. Older citizens turn out in higher proportions than do those who are younger. They do so because they have more interest in the election, more concern over the outcome and how it might affect them, and in some cases, more time to become involved. In addition, older people tend to have greater economic interests and ties to the community in which they live, two other reasons for participating. For many of them, too, voting is habitual.

The contrast in turnout between the youngest eligible to vote and citizens age sixty-five or older is significant. In the 2002 midterm elections, 31 percent of those born in 1975 or later (twenty-seven-years-old or younger) voted, compared to 78 percent of those born in 1926 or earlier (age seventy-six or older). In 2004, these figures were 65 percent for the youngest group, compared to 71 percent for those seventy-eight and older and 85 percent for those between sixty-two and seventy-seven.[35] In the 2006 midterm elections, about 24 percent of the eligible electorate was younger than thirty years of age.[36]

With education and income levels rising and with more of the population aging, one would expect turnout to be increasing. On balance, however, it has not been. Turnout has declined since the 1960s, and that decline has affected most population groups. The primary exception is African Americans living in the South who have voted in greater numbers as discriminatory electoral practices have been reduced or eliminated.[37] Most scholars believe that without the increase in education and income, turnout would have declined even further.[38]

The demographic distinctions between voters and nonvoters have resulted in an electorate that is not representative of the general population. Overrepresented are the more educated, higher-income, older members of society; under-represented are the younger, poorer, and less educated people. Moreover, the unrepresentative character of the electorate is even more pronounced in the nomination contests than in the general election.

THE CONSEQUENCES OF NOT VOTING

Does it *matter* that so many of those eligible to vote do not do so? Most observers believe that it does, even though they concede that the outcome of most elections and the policies of newly elected officials would probably be the same even if a greater number of nonvoters participated. Post-election surveys of voters and nonvoters show little difference in their candidate selection, policy preferences, and political attitudes.[39] The findings suggest that nonvoters in retrospect and after the election say that they support the candidates in roughly the same proportion as do voters. Moreover, the policy positions of voters and nonvoters are also similar.[40] Although nonvoters do tend to be slightly more liberal than voters, the ideological differences between them do not appear to be great enough to have a major impact on public policy.[41]

If the results of the election probably wouldn't change with more people voting, then what's the big fuss about nonvoting?[42] The answer lies in the link that voting forges between citizens and their elected representatives. Nonvoting weakens that link; it creates a representational gap between the general public and the voting electorate.

THE IMPACT OF VARIATIONS IN TURNOUT

Unequal Representation

The decline in voting has been greatest among "those less likely to vote in the first place,"[43] which are those at the lower end of the socioeconomic scale. This decline has produced and extended a class bias in voting as well as in other aspects of electoral activity, such as contributing money to the candidates and parties, attending rallies, and volunteering time.

Those who are most disadvantaged, who have the least education, and who need a change in conditions the most actually participate the least. Those who are the most advantaged, who benefit from existing conditions and presumably from public policy as it stands, vote more often. These trends in voting behavior work to reinforce, even to perpetuate, the status quo.

The tendency of higher-income, well-connected, older Americans to get involved and to vote has naturally encouraged candidates seeking office to address "their" issues, be they taxes, healthcare, or pensions, rather than issues in which the poor and the young might have more interest and concern.

The differential in turnout advantages the political party that attracts more of the people who fall into the higher participating groups. In recent years this has been the Republican Party. All things being equal, the GOP will turn out a higher percentage of its partisan identifiers than will the Democratic Party.

If the issues are geared to those who vote, then it follows that elected officials are more like to make policy decisions that reflect the interests and desires of those who elected them rather than those who voted against them or stood on the sidelines. And they do.

Research by prominent political scientists provides empirical evidence that political activity enhances representation.[44] In other words, those who are more active and tend to vote more regularly tend to reap the benefits of their participation in the political process. They select like-minded individuals, communicate their beliefs and desires to them, and use the threat to defeat them in the next election to persuade their representatives to support their interests.[45] It is more likely that their policy issues will be addressed and probably in a manner that works to their economic or social self interests.

Having the will and resources to affect political activity allows the advantaged to maintain and even extend their advantage. The American Political Science Association's Task Force on Inequality and American Democracy put it this way:

> The privileged participate more than others and are increasingly well organized to press their demands on government. Public officials, in turn, are much more responsive to the privileged than to average citizens and the least affluent. Citizens with lower or moderate incomes speak with a whisper that is lost on the ears of inattentive government officials, while the advantaged roar with a clarity and consistency that policy-makers readily hear and routinely follow. The scourge of overt discrimination against African-Americans and women has been replaced by a more subtle but potent threat—the growing concentration of the country's wealth and income in the hands of the few.[46]

In short, economic inequality extends political inequality, which in turn is reflected in public policy decisions. It is a vicious cycle, one that is difficult to break. To do so would require that the disadvantaged organize and increase their level of participation and that the advantaged share more equitably the benefits they receive.

Increased Difficulties Governing

Low turnout produces other problems for a democratic electoral process. It can make the meaning of the election less clear, the claim of a public mandate more problematic, and the task of fulfilling campaign pledges and promises more difficult. It also can have a negative impact on building and maintaining a majority coalition for governing. The fewer the people voting, the smaller the proportion of the population who will be initially supportive of the newly elected government and the more difficulty that those in elective positions may encounter in gaining support for their policy and legitimacy for their actions.

Low turnout can become a policy issue. One of the cornerstones of U.S. foreign policy since the end of World War II has been the promotion of and support for democratic institutions and processes. The failure of a majority of Americans to vote undercuts the credibility of this policy goal. Compare voter turnout in the United States with those of other democratic countries as shown in Table 2.4. Since 1945, the average turnout in Western Europe has been 77 percent of the voting-age population; it has been consistently lower in the United States, even as a percentage of registered voters.[47]

Some scholars actually see benefit in having a significant proportion of the electorate not voting on a regular basis. They claim that disinterest and inac-

TABLE 2.4 **International Voter Turnout in Selected Countries**

Country	Year	Type of Election	Turnout of Registered Voters (percentage)	Voluntary (V) or Compulsory (C) Voting	Rest Day (R) or Workday (W)
Australia	2004	Parliamentary	94.6	C	R
Austria	2004	Presidential	70.8	V	R
Belgium	2005	Parliamentary	90.5	C	R
Brazil	2005	Referendum	78.2	C	R
Canada	2004	Parliamentary	61.2	V	W
Chile	2005/6	Presidential*	87.7/87.1	C	W
Denmark	2005	Parliamentary	84.4	V	W
Finland	2003	Parliamentary	69.7	V	Bˆ
Germany	2005	Parliamentary	77.7	V	R
Greece	2004	Parliamentary	76.5	C	R
India	2004	Parliamentary	57.7	V	Bˆ
Iran	2005	Presidential*	62.7/59.8	V	R
Iraq	2005	Parliamentary	79.6	V	W
Israel	2003	Parliamentary	67.8	V	W
Mexico	2003	Legislative	41.7	C	R
Poland	2005	Presidential*	49.7/51.0/78.7	V	R
	2005	Parliamentary	40.6	V	R
Russia	2003	Parliamentary	55.7	V	R
South Korea	2004	Parliamentary	60.0	V	W
Spain	2004	Parliamentary	77.2	V	R
Switzerland	2003	Parliamentary	45.4	V	R
Ukraine	2004	Presidential*	74.2/81.1	V	R
United Kingdom	2005	Parliamentary	61.4	V	W
United States	2002	Legislative	69.0	V	W
United States	2004	Presidential	89.0	V	R

* More than one round.
Bˆ = Election conducted over more than one day.

Source: "Electionguide.org: voter turnout," www.electionguide.org/turnout 2003 (also 2004 and 2005); U.S. Census Bureau, News Releases, July 28, 2004, and May 26, 2005, www.census.gov/Press-Release/ www/releases/archives/voting/002278.html and www.census.gov/Press-Release/www/releases/archives/ voting/004986.html.

tivity enhances the quality of those who participate, mutes political conflict, promotes social stability, and implicitly provides support for public policy decisions by not challenging those decisions or holding policymakers accountable.[48] In this sense, apathy can be viewed as satisfaction with existing conditions; otherwise, it is argued, people would be more likely to protest in the streets and at the ballot box. Those who support this position point to the fact that bad times and discontent normally bring out a larger vote than do good times and public contentment.[49]

Most democratic theorists, however, do not subscribe to the belief that apathy is a positive social trait. Rather, they see it as an illness, a symptom of discontent within the political system by a significant segment of the population.[50]

POSSIBLE SOLUTIONS TO THE NONVOTING PROBLEM

Lower the Costs of Voting

What can be done about the problem of nonvoting? Describing the problem, the reasons people give for not voting, and the factors that influence turnout is easier than solving the problem of a sizable proportion of the eligible population not voting. Congress has dealt with the issue in two ways. First, it has enacted laws to remove or ease legal hurdles to voting, such as the "motor-voter" bill, which was designed to make registration easier, more accessible, and less time-consuming. Congress hoped that the proportion of the population who did not vote because they are not registered would decrease—perhaps by as much as 8 or 9 percent.[51] Although voter registration has increased steadily since the act went into effect in 1994, the percentage of the registered population has declined and turnout has remained anemic.[52] However, it might be even lower had the motor-voter bill not been enacted into law.

Similarly, the Help America Vote Act (2002) also was designed to improve the accuracy of registration lists, vote tabulation methods, and provide better oversight of the decisions state and local electoral officials make on election day. Turnout did increase in 2004, but whether it was the consequence of this legislation is unclear.

What else can Congress and the states do to reduce the personal costs of voting, costs measured in time, effort, and perhaps lost wages? One way to make it easier for people to find the time to vote is to hold elections on a nonworkday, a holiday, or a Sunday. The United States is one of the few democracies that still conduct elections on a workday (see Table 2.4). Although employers are required by law to give their employees time to vote, and not penalize them financially for doing so, some people still find it difficult to take the time off.

Making election day a holiday would make it easier for more people to vote. However, there would be opposition to such a proposal. Some businesses would lose money by being closed or forced to pay employees extra for working on a holiday. Schools would be closed, thereby increasing the burden on single parents. And some people employed in essential or recreational services, such as police, fire, hospital, or even restaurant employees, would still have to work.

A second and somewhat less costly alternative would be to combine election day and Veterans Day, a proposal made by the Federal Election Commission in 2001. However, veterans groups might object to partisan politics replacing the *raison d'etre*—the holiday that memorializes those who fought and died in defense of their country.

Instead of being held on a holiday, elections could be held on a Sunday, as they are in many European countries. But Sunday elections would compete with religious services, recreational activities, and family events.[53] Besides, many people work on Sunday. Under the circumstances, it is not clear whether turnout would increase all that much if elections were held on a Sunday or whether the American people would support such a change. Turnout could conceivably decrease.

Another possibility would be to extend the time people have for voting. Although most states keep their voting places open for at least twelve hours, some allow their citizens to vote up to twenty-one days before the election. Others permit "no-fault" absentee ballots so that people can vote by mail without having to certify that they will be out of the state at the time of the election. Oregon has gone even further. In 1998, voters in that state approved a ballot initiative that requires voting by mail ballot. Voting over the Internet also may be a possibility in the not-so-distant future, if the security and integrity of the voting system can be properly maintained.

Another change that might facilitate voting would be redesigning the form and shape of the ballot. Some states still use a party-column ballot, in which all of a party's candidates are listed together below the party's label. Partisans have no difficulty discerning their candidates. The office-column ballot, on which candidates are listed by the position for which they are running, may confuse people not familiar with the names of all the candidates. In addition, ballots also may contain complex policy initiatives on which voters are asked to decide quickly so as not to delay those waiting in line to vote.

Extending the time for voting and making it simpler to vote might increase turnout, but how much? It is unlikely that the elimination of these institutional barriers would substantially increase voter turnout. More extreme measures may be necessary to achieve this objective.

Increase the Costs of *Not* Voting

The most far-reaching and controversial proposal for increasing the proportion of the population who votes is simply to require voting as an obligation of citizenship and to fine those who fail to do so. After all, there are other citizen obligations mandated by law that have penalties for noncompliance, obligations such as reporting for selective service, paying income taxes, and serving on juries. Should voting be treated any differently from these other citizen responsibilities? For several democratic countries, the answer is "no." Australia, Belgium, Chile, and Italy have mandatory voting systems, and their turnouts are 90 percent or more (see Table 2.4).

Requiring all citizens to vote would convert equality in theory to near-equality in practice. Moreover, it would reduce the distinction between the electorate and the population. Government officials would have to be more responsive to the entire adult population rather than to just a portion of their electoral constituency. With mandatory voting, the poor, less educated, less informed, and less partisan would be better represented than they are today.

But mandatory voting also could result in a less informed and perhaps less intelligent electoral decision. It could reduce the quality of the electorate's judgment. Besides, there would undoubtedly be strong opposition to such a proposal. Some argue that mandatory voting would prevent people from protesting the choices they have by boycotting the election. Others claim that mandatory voting is undemocratic, that a democracy that prides itself on personal liberty should allow its citizens the right to decide whether or not they wish to vote.

Enhance the Incentives for Voting

With individual choice a value and voting a basic right, those interested in expanding participation have suggested other ways to encourage more people to become engaged in the electoral process. These include engaging in media campaigns in which prominent citizens urge others to get involved; better civic education in schools and communities, in which the responsibilities of citizenship are stressed; and bipartisan informational campaigns by parties and nonpartisan groups that would tell people why they should get out and vote. However, these so-called bipartisan efforts have themselves become controversial because they have been used by parties and groups to further their own political agendas and circumvent campaign finance regulations.

More effective grassroots organizing might help motivate more people to vote. However, such an expenditure of time, money, and effort by the political parties cannot be legislated by Congress or the states. More competitive elections also should improve turnout, but the parties have little motivation for decreasing their number of safe seats. Holding fewer elections might boost turnout as well, but such a proposal would require longer terms of office, a proposition that a cynical and distrustful public is unlikely to support. Gaining better representation for those in the minority in electoral districts might encourage more people to vote, but to achieve this representation would probably involve a fundamental change in the electoral system, a move from single-member districts and plurality voting to multimember districts and proportional voting.

Other ideas include shortening the election cycle, limiting negative campaigning, instituting voluntary codes of conduct for candidates, and providing more and better information about the candidates and their positions. But instituting such changes might run up against the First Amendment protections of freedom of speech and of the press and are thus not likely to be legislated by Congress or upheld by the federal judiciary.

The bottom line is that citizens' attitudes about politics and government need to be changed if voter turnout is going to be significantly increased. There's no easy way to accomplish this objective. In fact, the events of recent years—the scandals in the Clinton and Bush administrations, the campaign finance issues of soft money, stealth campaigns by nonparty groups, and concentrated expenditures in the key battleground states have intensified, rather than alleviated, public cynicism and mistrust of politicians. In short, nonvoting remains an attitudinal problem, one that is not likely to go away soon.

Getting people to the polls is only part of the problem; getting them to vote properly is another. Voting procedures need to be simplified, and the tabulation of votes needs to be improved. Suggestions include eliminating confusing ballot designs, replacing aging voting machines and punch cards with optical scan equipment, allowing voters who accidentally spoil their ballots to get new ones, and having election officials explain how to vote to those who have difficulty doing so.

In the aftermath of the 2000 election controversy, the state of Florida revised its electoral procedures.[54] Bills were introduced in Congress to set a uniform national closing time for polls (which was not enacted), to provide federal assistance to the states to update their voting equipment (which was part of the Help America Vote Act), to reduce discriminatory practices by having the Justice Department more vigorously enforce the 1965 Voting Rights Act, as well as to reform campaign finance laws (see chapter 5), and reduce fraudulent voting practices.

SUMMARY: SUFFRAGE AND TURNOUT DILEMMAS IN A NUTSHELL

The U.S. electoral system wasn't designed to be a participatory electoral democracy, but it has become one. In theory, today there is universal suffrage; in practice, most people do not vote on a regular basis. In theory, every adult citizen has an equal opportunity to participate; in practice, those with greater resources are in a better position to do so. In fact, their educational and economic advantages are both motivations for and consequences of voting. In theory, elected officials are supposed to be responsive to all the people; in practice, they tend to be more accessible and responsive to those who elect them, or so the public perceives.

Although low turnout is thought to be undesirable in and for a democratic political system, the remedies lawmakers have proposed and instituted to deal with the problem have not worked nearly as well as their sponsors had hoped. Removing the institutional barriers to voting should have increased substantially the proportion of the electorate that votes, but with the exception of African Americans living in the South, it hasn't. Lifting federal campaign restrictions for the solicitation and expenditure of money used to get out the vote, engaging in bipartisan educational efforts, and strengthening the parties' grassroots organizations should have increased turnout, but with the exception of the 2004 presidential election, it really has not done so. What it has done is to undercut the federal contribution and spending limits, thereby contributing to the public perception that money influences election outcomes.

The problem of nonvoting has resisted easy solutions. It is as much an attitude problem as anything else. Changing attitudes is difficult. Legislation alone cannot do so. It will require a major effort by those in and outside of government to reconstitute the civic culture and reestablish trust between the voters and their elected officials. There are no easy and quick fixes to the root causes of the nonvoting problem: public alienation and cynicism.

Now It's Your Turn

Discussion Questions

1. Can the public's will be expressed in an election if everyone—or most people—do not vote?
2. Should voting be an obligation of citizenship? If so, should that obligation be enforced by penalties for those who do not meet it by voting?
3. Should people with little interest in the election and information about it be encouraged to vote?
4. Should registration be eliminated as a precondition for voting?
5. Should voting rules in presidential elections continue to be set by the states and counties, or should they be established by the federal government?
6. Should the Constitution be amended so that federal government conducts all federal elections?
7. Should election day be a holiday or nonworkday, such as Sunday?

Topics for Debate

Challenge or defend the following statements:

1. Universal suffrage is neither necessary nor desirable.
2. Nonvoting is really not a major problem for American democracy.
3. Literacy tests should be instituted in a nondiscriminatory manner to ensure that voters have sufficient information about the candidates and issues to make an informed judgment on election day.
4. States should abolish polling booths and permit voting from home via mail, the Internet, or telephone over a designated period of time, not to be less than twenty-four hours.
5. The right to vote should not be abridged by conviction for a crime.

Exercises

1. Rock the Vote, a public interest organization dedicated to increasing voter turnout, particularly among younger citizens, ran a public relations campaign during the last presidential election to increase electoral awareness, to provide potential voters with more information about the candidates and their campaigns, and, most important, to get more people registered to vote. It plans to run another educational campaign during the next election. If that organization asked you for advice on such a campaign, what would you say?
   a. To whom should it direct its campaign?
   b. What should its principal appeal be, and how should it be articulated to achieve maximum impact?
   c. Should the content of that appeal change over the course of the campaign?
   d. What should be the principal means of communication?
   e. In addition to a public appeal, what else could the group do to enhance its educational efforts and achieve its principal objectives?

2. The National Commission on Federal Election Reform has proposed making election day a national holiday, establishing statewide systems of voter registration, replacing punch cards with ballots that can be optically scanned, and banning election-night predictions on the major networks until voting is completed within the continental United States. Assess each of these recommendations on the basis of
   a. its likelihood of increasing voter turnout,
   b. its costs to the governments that run the elections and to individuals who vote in them,
   c. its advantage or disadvantage to each of the major parties and to third parties and independent candidates.

   On the basis of your assessment, indicate which (if any) of the recommendations of the commission you support and which (if any) you oppose.

INTERNET RESOURCES

- Common Cause: www.commoncause.org
  A public interest group concerned with electoral reform, media and democracy, and accountability in government.
- Democracy Network: www.dnet.org
  A public affairs organization, sponsored by the League of Women Voters, which provides a range of information on candidates and issues.
- Electoral Assistance Commission: www.eac.gov
  Created by the Help America Vote Act, this national commission

allows people to download a national voter registration form and provides information on where to send it. It also collects useful data on registration and turnout.

- League of Women Voters: www.lwv.org
An established public interest group that publishes books and pamphlets on election activities, including information about the candidates and ballot initiatives. The league also lobbies Congress for campaign reform.
- Public Citizen: www.citizen.org
A public interest group, started by citizen activist Ralph Nader, that is concerned with the rules and procedures that govern elections in the United States. Openness of government and accountability of those in office are also major goals.
- Project Vote Smart: www.vote-smart.org
Another public interest group dedicated to educating the electorate, particularly younger voters, on the issues, the candidates, and the records of public officials; the group distributes free citizen tool kits and lots of information on-line.
- Rock the Vote: www.rockthevote.org
Getting young people to register and vote is the primary goal of this public interest organization. Its Web site provides a short form that can be used to begin the registration process. Rock the Vote will even remind those who registered through its site to vote on election day.

SELECTED READINGS

American Political Science Association Task Force Report. "American Democracy in an Age of Rising Inequality," *Perspectives on Politics* 2 (December 2004): 651–666.

Bennett, Stephen Earl, and David Resnick. "The Implications of Nonvoting for Democracy in the United States." *American Journal of Political Science* 34 (1990): 771–803.

Burnham, Walter D. "The Turnout Problem." In *Elections American Style,* A. James Reichley, ed. Washington, D.C.: Brookings Institution, 1987.

Conway, M. Margaret. *Political Participation in the United States,* 3rd ed. Washington, D.C.: CQ Press, 1999.

Gant, Michael M., and William Lyons. "Democratic Theory, Nonvoting, and Public Policy." *American Politics Quarterly* 21 (1993): 183–204.

Jackson, Robert A. "A Reassessment of Voter Mobilization." *Political Research Quarterly* (1996): 331–349.

Leighley, Jan E. *Strength in Numbers? The Political Mobilization of Racial and Ethnic Minorities*. Princeton: Princeton University Press, 2001.

McDonald, Michael, and Samuel Popkin. "The Myth of the Vanishing Voter," *American Political Science Review* 95 (December 2001): 963–974.

Pew Research Center for the People and the Press. *Deconstructing Distrust*. Washington, D.C.: Pew Research Center for the People and the Press, 1998.

Piven, Frances Fox, and Richard A. Cloward. *Why Americans Don't Vote*. New York: Pantheon, 1988.

Rosenstone, Steven J., and John Mark Hansen. *Mobilization, Participation, and Democracy in America*. New York: Macmillan, 1993.

Schlozman, Kay Lehman, "Citizen Participation in America: What Do We Know? Why Do We Care?" In *Political Science: The State of the Discipline*, Ira Katznelson and Helen V. Milner, ed. New York: W. W. Norton, 2002.

Skocpol, Theda, and Morris P. Fiorina, eds. *Civic Engagement in American Politics*. Washington, D.C.: Brookings Institution, 1999.

Teixeira, Ruy A. *The Disappearing American Voter*. Washington, D.C.: Brookings Institution, 1992.

Verba, Sidney, Kay Lehman Schlozman, and Henry E. Brady. *Voice and Equality: Civic Voluntarism in American Politics*. Cambridge, Mass.: Harvard University Press, 1995.

Wolfinger, Raymond E., and Jonathan Hoffman. "Registering and Voting with Motor Voter," *PS* 34 (March 2001): 85–92.

Wolfinger, Raymond E., and Steven J. Rosenstone. *Who Votes?* New Haven, Conn.: Yale University Press, 1980.

NOTES

1. Noncitizens, such as legal and illegal immigrants who are residents of the United States, also have a stake in the system. They have common interests, needs, and obligations, including the payment of taxes on income earned in the United States. They are not afforded voting rights, however, until they become naturalized citizens. For illegal aliens, especially, it is often difficult to meet the legal requirements for citizenship.

2. For an excellent study of turnout since the beginning of the Republic, see Walter Dean Burnham, "The Turnout Problem," in *Elections American Style*, A. James Reichley, ed. (Washington, D.C.: Brookings Institution, 1987), 97–133.

3. In every southern state, a majority of eligible African Americans were *not* eligible to vote until the mid- to late 1960s. Earl Black and Merle Black, *The Vital South: How Presidents Are Elected* (Cambridge, Mass.: Harvard University Press, 1992), 217.

4. Susan Welch et al., *American Government*, 3rd ed. (St. Paul, Minn.: West, 1990), 196.

5. Michael X. Delli Carpini and Ester R. Fuchs, "The Year of the Woman? Candidates, Voters, and the 1992 Elections," *Political Science Quarterly* 108 (Spring 1993): 30.

6. Two years later, the Supreme Court extended this prohibition to the election of state and local officials. It did so through its interpretation of the Fourteenth Amendment's equal protection clause, which holds that every person's vote should be equal: one person–one vote.

7. Benjamin I. Page and Robert Y. Shapiro, *The Rational Public: Fifty Years of Trends in Americans' Policy Preferences* (Chicago, University of Chicago Press, 1992), 166.

8. Frank Newport, "Americans Support Proposal to Eliminate Electoral College System," Gallup Poll, January 5, 2001, www.gallup.com/content/default.aspx?ci=2140, and Darren K. Carlson, "Public Flunks Electoral College System," Gallup Poll, November 2, 2004, www.gallup.com/contents/default.aspx?ci=13918.

9. NAACP Legal Defense and Educational Fund, "Democracy for All: Ending Felon Disfranchisement," www.naacpldf.org/content/pdf/felon_free/Felon_Disfranchisement_Q&A.pdf.

10. Michael P. McDonald, "Every Eligible Voter Counts: Correctly Measuring American Turnout Rates," www.brookings.edu/views/Papers/20040909mcdonald.pdf.

11. Janelle Carter, "Election Panel Submits Report to Bush," *Associated Press,* July 31, 2000.

12. U.S. Commission on Civil Rights as reported in Robert E. Pierre and Peter Slevin, "Florida Vote Rife with Disparities, Study Says," *Washington Post,* June 5, 2001, A1.

13. "Votes of Poor More Likely Uncounted," *Associated Press,* July 9, 2001, http://dailynews.yahoo.com/n/ap/20010709/ts/voter_study_1.html.

14. Robert F. Kennedy Jr. alleged in an article published in *Rolling Stone* that Bush's victory in 2004 was fraudulent. Kennedy cites numerous irregularities from absentee ballots not received to Democratic registration materials being destroyed to more than one million ballots voided. He also claims that 350,000 Democratic voters in Ohio were prevented from casting their ballots or having them counted. This number would have been sufficient to reverse the official results in that state. From www.rollingstone.com/news/story/10432334/was_the_2004_election_stolen.

Other irregularities also were reported. In the governor's race in the state of Washington, a race that was decided by 129 votes, it was alleged that ineligible ex-felons voted, as well as people who voted in the name of a deceased person. In Wisconsin, one hundred people were alleged to have voted twice. From "Building Confidence in U.S. Elections," *Report of the Commission on Federal Election Reform,* September 2005, 4.

15. According to American University's Center for the Study of the American Electorate, 39.7 percent of eligible voters cast ballots in 2002 and 40.4 percent in 2006. Zachary A. Goldfarb, "Politics," *Washington Post,* November 10, 2006, A13.

16. Rhodes Cook, "Democratic Primary Turnout: Comparing 2004 with Previous Highs," www.rhodescook.com/primary.analysis.html, and Chris Cillizza and Zachery A. Goldfarb, "Primary Turnout Low," *Washington Post,* October 8, 2006, A5.

17. Frances Fox Piven and Richard A. Cloward argue that ethnic and religious identities reinforced partisan loyalties to mobilize the vote, particularly among the working class. Similarly, sectional issues and party competitiveness also contributed to the high turnout in the nineteenth century. Frances Fox Piven and Richard A. Cloward, *Why Americans Don't Vote* (New York: Pantheon, 1988), 26–29.

18. Keith Melder, *Hail to the Candidate* (Washington, D.C.: Smithsonian Institution Press, 1992), 69–100, and Gil Troy, *See How They Ran* (New York: Free Press, 1991), 20–30.

19. The influx of immigrants, first predominantly from northern Europe during the period from 1840 to 1860, and later from southern Europe from 1880 to 1910, provided fertile ground for parties to recruit new partisans by providing them with social services and other benefits in exchange for their support.

20. American National Election Studies, "Voter Turnout 1948–2004," www.electionstudies.org/nesguide/toptable/tab6a_2.htm.
21. Pew Research Center for the People and the Press, "Voter Turnout May Slip Again," July 13, 2000.
22. Ibid.
23. *Retro-Politics* (Washington, D.C.: Pew Research Center for the People and the Press, November 1999), 139.
24. Princeton Survey Research Associates, national survey conducted October 21 to November 2, 1996.
25. Martin P. Wattenberg and Craig Leonard Brians, "Negative Campaign Advertising: Demobilizer or Mobilizer," *American Political Science Review* 93 (December 1999): 891–899.
26. Steven Finkel and John Greer, "A Spot Check: Casting Doubt on the Demobilizing Effect of Attack Advertising," *American Journal of Political Science* 42 (April 1998): 573–595, and Kim Fridkin Kahn and Patrick J. Kenny, "Do Negative Campaigns Mobilize or Suppress Turnout?" *American Political Science Review* 93 (December 1999): 877–889.
27. Massachusetts Institute of Technology and California Institute of Technology, "Voting: What Is and What Could Be," report issued July 17, 2001, and "Caltech-MIT Team Finds 4–6 Million Votes Lost in the 2000 Election. Nationwide Reforms Outline in Report," MIT news release, July 16, 2001, www.mit.edu/newsoffice/2001/voting2.htm.
28. Martin P. Wattenberg, "Getting Out the Vote," *Public Perspective* (January/February 2001): 16–17.
29. Pew Research Center for the People and the Press has conducted polls over the last decade that show declining trust and confidence in government. These results were collected in *Deconstructing Distrust,* which Pew published in 1998 and updated in "Public Votes for Continuity and Change in 2000," February 25, 1999. Another contemporary survey, this one by the Center on Policy Attitudes, found strong support (74.5 percent) for the proposition that "the government is pretty much run by a few big interests looking out for themselves." Found in "Expecting More Say: The American Public on Its Role in Government Decisionmaking," May 10, 1999.
30. Angus Campbell et al., *The American Voter* (New York: Wiley, 1960), 102.
31. The term "social connectedness" was used by Ruy A. Teixeira in *The Disappearing American Voter* (Washington, D.C.: Brookings Institution, 1992), 36–37, to describe the degree to which a person has ties to the community. The stronger the ties, the greater the motivation for voting.
32. Ibid. See also Scott Keeter, "Politics and the 'DOTNET' Generation," Pew Research Center for the People and the Press, May 30, 2006, www.pewresearch.org/obdeck/?ObDeckID=27.
33. Raymond E. Wolfinger and Steven J. Rosenstone, *Who Votes?* (New Haven, Conn.: Yale University Press, 1980), 13–26.
34. National Election Studies, "Voting Turnout, 1948–2004," www.electionstudies.org/nesguide/2ndtable/t6a_2_2.htm.
35. Ibid.
36. Jason Szep, "Youth Turnout in Election Biggest in 20 Years," Reuters News Agency, November 8, 2006, http://uselections.uk.reuters.com/top/news/usaNO8342322.
37. Teixeira, *The Disappearing American Voter,* 80.
38. Paul R. Abramson, John H. Aldrich, and David W. Rohde, *Change and Continuity in the 2004 Elections* (Washington, D.C.: CQ Press, 2006), 95.
39. Teixeira, *The Disappearing American Voter,* 95.

40. Stephen Earl Bennett and David Resnick, "The Implications of Nonvoting for Democracy in the United States," *American Journal of Political Science* 34 (1990): 771–802, and Michael M. Gant and William Lyons, "Democratic Theory, Nonvoting, and Public Policy," *American Politics Quarterly* 21 (1993): 183–204.

41. Teixeira, *The Disappearing American Voter,* 100.

42. Thomas E. Cavanaugh argues that elections have to be close and that the likely nonvoters who do cast ballots have to be disproportionately favorable to one candidate for the outcome to be changed. See Thomas E. Cavanaugh, "When Turnout Matters: Mobilization and Conversion as Determinants of Election Outcomes," in *Political Participation and American Democracy,* William J. Crotty, ed. (New York: Greenwood Press, 1991), 89–112.

43. Teixeira, *The Disappearing American Voter,* 72–74, 80.

44. Sidney Verba, Kay Lehman Schlozman, and Henry E. Brady, *Voice and Equality: Civic Voluntarism in American Politics* (Cambridge, Mass.: Harvard University Press, 1995).

45. John D. Griffin and Brian Newman, "Are Voters Better Represented?" *Journal of Politics* 67 (November 2005): 1206–1227.

46. "American Democracy in an Age of Rising Inequality," Task Force on Inequality and American Democracy of the American Political Science Association, 2004, 1.

47. International Institute for Democracy and Electoral Assistance, "Voter Turnout," www.idea.int/vt/findings.cfm.

48. This argument was advanced by Bernard Berelson, Paul F. Lazerfeld, and William McPhee in their book, *Voting* (Chicago: University of Chicago Press, 1954). See also Lester Milbrath, *Political Participation* (Chicago: Rand McNally, 1965).

49. Blame tends to be greater than credit. Political scientists have found that people seem more motivated to turn out to vote during bad times than during good ones. See Howard Bloom and H. Douglas Price, "Voter Response to Short Run Economic Conditions: The Asymmetric Effects of Prosperity and Recession," *American Political Science Review* 69 (1975): 1240–1254, and Morris P. Fiorina, "Economic Retrospective Voting in National Elections: A Microanalysis," *American Journal of Political Science* 22 (1978): 426–433.

50. See "Why Don't Americans Trust the Government," *Washington Post,* Kaiser Family Foundation, and Harvard University, 1996, and *Deconstructing Distrust* (Washington, D.C.: Pew Research Center for the People and the Press, 1998).

51. Teixeira, *The Disappearing American Voter,* 106–147, and Wolfinger and Rosenstone, *Who Votes?* 73.

52. "The Impact of the National Voter Registration Act, 2003–2004," Election Assistance Commission, Report to Congress, June 30, 2005, 2.

53. Moreover, churches are often polling and voting stations in the United States.

54. The new Florida law provided $24 million to modernize voting machinery at the county and precinct level, $6 million for voter education efforts, and $2 million to create a registration database for the state. In addition, the legislation standardized recount procedures and provided for provisional ballots in the cases in which there are registration disputes.

chapter 3

How Representative Are American Elections?

Did you know that. . .

- the constitutional system was designed to protect the rights of minorities, and the electoral system has evolved to reflect the influence of majorities (or at least pluralities)?
- drawing the shape of a legislative district to advance the party in power is an old American tradition that goes back more than two hundred years?
- for most of U.S. history, the Supreme Court regarded the drafting of legislative districts as a political, not a judicial, issue and thus stayed away from this type of representational question?
- the redrafting of congressional districts to gain more representation for African American and Latino voters in the 1990s contributed to increasing the number of conservative Republican members of Congress?
- the Electoral College was originally designed to ensure that the most qualified, not necessarily the most popular, candidates were selected as president and vice president?
- sixteen states currently have laws that place limits on the number of terms their state legislative representatives can serve?
- women make up 52 percent of the electorate but a relatively small percentage of members of Congress and state legislators?
- more than half of the members of the House of Representatives face no real opposition in their quest for renomination?
- twenty-nine members of the House ran unopposed in the 2004 general election, and 129 others won with more than 70 percent of the vote?
- half of the Senate had no opposition in their bid for renomination, and more than one third received 65 percent of the vote in their last election?
- groups that are less well represented in government support a stronger role for government than do those that are better represented?

Is this any way to run a democratic election?

I n a representative democracy, all citizens are entitled to have their interests represented. Is the U.S. electoral system, in which candidates are chosen by plurality vote in single-member districts, fair and equitable for all groups in the society? Many people say "no." They claim that the system overrepresents the majority and underrepresents the minority.

This chapter addresses the issue of representation. It examines how the electoral system affects the representative character of government. Beginning with a discussion of the concept of representation, the chapter then turns to the relationship between the structure of elections and the type of representation that this structure produces. In the process, the discussion focuses on those who have benefited from this representational struggle and those who have not and on the impact representation may have on attitudes toward government and public policy outcomes. The chapter also explores the necessity and desirability of imposing legal qualifications for office and their effect on a democratic electoral process.

THE CONCEPT OF REPRESENTATION

The concept of representation is central to the democratic belief that government should reflect the values and policy preferences of its citizens. This belief became the principal justification for the American Revolution. "Taxation without representation is tyranny!" was the rallying cry of those who wanted their representational rights as English citizens restored.

Although the issue for the colonists was their lack of representation in Parliament, for the framers it was devising a system that would permit diverse representation but not reflect every mood of the masses, much less convert those moods into public policy. By overlapping constituencies between the federal government and the states and within the federal government itself, the delegates at the Constitutional Convention hoped to achieve both state and popular representation without domination by a single interest, region, or group. To do so, they designed a system in which parts of the polity were better and more effectively represented than was the polity as a whole. Their artful constitutional framework has shaped the representational character of the American electoral system ever since.

The Constitution gave the states the authority to determine how their representatives would be chosen. Most used their discretion to create institutions that paralleled those of the national government in which representatives were chosen from clearly defined geographic areas. Within these areas, voters selected candidates directly by popular vote or indirectly by voting for state legislators who in turn selected the state's senators and presidential electors.

How the election was to be conducted, voter eligibility determined, and candidates chosen were left to the states to decide. The Constitution specifies only a few qualifications for federal office: a minimum age, a geographic residence requirement at the time of election, citizenship for a specified number of years, and, in the case of the president, being both native born and a fourteen-year resident of the United States before the election. The Constitution also prohibits religious tests as a condition for holding public office.

Types of Representation

In choosing their representatives, the states selected candidates from their pool of eligible voters: initially, white, male Christians who owned property. Most elected officials were better educated than the average male citizen and usually prominent in the community. As the country became more diverse and as suffrage expanded, so too did the acceptable qualifications for being elected to office. However, what qualifications were deemed acceptable changed much more slowly than did the composition of the electorate. Even today, most of the initial dominant characteristics still prevail: white, male, with above-average education and income.

Herein lies part of the representational dilemma for the United States. If one purpose of representation is to reflect the needs and interests of the society as a whole, then how can a government dominated by white males provide fair and equal representation?

Many say that it cannot. They argue that only a person who shares the characteristics of a particular constituency can effectively represent it. Knowing how it feels to live in the constituency, having interests and needs similar to those of the people who reside there, and sharing the values, political beliefs, and perceptions of these residents are keys to effective representation. Taken to its obvious conclusion, this argument contends that the best representative for most people most of the time is a person who resembles them demographically and attitudinally.

It follows that the composition of government also should reflect the composition of society if the government is to be representative of that society. In other words, if a particular group, such as African Americans, constitutes a certain proportion of the voting-age population, about 13 percent, then it should constitute a similar proportion of the government. When Bill Clinton promised in his 1992 campaign to appoint an administration as diverse as America, he was subscribing to this tenet of equal and fair representation for all.

Getting their fair share has become a goal of underrepresented groups and a hot-button political issue for them. Not only do the underrepresented want their needs addressed, their interests satisfied, and their values incorporated into public policy decisions, but they also want to be represented in the institutions in which their own people, people who have their demographic and in some cases attitudinal characteristics, make decisions. They see representation as a symbol of equality.

In addition to **descriptive representation**, or how well the government reflects the composition of society, there is also the issue of **substantive repre-**

sentation, which is how well public policy decisions reflect the values, interests, and desires of the various groups that comprise American society. Whereas descriptive representation is reflected in the *who* of government (the people who make the decisions), substantive representation is reflected in the *what* of government (public policy and its impact). This distinction arises in part because it is possible for a person who reflects the demographic characteristics of a particular group to hold beliefs that don't reflect the dominant sentiment of that group. To use a few extreme examples, do the beliefs and decisions of Justice Clarence Thomas or former Republican representative J. C. Watts of Oklahoma better reflect those of the African American community than do those of Democratic senator Ted Kennedy of Massachusetts or House Speaker, Nancy Pelosi, a Democrat from California?

Although substantive representation is more difficult to evaluate than descriptive representation, it is every bit as important. Not only do people want to see their own reflection in government, they also want that government to be responsive to their needs and interests.

Roles of Representatives

How to achieve equitable representation is an important issue; what role representatives should play in office is another. People want their representative to serve their constituency and the nation. But serving both may be difficult if the interests of the constituency and nation diverge. For example, members of Congress have increasingly earmarked special projects for their districts while complaining about the size of the annual budget deficit. They provide short-term fixes for their constituents' needs that exacerbate longer-term problems for the country. During the period in 2006 when gasoline prices spiked, a group of senators proposed a $100 tax rebate to help consumers, particularly those with limited incomes who have to commute considerable distances to work. Had the plan been approved, it would have provided short-term relief but it also would have maintained demand, which might have pushed prices higher, let alone increased the pollution from automobile travel.

There are other representational issues: disagreements among constituents as well as differences in the intensity of their feelings and disagreements between constituents and their elected representatives. What should an elected representative do if these differences persist?

There are basically two schools of thought about what the representative's proper role should be. The democratic school perceives the representative as a **delegate** of the people and, as such, duty bound to discern and reflect the majority opinion. If there is a consensus, the representative should follow it; if there isn't, then a representative may be able to exercise more personal discretion in deciding what to do, particularly if that representative has the information and expertise to make an informed judgment.

The other representational role is that of a **trustee**, a person charged with using the information and expertise at his or her disposal to make the best possible decision. Edmund Burke put it this way in a speech to the people of Bristol who elected him to Parliament:

> Parliament is not a congress of ambassadors from different and hostile interests, which interests each must maintain, as an agent and advocate, against other agents and advocates; but Parliament is a deliberative assembly of one nation, with one interest, that of the whole—where not local prejudices ought to guide, but the general good, resulting from the general reason of the whole. You choose a member, indeed; but when you have chosen him he is not a member of Bristol, but he is a member of Parliament.[1]

Those who favor a trustee role believe that the public have neither the desire, ability, or the knowledge to focus on policy matters, much less make policy statements. This is why they elect representatives to make policy decisions for them. Representatives have greater interest and desire (as indicated by their candidacy) in public policy and, hopefully, the knowledge and ability to do the job effectively. Moreover, this school of thought sees legislative institutions as deliberative bodies in which the deliberation itself should impact on a representative's policy judgments.

The American people are ambiguous about the role they want their representatives to play. They prefer leaders to followers, but they also want their leaders to stay in touch with popular sentiment. They expect their elected officials to look out for their interests, but they also think that their representatives are too sensitive to special interests, and they believe that most members of Congress are too parochial for the good of the country, but they keep reelecting most of them.

People think that elected officials would make better decisions if they did what most of the people want, but they do not believe that officials do so most of the time.[2] Moreover, they are also skeptical of public opinion polls as accurate measures of public opinion. Most people do not understand how a poll of about one thousand people can accurately measure the sentiment of an entire country.[3] Their skepticism about polling extends to the motivation that prompts officials to rely on them. More people believe that those in government use polls to stay popular and get reelected than because they want to give the public a say in what the government does.[4]

Contemporary political developments have been pushing elected representatives closer to their constituents than in the past. Candidates for office make representational promises that they are expected to fulfill. Failure to do so is frequently the subject of media attention and can become a campaign issue if the incumbent stands for reelection. Getting reelected is believed to be a primary motivation for legislators when they make policy judgments. Legislative offices are devoting more staff, more time, and more resources to servicing constituency needs. Members of Congress have received greater allowances for home travel, and even the legislative calendar has been adjusted to permit representatives to spend more time in their home districts.

Nonetheless, the use of public opinion polls and focus groups to dig more deeply into the opinions and attitudes of the populace; the development of rapid and easy communication by e-mail, fax, and telephone; and the growth and professionalization of interest groups have all kept legislators more closely in touch with their constituents than they were in the past. Similarly, the expansion of local news programming has allowed constituents to become better informed about the behavior of their representatives and has created the perception among legislators that their words and actions are increasingly visible to the folks back home. Frequent elections keep these officials accountable. All of these linkage mechanisms are consistent with a democratic political system, although the low level of public information and the absence of dominant constituency opinions on many issues give officials considerable discretion in making public policy choices.

THE STRUCTURE OF ELECTIONS AND THE UNDERREPRESENTATION OF MINORITIES

How elections are structured shapes the representative character of the American political system—particularly its descriptive representation. The boundaries of legislative districts, the number of officials selected within them, and the procedure by which the winner is determined all affect the character of representation.

As noted in chapter 2, rules and procedures aren't neutral. The plurality voting system in single-member districts disproportionately benefits those in the majority. It also benefits the two major parties at the expense of third parties and independent candidates. Similarly, the way the Electoral College operates today favors the large states and groups within them.

Plurality Voting in Single-Member Districts

The Constitution does not prescribe single-member districts. What it does require is a reapportionment, every ten years, of the members of the House of Representatives on the basis of the national census. States gain or lose seats depending on how their proportion of the population compares to that of the country as a whole. There is one proviso, however, that every state must have at least one representative in the House.

Although the Constitution does not specify how the seats are to be allocated within the states, a single-member district system has generally prevailed since the Constitution was ratified. In such a system, the state drafts the boundaries of its legislative districts, and each district is represented by one legislator selected on the basis of the popular vote.

A voting system in which the candidate with the most votes wins favors those in the majority. It does so within each district as well as cumulatively among the districts within the state. It is difficult for a minority to gain representation unless it constitutes a majority or near majority within a district.

The best evidence to support the proposition that a system in which the plurality winner in single-member districts hurts minority groups is the composition of legislative bodies today. Take Congress, for example. Table 3.1 shows the percentages of African Americans, Latinos, and Asian Americans in

TABLE 3.1 **Minority Members of Congress, 1985–2007 (percentages)**			
Congress/Year	African Americans	Hispanics	Asian Americans
House of Representatives			
99th/1985	4.4	2.5	1.1
100th/1987	5.1	2.5	1.4
101st/1989	5.3	2.5	1.4
102nd/1991	5.7	2.3	1.1
103rd/1993	8.7	3.9	1.6
104th/1995	9.0	4.1	1.6
105th/1997	8.5	4.1	1.4
106th/1999	9.0	4.4	1.6
107th/2001	8.3	4.4	1.6
108th/2003	8.5	5.3	1.1
109th/2005	9.1	5.3	1.1
110th/2007	9.1	5.7	1.4
Senate			
99th/1985	0	0	2
100th/1987	0	0	2
101st/1989	0	0	3
102nd/1991	0	0	2
103rd/1993	1	0	2
104th/1995	1	0	2
105th/1997	1	0	2
106th/1999	0	0	2
107th/2001	0	0	2
108th/2003	1	0	2
109th/2005	1	2	2
110th/2007	1	3	2

Source: U.S. Census Bureau, *Statistical Abstract of the United States: 2006,* Table 395; *Members of Congress: Selected Characteristics, 1985–2003;* and updated by author.

Congress since 1985. Although African Americans constitute 12.7 percent of the voting-age population; Latinos, 14 percent (and growing); and Asian Americans, around 4 percent, these groups have traditionally been underrepresented in Congress, although more so in the past than at present.[5]

Not only has the underrepresentation of minority groups become a political issue, but it also has become a legal one, because the Fourteenth Amendment requires that states not deny their citizens equal protection of the laws. Equal protection, in turn, implies equal influence on and representation within the body that makes the laws.

Not until the 1960s, however, did the judiciary begin to address constitutional issues associated with minority representation. In 1962 the Supreme Court decided in the case of *Baker v. Carr* (369 U.S. 186) that malapportioned state legislatures may violate the equal protection clause of the Fourteenth Amendment. The Court's judgment that legislative districting can be a judicial matter, not simply a political one, opened the floodgates to suits by those who believed that the size and shape of their districts discriminated against them and denied them equal representation.

In cases arising from these lawsuits, the Supreme Court ruled that all districts that elect representatives, except for those for the U.S. Senate and the Electoral College, had to be apportioned on the basis of population according to the one person–one vote principle.[6] Additionally, the Court said that the size of congressional districts within a state cannot vary very much in size.[7]

The configuration of districts, however, wasn't subject to judicial scrutiny until 1986, when the Supreme Court ruled in the case of *Davis v. Bandemer* (478 U.S. 109) that partisan gerrymandering, the drafting of the boundaries of legislative districts to benefit the party in power, could also become a constitutional issue if it denied some people equal representation.

By the 1980s, the battle over representation had spread to all institutions of the national government. Congress got involved when it amended the Voting Rights Act in 1982 to encourage states to create districts in which racial and ethnic minorities were in the majority. Subsequently, the Justice Department pressured the states to follow the dictates of the legislation after the 1990 census and legislative apportionment were completed.

The redrafting of state congressional districts resulted in an increase in minority representation in Congress (see Table 3.1), but it also contributed to a more Republican, more conservative Congress for the next decade. Most of the newly crafted districts were in the South and Southwest. Because African Americans and Latinos are predominantly Democratic, concentrating them in so-called majority-minority districts resulted in more conservative, "whiter" districts in other parts of the state that benefited the Republicans at the expense of the Democrats.

The gain in GOP seats helped the Republicans win control of Congress in 1994 and allowed them to institute their more conservative policy agenda, which was opposed by the minority groups that the voting rights legislation was designed to help. Thus, in effect, the establishment of more districts in which a minority within the state became a majority within a district improved the descriptive representation for these minority groups but adversely affected their substantive representation.[8]

Legal challenges to these new minority districts were quickly initiated by Democrats and others who believed that they amounted to racial gerrymandering. A divided Supreme Court agreed. By a majority of only one, the Court held that race could not be a primary factor in drafting the boundaries of legislative districts.[9] The Court's decision was seen as a major setback for those desiring greater minority representation of elected officials.

Not only does minority underrepresentation contribute to a racial and ethnic bias, it also reinforces economic inequality within the political system given the lower levels of income and higher levels of unemployment among the two largest minority groups, African Americans and Hispanics. As noted in the previous chapter, economic inequality is evident in elections as well as in pressures on government.

In short, single-member districts with winner-take-all voting work to favor the demographic and partisan majorities in those districts. Aspiring politicians have to run on the Democratic or Republican labels if they are to have a reasonable chance of being elected in competitive districts. In noncompetitive ones, they have to vie for the nomination of the dominant party, whose primary is effectively equivalent to the general election.

Sometimes, to improve their chances, Democratic and Republican candidates in the general election seek a third-party endorsement to get an extra line on the ballot and garner support from those who do not identify with either of the major parties. But rarely does a candidate who is endorsed only by a third party, or who runs as an independent, win. As of this writing, there are only a very few members of Congress who have been elected as independents, and all but one had a major party affiliation before declaring themselves independent.

Improving Minority Representation

What can be done to improve demographic and partisan minority representation? There are several answers, but none of them affords much immediate hope of rectifying the representational problem for certain groups. The principal structural change that would contribute to minority representation would be to create multimember districts and use a proportional system of voting in which candidates are chosen roughly in proportion to the vote they or their parties receive.[10]

Many countries, especially those with a parliamentary system of government, such as Brazil, Israel, and Spain, have proportional voting. Others, such as Italy, Japan, and Mexico, mix proportional and plurality voting systems for their legislative representatives. (Table 3.2 lists the electoral systems of other democratic countries.)

TABLE 3.2 **Electoral Systems of Various Democratic Countries**	
Country	System of Representation
Australia	Single-member districts (SMD) but uses proportional representation (PR) for senate elections
Austria	Proportional representation
Belgium	Proportional representation
Canada	Single-member districts
France	Single-member districts
Germany	Combination of SMD and PR
Greece	Proportional representation
Ireland	Proportional representation
Israel	Proportional representation
Italy	Combination of SMD and PR
Japan	Combination of SMD and PR
S. Korea	Combination of SMD and PR
Mexico	Combination of SMD and PR
Slovakia	Proportional representation
South Africa	Proportional representation
Spain	Proportional representation
Sweden	Proportional representation
United Kingdom	Single-member districts
United States	Single-member districts

Source: Data from "Voting in Major Democracies." Copyright © 1999 The Center for Voting and Democracy.

Some of the states in the United States use proportional voting in multi-member districts to choose state legislators and city council and school board members. Its principal advantage is that demographic and partisan minorities can gain representation roughly in proportion to their strength within the electorate. It also encourages turnout, because representation is allocated according to the proportion of the vote that parties or candidates receive, thereby motivating all parties to try to maximize their vote. In noncompetitive, single-member districts, there is much less incentive to turn out to vote.

A proportional election might require more complicated voting instructions and more complex ballots, however. It also could make it easier for candidates and parties with extreme political views to gain representation in government. In Israel, which has a proportional representation system, the small religious parties, some of which have strong fundamentalist beliefs, have exercised disproportional power because their support has been necessary to the formation of a governing majority.

The main disadvantage of a proportional system is that it is much less likely that one party will constitute a legislative majority. This forces the leader of the party with the most seats to try to form a governing coalition with other parties. A multiparty coalition is more fragile than a coalition composed of a single party. A vote against the government on a major issue frequently topples the governing coalition and either forces new elections or requires a new person to try to form a viable government. It is also harder to pinpoint accountability in a multiparty government.

The other way to achieve fairer and more equal representation for minorities is to eliminate the allegiances and attitudes (some consider them biases and prejudices) that favor the majority. Although there is some evidence that the race, ethnicity, and religion of a candidate are not as important to today's voters as they were a decade or two ago, major attitudinal change within the population as a whole takes time and, judging by the demographic composition of elected public officials, has a long way to go.

AMERICAN POLITICS AND THE UNDERREPRESENTATION OF WOMEN

Women are a majority of the U.S. population today, composing almost 52 percent of the voting-age population. They are also a majority of the electorate, although this is of more recent origin. Women won the right to vote in 1919, but it took another sixty years for them to vote in equal proportion to men. Today, the proportion of women voting is actually slightly higher than that of men. Yet women represent a substantially lower proportion of members of Congress and of state legislative and top executive officials than do men. Why? (See Table 3.3.)

TABLE 3.3 **Women in Elective Office, 1975–2007 (percentages, rounded)**																
Level of Office	\	\	\	\	\	\	\	Year								
	1975	1977	1979	1981	1983	1985	1987	1989	1991	1993	1995	1997	1999	2001	2003	2005 2007
Congress	4	4	3	4	4	5	5	5	6	10	10	11	12	14	14	15 15
Statewide executive	10	10	11	11	11	14	14	14	18	22	26	26	28	27	26	27 27
State legislature	8	9	10	12	13	15	16	17	18	21	21	22	23	22	22	23 24

Source: Center for American Women and Politics, Eagleton Institute of Politics, Rutgers University. www.cawp. rutgers.edu/Facts3.html.

For most of the nation's existence, men dominated politics, and that domination to some extent still exists. It will take time for women to gain the electoral positions or professional status from which they can more successfully seek office. Moreover, women, who still take time off from their careers far more often than do men to raise a family, are disadvantaged politically for doing so. Finally, the incumbency advantage in congressional elections, so evident in the last several decades, has reduced electoral competition and extended the advantage of current elected officials, who are predominantly male. Nonetheless, women have made gains in recent years, as indicated in Table 3.3, and they are likely to continue to do so in part because they constitute a majority of the electorate and tend to be more supportive of women candidates than are men.

THE ELECTORAL COLLEGE SYSTEM AND THE OVERREPRESENTATION OF LARGE STATES

The Electoral College system also creates a representational bias. Initially designed as a dual compromise between the large and small states and between proponents of a federal structure and of a more centralized national government, it provided an alternative to other methods considered for choosing the president in accordance with a republican form of government: legislative selection or a direct popular vote. The framers did not want Congress to select the president because they feared that would jeopardize the executive's independence. Nor did they want the people to do so because they lacked faith in the average person's capacity to make an informed judgment and in the states' ability to conduct fair and honest elections. Moreover, the delegates at the Constitutional Convention wanted a leader, not a demagogue, a person selected on the basis of personal qualifications, not popular appeal. Finally, they hoped that their electoral system, which had electors voting at the same time in their respective states, would limit the potential for cabal, intrigue, and group dominance over the election outcome. Given the state of communications in 1787, distance provided safety, or so the framers thought.

According to the original plan, states would be allocated electors in proportion to their congressional representation in the House and Senate, thereby giving some advantage to the smallest states because of their equal representation in the Senate, an advantage that remains in place today. Wyoming, the least populous state, has a population that is only 1.5 percent that of California's but has electoral votes equal to 5.6 percent of its neighbor to the west. Other inequities result from the apportionment of House seats. Montana's population is twice that of Wyoming's, yet both states have the same representation in the Electoral College.

The original plan also allowed the states to choose their electors in any manner they saw fit. In the first election, in which ten states participated, half of them had their legislatures select the electors, the others chose them in some form of popular vote. After the electors were selected, the Constitution stated that they meet in their respective states and vote for two people, at least one of whom could not be an inhabitant of their state.

The person with the most votes would be president, provided the plurality winner had a majority[11]; the person with the second-most votes would be vice president. In this way the framers hoped to ensure that the two most qualified people would be chosen for the top two offices.

The system worked according to the original design for the first two elections in 1788 and 1792. Washington was the unanimous choice of the electors, but there was no consensus on the other candidate. John Adams, the eventual second choice, benefited from some informal caucusing prior to the vote.

Partisanship and Winner-Take-All Voting

The development of the party system in the mid-1790s transformed voting in the Electoral College. Instead of making an independent judgment, electors exercised a partisan one. They became partisan agents. Selected on the basis of their loyalty to a party, they were expected to vote for its candidates. And with a very few exceptions, they have. Since 1787, there have been only 11 "faithless electors" (out of a total of 21,915) who did not vote for their party's nominee as was expected. None of these errant votes affected the respective election's outcome.[12]

In the early part of the nineteenth century, there was a movement in many of the states to directly elect the electors. In 1800, ten of the fifteen states had their legislatures choose the electors. By 1832, all but South Carolina elected them by popular vote. That state began to do so in 1864.

The popular selection of electors made the Electoral College more democratic than it had been and was intended to be. However, the movement of states to a **winner-take-all system**, in which partisan slates of electors competed against one another, created a plurality-rule scenario. It also created advantages for some states and disadvantages for others.

The large states, whose electoral votes are magnified by winner-take-all voting, benefit the most. Within these states, groups that are geographically concentrated and unified in their voting behavior also are helped because they can exercise an influence disproportionate to their numbers. Moreover, these groups tend to get candidates to focus on their issues and the positions they favor: Cubans living in Florida want to maintain sanctions on the regime of Fidel Castro, Jews in New York want aid and support for Israel, and Hispanics in the Southwest are concerned about immigrant rights and a guest worker program. The list goes on.

If the large states were equally competitive, the electoral system would encourage candidates to concentrate their campaigns in these states. The seven largest states combined have 36 percent of the entire electoral vote. But some of these states are not as competitive as some of the middle-size and smaller ones. And in this age of polling and targeting, candidates concentrate their campaigns, advertising, and voter mobilization efforts in states that are the most competitive. At the beginning of an election cycle, this can be as many as one third of the states; by the end that number is reduced to single digits. In 2000 and 2004, the five major battleground states that received the most attention and campaign activities were Florida, Michigan, Ohio, Pennsylvania, and Wisconsin.

Concentrated campaigning makes strategic sense, but it also undercuts the democratic and national character of presidential elections. It undermines the democratic process by discouraging turnout in the non-battleground states and by neglecting or downplaying the issues and interests of people who live in those states. It makes a mockery of the only national election in the United States for the only nationally elected public officials, the president and vice president. If that election were truly national, then the campaigns should be national as well, and the parties should devote their efforts to getting all eligible voters out to vote, not just those in the key battleground states. Moreover, to create or sustain a national agenda, a national mandate, and a national coalition for governing, it is necessary to think in national terms on issues, make national appeals, and mount a national campaign effort with candidate appearances, advertising, and grassroots activities in all of the states.

In addition to the unequal representation in the Electoral College, made worse by the general ticket system that produces a winner-take-all outcome in forty-eight of the fifty states and the District of Columbia, and an unequal campaign effort that focuses increasingly on the key battleground states, the Electoral College system also can produce an undemocratic result. Three times in American history, in 1876, 1888, and 2000, the winning candidate did not receive a plurality of the vote.[13] Many more times, the shift of a relatively small number of votes in a few states would have changed the outcome of the election.

The most likely situation in which the candidate with the most popular votes would lose in the Electoral College is that of very close competition between the major parties, along with a strong third-party candidate who captures sufficient electoral votes to deny the leading candidate a majority. The elections of 1968, 1992, and 2004 could have produced such a scenario but did not. The election of 2000 did.

Table 3.4 indicates the six states in which the winning candidate's margin of victory was less than the votes that third-party candidates Ralph Nader and Pat Buchanan received. According to the Voter News Survey exit poll, 47 percent of Nader voters said they would have voted for Gore, 21 percent for Bush, and 30 percent indicated that they would not have voted at all. Although Buchanan received a much smaller vote than Nader, most of his supporters indicated that they would have voted for Bush. Thus, had Nader not run, Gore would have won Florida (although probably not New Hampshire) and, with Florida's twenty-five electoral votes, he would have won the election. Had Buchanan not run but Nader remained in the race, Bush would have likely

TABLE 3.4 **The Potential Impact of Third-Party Candidates on the 2000 Presidential Election**

States	Nader Vote	Bush's Margin	Number of Electoral Votes
Florida	97,488	537	25
New Hampshire	22,188	7,211	4
	Buchanan Vote	Gore's Margin	
Iowa	5,731	4,144	7
New Mexico	1,392	366	5
Oregon	7,063	6,765	7
Wisconsin	11,471	5,708	11

Source: Federal Election Commission, "2000 Presidential General Election Results by State," www.fec.gov/pubrec/fe2000/2000presge.htm.

picked up three to four additional states. Had they both not run, Gore would have been advantaged because of the size of the Nader vote and probably would have been elected.

If the Electoral College provides unequal representation to the states, if this system encourages the candidates to mount highly concentrated campaigns in only a few of the states, and if the election can result in an undemocratic outcome, then why keep it?

Supporters contend that it has worked reasonably well. It has been decisive and reflective of the popular vote most of the time, even enlarging the winning candidate's margin of victory in the Electoral College. They claim that the system reflects the country's federal structure, requires the winner to have support across the country, protects concentrated minorities, and compartmentalizes and thereby reduces the impact of fraudulent voting practices.

Opponents note that the system has not worked as the framers intended since the two-party system developed, and has produced three non-plurality winners and close calls in several other elections. They contend that it was never based on the principle of federalism, nor would its demise affect the federal character of the United States, and that its benefits to any one group are offset by the disadvantages to other groups, including other minorities, thereby undermining the principle of equal protection of the laws.

Nor do its opponents perceive the electoral system as more likely to contain the evils of cabal, intrigue, and voter fraud. On the contrary, they argue, the more complex the electoral system, the more likely it is to be subject to deals among the electors and those who support them; the smaller the electoral unit, the more likely a dispute over relatively few votes could make a difference. They point to Florida in 2000 as an example. In the national popular vote, Gore won about 540,000; in Florida, the final tally gave Bush a 537-vote victory. Which of these two situations, the national vote or the Florida vote, is more likely to result in controversy?

Reforming the Electoral College System

What are the options? Most Americans favor a direct popular vote. Gallup polls preceding the last two presidential elections report that 61 percent of the population supports a constitutional amendment to elect the president by direct popular vote; thirty-five percent oppose such an amendment.[14] There is a partisan cleavage in the support for this reform, with 73 percent of Democrats and 66 percent of independents in favor but only 46 percent of Republicans.[15]

In 1969, the House of Representatives voted for a constitutional amendment to directly elect the president, but the Senate did not follow suit. In 1979, fifty-one Senators supported a joint resolution for a direct popular vote, not the two thirds necessary for a constitutional amendment. Since then, members of Congress have repeatedly introduced direct election amendments, but to no avail.

The tradition of the Electoral College, the reluctance of states that are advantaged to change it, and the Republican Party's hesitancy, based in part on philosophy, the beliefs of its partisans, and the increasing number of Hispanics coming into the electorate and their current inclination to vote Democratic, have thus far prevented a direct election amendment from being passed by Congress and put to the states for a vote. Even in the aftermath of the controversial 2000 election, Florida vote, and Supreme Court decision, Congress, controlled by the Republicans, did not even hold public hearings on such a change.

Congress's reluctance to address the issue, combined with the increasing public dissatisfaction with the Electoral College and the way campaigns are conducted within it, have prompted a variety of citizen proposals for changing the current system. One of the most innovative is a state-based plan for electing the president by a national, popular vote. States would enter into an interstate compact in which they would agree to join together to pass identical laws that awarded all of their electoral votes to the presidential candidate who received the most popular votes in the country as a whole. The compact would not take effect, however, until it was agreed to by enough states to cast a majority of the electoral votes, thereby ensuring that the candidates with the most popular votes would win in the Electoral College.[16] The practical merits of this proposal are that it does not necessitate a constitutional amendment, which is unlikely at this time, and would continue to allow the states to retain the authority for determining their electors and how they voted.

A direct election of the president and vice president would certainly be consistent with a democratic election process; it would encourage turnout across the country, not just in the battleground states; it would prevent a discrepancy between the popular vote and the electoral vote; and it would force the candidates to campaign in population centers, appeal to urban-suburban interests, and provide a national agenda and more justification for claiming a national mandate.

Critics, however, see a direct, popular vote, particularly a close one, as more likely to nationalize and thereby aggravate such problems as voter (in)eligibility, possible vote fraud, and vote tabulation errors like the ones in Florida in 2000. A national election would probably cost more and might take longer. Less populated rural areas, particularly in the Mountain states and the Midwest, might be neglected. An election decided primarily by voters concentrated on the Atlantic and Pacific coasts would not provide the geographic balance and federal character that the current system provides.

Finally, a plurality winner might not receive a majority of the votes as the Electoral College requires today. In seven out of the twenty-five elections in the twentieth century and one out of two in the twenty-first century, the winner did not receive 50 percent of the popular vote. One way to deal with this problem is to have a run-off election between the top two candidates if neither receives a majority. Another is to have Congress select the winner from the top two vote-getters, and a third alternative would be to elect the plurality winner, provided that candidate received at least 40 percent of the total vote.[17] Only Abraham Lincoln in 1860 fell below this percentage. In a four-candidate contest, he received 39.8 percent of the vote.

Other proposals, such as allocating a state's electoral votes in proportion to the popular vote that the candidates received in that state, have been advanced. Known as the **proportional plan**, such a voting system would more closely reflect the diversity of views across the country and encourage turnout among the population, but it also might result in a proliferation of votes among different candidates and parties, thereby making it more difficult for any one to get a majority. Third-party and independent candidates would exercise more influence under a proportional voting system. Moreover, unless all the states move to such a system those that allocate their electoral votes in proportion to their popular votes would be disadvantaged. Candidates would not concentrate their efforts on proportional voting states because the payoff in electoral votes would be much smaller than in winner-take-all states— a principal reason that Colorado voters rejected a proportional voting initiative in 2004.

Another option, known as the **district plan**, currently is used in the states of Maine and Nebraska. This option gives two at-large electoral votes to the candidate who wins the popular vote in the state and one electoral vote to the candidate who wins the vote in each legislative district in the state. A district plan for allocating electoral votes would produce closer presidential elections than the current system, but it also might align the presidential election more closely to that of Congress, particularly the House of Representatives. Moreover, the uncompetitive nature of most congressional districts would not provide incentives for candidates to campaign in these districts nor would it motivate people living within them to vote. Thus far in both states that use the district voting system, the same party has won the statewide and district votes.

Table 3.5 lists the Electoral College vote since 1960 under the present system and the vote that would have resulted if each of the other systems had been employed on a national level. The results of only one of these elections would have changed. Under both the proportional and the district systems, Nixon probably would have defeated Kennedy in 1960.[18] In 1976 Carter and Ford would have tied under the district plan, but a Democratic Congress probably would have selected Carter anyway. In 2000 Bush wins in every voting system except direct election.

Despite the results in 2000, the present Electoral College system, with its winner-take-all voting in forty-eight of the fifty states, has tended to enlarge the winning candidate's margin of victory, thereby giving the victor a larger mandate for governing than that candidate would otherwise have. However, acting on the basis of such a mandate can be hazardous as President George W. Bush discovered in 2005 when his second-term domestic agenda priorities of Social Security privatization and immigration reform met with public and congressional opposition. The current system also has compartmentalized voting problems although in 2000 that compartmentalization extended the indecisive outcome for five weeks.

CONSEQUENCES OF REPRESENTATIONAL BIAS

Representational inequalities have contributed to public policy outcomes that favor those who are already economically and educationally advantaged. It also affects their attitudes toward government. It would be expected that those who perceive of themselves as less well represented in government would be more critical and less trusting of that government. And they are.[19]

Differences in perceptions of what government should do are also apparent. Although two out of three Americans believe that the government is doing too little to address the issue of poverty in the United States, a higher percentage of African Americans (85 percent) share this belief than non-Hispanic whites (64 percent).[20] Similarly, a recent Gallup Poll found majority and minority populations differing over the role the government should play in improving the economic and social position of those in the minority (as indicated in Table 3.6).

Demographic differences are also apparent in the policy priorities that people think government should have. Although there is a general consensus that government should help the needy (57 percent), there is partisan disagreement over the extent to which the government should do so. Democrats are more supportive of a larger government role (68 percent) than are Republicans (46 percent).[21] In general, men assign a lower priority to government's involve-

TABLE 3.5 **Voting for President, 1956–2004: Four Methods for Aggregating the Votes**

Year		Electoral College	Proportional Plan	District Plan	Direct Election
1956	Eisenhower	457.0	296.7	411.0	57.4
	Stevenson	73.0	227.2	120.0	42.0
	Others	1.0	7.1	0	0.6
1960	Nixon	219.0	266.1	278.0	49.5
	Kennedy	303.0	265.6	245.0	49.8
	Byrd	15.0	5.3	14.0	0.7
1964	Goldwater	52.0	213.6	72.0	38.5
	Johnson	486.0	320.0	466.0	61.0
	Others	0	3.9	0	0.5
1968	Nixon	301.0	231.5	289.0	43.2
	Humphrey	191.0	225.4	192.0	42.7
	Wallace	46.0	78.8	57.0	13.5
	Others	0	2.3	0	0.6
1972	Nixon	520.0	330.3	474.0	60.7
	McGovern	17.0	197.5	64.0	37.5
	Others	1.0	10.0	0	1.8
1976	Ford	240.0	258.0	269.0	48.0
	Carter	297.0	269.7	269.0	50.1
	Others	1.0	10.2	0	1.9
1980	Reagan	489.0	272.9	396.0	50.7
	Carter	49.0	220.9	142.0	41.0
	Anderson	0	35.3	0	6.6
	Others	0	8.9	0	1.7

ment in healthcare, education, and the concerns of the elderly than do women.[22]

Finally, there are variations in attitudes toward government power: individuals who are white, male, and Republican are more likely to believe that the government has too much power; conversely, women, minorities, and poorer, less educated people believe that the government should exercise more power.

TABLE 3.5 **Voting for President, 1956–2004: Four Methods for Aggregating the Votes** *(continued)*				
Year	Electoral College	Proportional Plan	District Plan	Direct Election
1984 Reagan	525.0	317.6	468.0	58.8
Mondale	13.0	216.6	70.0	40.6
Others	0	3.8	0	0
1988 Bush	426.0	287.8	379.0	53.4
Dukakis	111.0	244.7	159.0	45.6
Others	1.0	5.5	0	1.0
1992 Bush	168.0	203.3	214.0	37.5
Clinton	370.0	231.6	324.0	43.0
Perot	0	101.8	0	18.9
Others	0	1.3	0	0.6
1996 Clinton	379.0	262.0	345.0	49.2
Dole	159.0	219.9	193.0	40.7
Perot	0	48.8	0	8.4
Others	0	7.3	0	1.7
2000 Bush	271.0	260.3	288.0	47.9
Gore	266.0*	260.0	250.0	48.4
Others	0	17.7	0	3.7
2004 Bush	286.0	275.2	317.0	50.7
Kerry	251.0†	258.3	221.0	48.3
Others	0	4.5	0	1.0

* One Democratic elector in the District of Columbia cast a blank ballot.
† One Democratic elector in Minnesota cast a vote for Edwards for president and Kerry for vice president.

Source: From *The Road to the White House, 2008: The Politics of Presidential Elections,* by Stephen Wayne. Copyright © 2008. Reprinted with permission of Wadsworth, an imprint of Thomson Learning: www. thomsrights.com. Fax 800-730-2215.

The former see the government as an inhibitor of individual initiative; the latter see it as an equalizer.

These findings carry over to government performance. Polls following the 2000 election indicated that a majority of African Americans believed that Bush stole the election, compared with only 17 percent of the white population.[23] African Americans also have been less satisfied than most Americans

---

TABLE 3.6 Role of Government in Helping Minorities

Question: "How much of a role, if any, do you think government should have in trying to improve the social and economic position of blacks and other minority groups in this country?"

	Major Role	Minor Role	No Role	No Opinion
National Adults				
June 2005	37	44	17	2
June 2004	40	45	14	1
Non-Hispanic Whites				
June 2005	26	52	21	1
June 2004	32	51	16	1
Blacks				
June 2005	71	21	6	2
June 2004	68	22	9	1
Hispanics				
June 2005	64	20	11	5
June 2004	67	21	8	4

Source: Gallup Poll, www.gallup.com/content/default/aspx?ci+1687&pg=4.

---

with the direction in which the country is heading, and they are much more disapproving of Bush's job performance than the country as a whole, especially in light of the government's tepid response to the victims of Hurricane Katrina.[24] Table 3.7 indicates the racial and gender differences on the government response and the racial overtones to the natural disaster.

What do these findings have to do with representational bias? The answer is that those at the lower end of the socioeconomic scale, who are less well represented, turn to government the most because they have nowhere else to go.[25]

LEGAL QUALIFICATIONS AND DEMOCRATIC OUTCOMES

In a democratic political system, people should be able to select the candidate of their choice. In the United States, however, legal qualifications for office can and do inhibit that selection. The most controversial qualification for office is term limits, which prevent the electorate from reelecting a popular and experienced incumbent who has served the maximum number of years prescribed by law. Term limits currently apply to the president and to state legislators in sixteen states. Many state constitutions limit governors' terms as well.

TABLE 3.7	**Racial Perceptions of the Government's Response to Hurricane Katrina**

Would the government's response have been faster if most victims had been white?

	Total	White	Black
Faster	26	17	66
Same	68	77	27
Don't know	6	6	7

Does the government's response show racial inequality is still a major problem?

	Total	White	Black
Yes	38	32	71
No	50	56	22
Don't know	12	12	7

Source: "The Black and White of Public Opinion," Pew Research Center for the People and the Press, October 31, 2005, www.people-press.org/commentary/display.php3?AnalysisID=121.

Term Limits

The Twenty-second Amendment, ratified in 1951, limits a president to a maximum of two elected terms in office, or to only one if the president serves more than half his predecessor's term. Lyndon Johnson, who became president after John F. Kennedy's assassination in November 1963, would have been eligible for two elected terms; Gerald Ford, who succeeded Richard Nixon in August 1974, was eligible for only one.

The movement for term limits, which peaked in the 1990s, was spurred by dissatisfaction with the performance of government and the behavior of public officials. The public's perception is that elected officials lose touch with the people who elected them, that they are unduly influenced by special interest lobbyists, that they become increasingly self-interested and self-promoting, and that they use the perquisites of their office to gain an unfair reelection advantage. Thus, the argument is that the only effective way to ensure turnover in office is to limit the terms of those elected.[26]

Those who support this argument contend that legislatures were initially designed to be popular assemblies in which concerned citizens represented their brethren to formulate and oversee public policy. The idea of an assembly composed of political professionals with job security gained through significant incumbency advantages is anathema to this original design and its intent to keep government close to the governed. Rotation in office keeps elected officials more in touch with the needs and interests of the electorate. It also creates more nonincumbency elections in which competition is stimulated and more voters turn out. It is argued as well that term limits prevent special interest groups from becoming too cozy with those in power and thus less likely to use their resources to "buy, rent, or influence" elected officials. The recent sandal in which Washington lobbyist Jack Abramoff provided benefits to members of Congress in exchange for their help in satisfying the public policy interests of his clients is a case in point.

The anti-term limits crowd contends that limits are unnecessary, undesirable, and undemocratic.[27] They are *unnecessary* because there is sufficient turnover in most legislatures. Critics argue that term limits are *undesirable* because they result in the election of less knowledgeable and less experienced public officials who lack the skills to be effective in office.[28] Inadequate information and understanding of the problem can result in unwise and ill-considered public policy decisions and on overdependence on staff—the so-called unelected representatives, who are not directly accountable to the electorate—and also may require longer learning periods during which government may not operate effectively.

Finally, opponents of term limits contend that they are *undemocratic* because they prevent the electorate from reelecting a particular representative who may have served well in office. Moreover, such limits remove the incentive for an incumbent to be responsive in his or her last term and may contribute to the phenomenon of declining influence in that term.

The Twenty-second Amendment is a good example of the negative impact term limits can have. The amendment that prohibits presidents from running for a third term weakens them as the second term progresses, particularly in their last two years. The term **lame duck** is frequently used to describe their predicament. As power flows away from them, they usually seek refuge in ceremony, travel, and speeches; concentrate on foreign policy; and make much more use of their unilateral instruments of executive authority.

Supporters of the amendment believe that the loss-of-power argument is overblown, and that presidents are reelected to continue their policies already in place, not to create a lot of new domestic programs. The greater danger, they contend, is that the cult of personality can upset the balance of power and effectively undercut the democratic electoral process as Republicans claim that it did when Franklin Delano Roosevelt was reelected in 1940 and 1944 after having served two full terms in office.

Some states also sought to impose restrictions on how long their members of Congress could serve. Not only did they believe that turnover would bring new ideas to government, but they also wanted to provide more electoral opportunities for their term-limited state legislators. The Supreme Court, however, ruled that state-imposed limits on members of Congress were unconstitutional because they added an additional qualification for eligibility to serve in Congress, thereby conflicting with Article I of the Constitution, which specifies only age and residence requirements for members of Congress. The Court's decision effectively derailed the term-limits movement.

Age, Residency, and Citizenship Requirements

In addition to term limits, there are several other constitutional qualifications that limit public choice. At the national level, these include minimum age and residency requirements for both candidates for Congress and the presidency, and a native-born requirement for president. Are such qualifications still necessary and desirable? Does it make sense to have a minimum age requirement but no requirement for maximum age? Ronald Reagan, the oldest president, suffered memory loss in his second term. Strom Thurmond, the oldest member of Congress, was reelected at the age of ninety-two and stood fourth in line for the presidency as president pro tempore of the Senate when the GOP controlled that body. About one third of the electorate thought that Senator Robert Dole's age of seventy-four was a factor that could affect their voting decision when considering the 1996 Republican presidential candidate.

The president has to be a native-born American. Being born in the United States might have been important in 1787, when the nation was young and patriotic ties to it were weak, but is it relevant today? Several prominent Americans have been precluded by this requirement from becoming president. They held high positions in government, were in the line of succession, and would have been considered qualified in every other respect, but they were born in other countries. Included among these individuals were secretaries of state Henry Kissinger (born in Germany) and Madeleine Albright (born in Czechoslovakia).

Similarly, what is the purpose of a residency requirement, particularly in an age of international commerce in which business executives employed by multinational corporations often have to spend considerable time living abroad? Although the Constitution mandates residence in a state before a person can represent that state, it is still possible to achieve residency by moving there and declaring residence at the time of the vote. Former attorney general Robert Kennedy and then first lady Hillary Rodham Clinton both moved to New York to be candidates for the U.S. Senate. Both were elected, although Kennedy hadn't lived in the state long enough to vote in the election in which he won.

SUMMARY: REPRESENTATIONAL DILEMMAS IN A NUTSHELL

American democracy rests on the concept of representative government. In such a government, all citizens have the right to be equally and fairly represented. But theory and practice diverge. Structural biases affect the representative character of the political system.

Plurality voting in single-member districts overrepresents majorities at the expense of minorities, but it also contributes to stability and accountability in government by maximizing the number of seats that the majority party holds. A proportional voting system in multimember districts increases minority representation, but frequently at the cost of coalition government.

Women are underrepresented but not as a consequence of structural bias. Their failure to achieve representation equal to their proportion of the population is largely a residue of the restrictions placed on women's suffrage before 1920, traditional voting prejudices, and differing gender career patterns.

Winner-take-all voting in the Electoral College inflates the clout of the large states and the cohesive groups within them. It also encourages candidates to concentrate their campaigns in the most competitive states (determined by historical voting patterns and current public opinion polling) and neglect most of the rest of the country. As a consequence, presidential elections are national, but presidential campaigns are not.

If states with more than half the electoral votes required their electors to vote for the national popular vote winner, an undemocratic result could not occur in the Electoral College. Under the current arrangement, however, it can and has. It also could occur if states were to apportion their electors on the basis of statewide and legislative district voting or on the proportion of the vote that candidates received in the state, although the results of the Electoral College vote would probably be closer than it has been in the winner-take-all system.

The underrepresentation of certain groups has been a source of discontent to them and has affected their attitudes toward government and public policy. Those who are economically disadvantaged and thus underrepresented in the electorate and in government tend to want a larger and more active government, particularly in the economic sphere, than those who have greater material resources and educational opportunities and thus tend to be well represented.

Electoral and representational outcomes also are affected by restrictions placed on eligibility. Of the term, age, and residency requirements that shrink the pool of eligible candidates, limits on tenure are the most controversial and seem to have the greatest impact on the functioning of government.

To address representational bias and the policy problems that flow from it, the majority has to be more cognizant of the need for minority representation and willing to adjust the electoral system or its voting behavior to achieve it. A tall order, to be sure.

Now It's Your Turn

Discussion Questions

1. Is it possible to have a democratic electoral system in which the majority decides and the minority is fairly represented?
2. If women constitute a majority of the voting-age population, why are fewer women than men elected to positions in government?
3. Is it important for a representative democracy to have demographic, issue, and ideological groups represented in proportion to their percentages in the population? If so, how can this representation be achieved? If not, why not?

4. Why do people who are "worse off," less well represented, and benefit the least from government want government to do more, whereas those who are "better off," better represented, and as a result, more likely to benefit from public policy today want government to do less in the economic sphere?
5. What consequences do you think a direct election of the president would have on the electorate, the electoral process, and government and public policy?
6. Are age, residency, and place-of-birth requirements consistent with a democratic electoral process in which the people are supposed to be able to choose their elected leaders?

Topics for Debate

Challenge or defend the following statements:

1. Descriptive representation is irrelevant and may be harmful to substantive representation and effective government.
2. The system of plurality voting in single-member districts is inconsistent with the Supreme Court's interpretation of the Fourteenth Amendment's equal protection clause.
3. The underrepresentation of women in elected positions does not adversely affect public policy.
4. The direct election of the president is neither necessary nor desirable.
5. Term limits are a good idea and should be imposed for all elected officials.
6. Age qualifications for office are unnecessary and undesirable and should be eliminated.

Exercise

A congressional committee is holding a hearing on how to improve representation in the national government. As an expert on representational issues, you've been invited to testify. Your assignment is to prepare and present your testimony. In your testimony, note the following:

1. how well the society is currently represented in the federal government and the public policy it makes today,
2. the principal groups that suffer representational bias,
3. the source of their representational problems and what it would take to fix them,
4. the pros and cons of changing the system to remove these representational problems (including any unintended consequences that might occur), and
5. your recommendation to the committee on what (if anything) it should propose to Congress as a legislative solution to the problem.

INTERNET RESOURCES

- Center for Voting and Democracy: www.fairvote.org
  Contains a wealth of information on various voting systems, especially proportional representation.
- National Popular Vote: www.nationalpopularvote.com
  A proposal and arguments for the direct election of the president accomplished by an interstate compact and not by a constitutional amendment.
- The Pew Research Center for the People and the Press: www.people-press.org
  Conducts surveys on public knowledge, attitudes, and opinions toward candidates, government, and the media.
- U.S. Term Limits: www.termlimits.org
  A Web site devoted to promoting term limits. It provides information on states who have legislated or had initiatives on term limits.
- Voter Information Services: www.vis.org
  Provides a database on congressional voting that can be downloaded for analysis.

SELECTED READINGS

Abbot, David W., and James P. Levine. *Wrong Winner: The Coming Debacle in the Electoral College.* New York: Praeger, 1991.

Best, Judith. *The Choice of the People? Debating the Electoral College.* Lanham, Md.: Rowman and Littlefield, 1996.

Glennon, Michael J. *When No Majority Rules: The Electoral College and Presidential Selection.* Washington, D.C.: CQ Press, 1993.

Guinier, Lani. *The Tyranny of the Majority.* New York: Free Press, 1994.

Hardaway, Robert M. *The Electoral College and the Constitution: The Case for Preserving Federalism.* Westport, Conn.: Praeger, 1993.

Jackson, John S., III, J. C. Brown, and David Bositis. "Herbert McClosky and Friends Revisited: 1980 Democratic and Republican Elites Compared to the Mass Public." *American Politics Quarterly* 10 (1982): 158–180.

Lublin, David. *The Paradox of Representation.* Princeton: Princeton University Press, 1997.

Malbin, Michael J., and Gerald Benjamin, eds. *Limiting Legislative Terms.* Washington, D.C.: CQ Press, 1992.

Nye, Joseph S., Jr., Philip D. Zelikow, and David King. *Why People Don't Trust Government.* Cambridge, Mass.: Harvard University Press, 1997.

Pitkin, Hanna F. *The Concept of Representation.* Berkeley: University of California Press, 1967.

Swain, Carol M. *Black Faces, Black Interests: The Representation of African Americans in Congress.* Cambridge, Mass.: Harvard University Press, 1993.

Warren, Mark E. *Democracy and Trust.* Cambridge: Cambridge University Press, 1999.

Will, George. *Restoration: Congress, Term Limits, and the Recovery of Deliberative Democracy.* New York: Free Press, 1992.

NOTES

1. Edmund Burke, "Speech to the Electors," *Burke's Politics,* quoted in Hanna F. Pitkin, *The Concept of Representation* (Berkley: University of California Press, 1967), 171.

2. In a national survey conducted for the Center on Policy Attitudes, people were asked if "elected officials would make better decisions if they thought more deeply about what they think is right." Almost 80 percent of the respondents said "yes." They were also asked, "When your Representative in Congress votes on an issue, which should be more important: the way voters in your district feel about that issue, or the Representative's own principles and judgment about what is best for the country?" A majority of 68.5 percent answered "the way voters feel." Steven Kull, "Expecting More Say: The American Public on Its Role in Government," Center on Policy Attitudes, May 10, 1999, 35. Frank Newport, "Americans Want Leaders to Pay Attention to Public Opinion, But Still Skeptical of Standard Sample Sizes Used by Pollsters," Gallup Poll, October 12, 2005, www.brain.gallup.com/content/default.aspx?ci=19138&pg=1.

3. "Polling and Democracy," *Public Perspective* (July/August 2001): 24. They also believe that public officials place too much attention on polls. Gallup Poll, "Public Opinion Polls," April 15, 1999, www.gallup.com/poll/indicators/indpolls.asp.

4. "Polling and Democracy," 23.

5. U.S. Census Bureau, *Statistical Abstract of the United States: 2006* (Washington, D.C.: Government Printing Office, 2006), Table 13: Resident Population by Sex, Race, and Hispanic Origin for 2004, 15.

6. *Reynolds v. Sims,* 377 u.s. 533 (1964).

7. *Wesberry v. Sanders,* 376 u.s. 1 (1964).

8. For an excellent discussion of this quandary, see David Lublin, *The Paradox of Representation* (Princeton: Princeton University Press, 1997).

9. *Shaw v. Reno,* 509 u.s. 630 (1993); *Miller v. Johnson,* 115 S.Ct. 2475 (1995); *Bush v. Vera,* 116 S.Ct. 1941 (1996), and *Meadows v. Moon,* 117 S.Ct. 2501 (1997).

10. Lani Guinier, a law professor and unsuccessful nominee for assistant attorney general for civil rights in the Clinton administration, argues in her book *The Tyranny of the Majority* (New York: Free Press, 1994) that only with cumulative voting in multimember districts can the minority hope to achieve fair and equal representation. Guinier's proposal is to give citizens as many votes as there are candidates and allow them to distribute their votes any way they choose. They could, for example, give all the votes to one of the candidates, perhaps a person who shares their demographic characteristics or attitudinal views, or they could divide them among several of the candidates. Guinier contends that such a system would accord with the one person–one vote principle but would not involve the state in racial districting. Without such a system, she contends that the prejudices of the majority will dominate. This proposal, which conservatives found alarming, forced Guinier to withdraw her nomination when she failed to obtain sufficient support in the Senate.

11. If no candidate received a majority, the House of Representatives would choose from among the top five candidates. The Twelfth Amendment later reduced this number to three when it provided for separate ballots for the president and vice president. In the event of a House election, voting would be by state, with each state delegation possessing one vote.

12. *Every Vote Equal: A State-based Plan for Electing the President* (Los Angeles: National Popular Vote Press, 2006), 85.

13. In 1876 a dispute over twenty electoral votes and the resolution of it by a congressionally established commission resulted in the election of Republican Rutherford B. Hayes, who had fewer popular votes than his opponent, Samuel J. Tilden. In 1888 Republican Benjamin Harrison received a majority of the electoral votes; his opponent, President Grover Cleveland, received a majority of the popular votes. In 2000 Republican George W. Bush won a majority of the electoral vote; Democrat Al Gore had a plurality of the popular vote.

14. Darren K. Carlson, "Public Flunks Electoral College System," Gallup Poll, November 2, 2004, www.gallup.com/contents/default.aspx?ci=13918.

15. Ibid.

16. *Every Vote Equal,* 243–274.

17. Two elections would be costly, might result in the candidate who came in second in the first round winning in the second, and would be time-consuming, thereby shortening the transition.

18. In Alabama and Mississippi, fourteen unpledged electors voted for Democratic senator Harry Byrd of Virginia.

19. *Deconstructing Distrust* (Washington, D.C.: Pew Research Center for the People and the Press, 1998), 20, and 2004 data from National Election Studies, www.umich.edu/~nesguide/nesguide/toptable/tab5a_1.

20. Rakshoa Arora, "Americans Dissatisfied with Government's Efforts on Poverty," Gallup Poll, October 25, 2005, www.gallup.com/content/default.aspi?ci=19138&pg=2.

21. Pew Research Center for the People and the Press, "The American Public Opinions and Values in a 51%–48% Nation," 22.

22. Pew Research Center, *Deconstructing Distrust,* 46.

23. Gallup Poll, "Seven out of 10 Americans Accept Bush as Legitimate President," July 17, 2001, www.gallup.com/poll/releases/pr010717.asp.

24. Gallup Poll, "With the Advent of Bush Administration, Blacks Have Become More Negative about All Three Branches of Government," July 10, 2001.

25. Representational bias is also a factor in perceptions of how much attention those in office pay to certain groups. In its surveys of public opinion, the Pew Research Center for the People and the Press found "striking differences among racial, gender, and income groups over the level of government attention afforded their own social groups and whether this amount was appropriate." Pew Research Center for the People and the Press, "The American Public Opinions and Values," 22.

26. For arguments in favor of term limits, see Mark Petracca, "Rotation in Office: The History of an Idea," in *Limiting Legislative Terms,* Michael J. Malbin and Gerald Benjamin, eds. (Washington, D.C.: CQ Press, 1992), 19–52, and George Will, *Restoration: Congress, Term Limits, and the Recovery of Deliberative Democracy* (New York: Free Press, 1992).

27. Malbin and Benjamin, *Limiting Legislative Terms,* 198–221.

28. John R. Hibbing, *Congressional Careers: Contours of Life in the U.S. House of Representatives* (Chapel Hill: University of North Carolina Press, 1991), 180, and John M. Carey, *Term Limits and Legislative Representation* (Cambridge: Cambridge University Press, 1996), 193–194.

chapter 4

Has Money Corrupted Our Electoral Process?

Did you know that. . .

- Richard Nixon spent six times as much money in his last race for the presidency in 1972 as he spent for his first in 1960?
- almost $4 billion was spent on the 2004 federal elections?
- the more money incumbents spend in the general election the more likely they are in trouble?
- despite the prohibition on the national parties raising soft money in the last presidential election, they still raised more money than they had in any other election cycle?
- the big contributors in the 2004 election were not by and large the same people and groups that made large soft money contributions four years earlier?
- there may be no causal relationship between campaign spending and electoral success?
- the party that controls Congress tends to receive a larger proportion of its funds from political action committees (PACs)?
- most people do not contribute to political campaigns; only about 11 percent of taxpayers today check off the box that allows $3 of their taxes to go to a Federal Election Campaign Fund?
- foreign governments and multinational corporations spend much more money lobbying elected officials than they do trying to influence the outcome of elections?
- people believe that members of Congress are more beholden to their large contributors than to their own electoral constituents?
- the Federal Election Commission is permanently immobilized by its partisan composition of three Democrats and three Republicans, which makes it difficult to resolve controversial partisan political issues?

Is this any way to run a democratic election?

MONEY AND DEMOCRATIC ELECTIONS

What does money have to do with democracy? The answer is "a lot" if it:

1. gives wealthy people and groups an unfair advantage in influencing the election;
2. affects who votes and how they vote;
3. conditions who runs for office and who does not;
4. affects information the electorate receives about the candidates and their issue positions;
5. affects public perceptions of how the electoral system is working, whether it is fair or unfair, and whether it contributes to effective government in a democracy.

Money can and does affect the democratic character of elections in the United States. If a basic tenet of an electoral democracy is the right of every adult citizen to have an equal opportunity to influence an election outcome, then the unequal distribution of resources within society threatens that right. Does the average citizen have the same opportunity to affect an election campaign as multibillionaires Bill Gates and George Soros do, or to run for office, as multimillionaires George W. Bush and John Kerry did in 2004? Do two equally qualified candidates have the same chance to win if one is wealthy and willing to use a personal fortune to advance his/her political ambitions while the other does not have the wealth to do so? Is everyone equally protected by the laws if some people are able to gain more access to policymakers by virtue of their campaign contributions and expenditures than those who cannot or do not contribute?

The difficulty in providing equal opportunities for all citizens stems in large part from the value Americans place on personal freedom and private property. The Constitution protects the right of people to use their own resources as they see fit, provided they do so legally. Moreover, the Supreme Court has equated campaign spending with freedom of speech. In 1976, in the case of *Buckley v. Valeo* (424 U.S. 1), the Court held that the independent expenditure of funds by individuals and groups in a political campaign is protected by the First Amendment, as is the advocacy of issues by party and nonparty groups. So how can campaign spending be restricted if doing so violates fundamental First Amendment rights?

Not only does the Constitution protect the rights of people and groups to express their feelings and "petition the government for grievances," but the electoral and governing systems are designed to allow them to do so, to enable those who feel most strongly about a candidate or issue to try to convince others of the merits of their deeply felt beliefs.

Should a democratic electoral system allow those with greater resources and more intense feelings to exercise more influence over the selection of candidates, the issue agenda for the campaign, the way the news media cover it, and the mobilization of the electorate? Should the giant companies of the communication industry be able to condition the scope, content, and "spin" of the information the electorate needs to make an informed voting decision? Should the mass media profit from the election campaign as they did in 2000 and 2004?

Most people are concerned about the influence that special interests and the press exercise on elections and government.[1] These perceptions, documented in recent public opinion polls, have contributed to and perhaps followed from a dissatisfaction about politics and politicians, elections and candidates, and government and public policy makers that Americans regularly express.[2] Discontent with government has been a persistent national problem since Watergate, and is a problem cited by Republicans and Democrats alike.[3] For many, money is the root of all evil, but it is also "the mother's milk of politics." Herein lies the dilemma for a democratic electoral process.

This chapter explores the impact of money on elections. It begins with a description of the rising costs of political campaigns, the problems associated with these costs, and how Congress has attempted to deal with them. It then assesses the intended and unintended consequences of recent election laws on the conduct of campaigns and the democratic character of the electoral system. Subsequent sections of the chapter deal with the relationship between money and electoral success, public perceptions of the money problem, and proposals for campaign finance reform.

CAMPAIGN FINANCE LEGISLATION AND ITS CONSEQUENCES

The costs of elections have skyrocketed in the last thirty years. In 1960 Richard Nixon spent about $10 million in his race for the presidency. Eight years later, he spent $25 million. Running for reelection against weak opposition in 1972, he spent more than $61 million. Since then, campaign expenditures have risen dramatically. The Center for Responsive Politics, a public interest group that tracks campaign spending, estimated that $2.2 billion was spent on the federal elections during the 1995–1996 election cycle, $3 billion during the 1999–2000, and almost $4 billion during 2003–2004.[4]

Various factors have contributed to this rapid increase in spending. The nomination process has become more competitive. Successful candidates now have to run in two elections, one for the nomination and one for the general election and must do so for longer periods of time. The techniques of modern campaigning—television advertising, survey research, direct-mail fund-raising, and grassroots organizing—have added to the costs.

The Federal Election Campaign Act

Fearing that the election process had become too expensive; that candidates had to spend too much time raising money; that they had become too dependent on large donors, who in turn, were exercising too much influence over the electoral and governing processes; and that money was being given secretly, and perhaps illegally, to candidates and parties, Congress went into action. Legislation was enacted in the 1970s to reduce the costs of elections, decrease dependence on large donors, and open contributions and expenditures to full public review. The Democratic Congress had an additional objective in passing this legislation—to reduce the Republican Party's financial advantage in elections.

The new laws were primarily directed at the presidential election, but some restrictions also were placed on congressional elections. The amount of money that individuals and groups could give to candidates for federal office as well as to the political parties was strictly limited. In addition, a restriction was placed on how much money candidates could contribute to their own campaigns. Federal subsidies and grants for major party presidential candidates and funds for the major parties were provided, and spending limits in the presidential campaign were established. The law also allowed corporations and labor unions, previously banned from contributing money, to encourage their employees, members, and stockholders to form political action committees (PACs) and contribute up to $5,000 per candidate per election.[5] A federal election commission, composed of six members, two appointed by the president and four by Congress, was set up to monitor and police election activities.

The Federal Election Campaign Act (FECA) was the first comprehensive law to regulate campaign finance activity and the first to provide partial public funding. Previous legislation had prohibited direct business and labor contributions but had done little to regulate the source and amount of campaign contributions and expenditures.

Prior to the 1970s the only public funding was at the state level, and it paid for the conduct of the election. In providing public subsidies, the United States followed the practices of several European countries that also subsidized candidates or their parties' elections. (Table 4.1 summarizes the grants and subsidies of other democratic governments.)

The FECA, scheduled to go into effect after the 1972 elections, was immediately challenged as unconstitutional. Critics charged that the limits on contributions and spending violated the constitutionally guaranteed right to freedom of speech, that the funding provisions unfairly discriminated against third-party and independent candidates, and that appointment of four of the commissioners by Congress violated the principle of separation of powers.

In 1976, the Supreme Court declared two parts of the law unconstitutional. Although the Court upheld the right of Congress to regulate campaign contributions for candidates for federal office, it held that independent spending by individuals and groups was protected by the First Amendment to the Constitution and thus could not be regulated. It also voided Congress's selection of four of the six election commissioners as an intrusion into the president's executive authority.

The Court's decision forced Congress back to the drawing board in the midst of another presidential election cycle. A new law was enacted at the start of the 1976 presidential nomination campaign. It retained the contribution and spending limits and public funding of the presidential campaign. But the funding was to be voluntary. Candidates did not have to accept government funds; if they did, they were limited in how much they could contribute or lend to their own campaign and how much that campaign could spend. The Federal Election Commission (FEC) was reconstituted with all six members, three Republicans and three Democrats, to be nominated by the president and appointed with the advice and consent of the Senate.

With limited money available, the candidates decided to spend the bulk of their resources on television advertising to reach the widest possible audience. As a consequence, much of the political paraphernalia that normally accompanies presidential campaigns—buttons, bumper stickers, campaign literature and the like—was missing or in short supply. Voter turnout continued to decline. Congress was concerned, with some justification, that the funding limitations, the emphasis on television advertising and on media-oriented events, and the drop in turnout were all related.

The 1979 Amendment and the Soft Money Loophole

An amendment to the law was enacted in 1979 that enabled the parties to raise and spend unlimited amounts of money for their voluntary efforts to promote voting through educational campaigns, get-out-the-vote drives, and other party-building efforts.[6] The only prohibition on the expenditure of soft money was that it could not be spent advocating a specific candidate's election.

The soft-money amendment created a gigantic loophole in the law, permitting, even encouraging, the solicitation of large contributions and the expenditure of these funds to help influence the outcome of the election. Unlike the "hard money" that was strictly regulated and reported, soft money was not regulated.

In the first two presidential elections after the soft money amendment was enacted, the Republicans enjoyed a financial advantage. Helped by negative reaction to the Carter presidency, Reagan's popularity among wealthy conservative donors and business interests, and subsequently, his own general popularity in 1984, the GOP raised $31 million in soft money, compared to only $10 million for the Democrats. But that was just the beginning.

The race for soft money increased exponentially in the 1990s. It did so as a consequence of a clever plan conceived by President Clinton's political advisers. Clinton needed to improve his public standing and image in the aftermath of the Republicans' victory in the 1994 midterm elections. To do so, the president's political strategists recommended an advertising campaign in which the president's moderate policy positions were contrasted with the more conservative Republican stands.

TABLE 4.1 **Public Subsidies to Political Parties and Candidates**

| Country | Recipient | Direct Subsidies | | | | Indirect subsidies |
		Interval	Basis	Eligibility	Specific grant/services	
Australia	Candidates, parties		Per vote	At least 4% of vote, must be registered with EC	Transportation, get out the vote, broadcasting	
Belgium	No direct subsidies	n/a	n/a	n/a	Broadcasting, encouragement of voting	
Canada	Candidates, parliamentary groups	Election	Per vote	Candidate: 15% of votes in district, parties must spend 10% of limit	Broadcasting, encouragement of voting	Tax credits
Denmark	Parliamentary groups	Annual	Per seat		Broadcasting, press and publications, women/youth groups	
France	Presidential candidates	Election			Bill posting, broadcasting, printing ballots, press/publications	Kickbacks of deputy salaries
Germany	Parties	Election	Per vote	5% for national party lists*	Broadcasting, subsidies to party foundations	Tax deductions
India	No direct subsidies	n/a	n/a	n/a	Broadcasting	
Ireland	No direct subsidies	n/a	n/a	n/a	Broadcasting	
Israel	Party groups	Annual, every election	Per seat	†	Broadcasting, get out the vote	
Italy	Parties, parliamentary groups	Annual, every election	Per vote		Broadcasting, education, women's and youth groups	Kickbacks of deputy salaries

					Tax benefits
Japan	Candidates	Every election			Transportation, publications, broadcasting, advertising, use of public halls	
Mexico	Parties	Annual, every election	Per vote	Party should obtain more than 1.5% of total ballot	Broadcasting	Tax exemptions
Netherlands	No direct subsidies	n/a	n/a	n/a	Broadcasting, get out the vote, party foundations, women/youth	Tax deductions
Poland	No direct subsidies	n/a	n/a	n/a	Broadcasting, use of public halls, printing/mailing, get out the vote	Limited tax exemptions for parties
Spain	Parties	Annual, every election	Per vote	Party must have won one electoral seat (at 3% threshold)		
Sweden	Parties, parliamentary groups	Annual	Per seat, per vote		Publications, encouragement of voting, broadcasting	
United Kingdom	Parliamentary groups	Annual			Publications, mailing, broadcasting, use of public halls	Gifts to parties exempt from inheritance tax
United States	Candidates in presidential primaries and elections	Election	Matching grant in primary, fixed sum in election from earmarked funds		Nomination costs, mailing, most states pay for voter registration/ballots	Tax credits and deductions

*0.5% of votes for national party lists of candidates, or 105 of first votes cast in a constituency if no regional list has been accepted.
† Had at least 1 MP in last parliament or has been recognized as a group by the legislature.

Source: Lawrence LeDuc, Richard G. Niemi, and Pippa Norris, eds., Comparing Democracies: Elections and Voting in Global Perspective (Thousand Oaks, Calif.: Sage, 1996), Table 5.1, 38.

Launched in the summer of 1995, the campaign was very expensive. In the first two months, almost $2 million was spent on it. Fearful that the continued expenditure of large sums of money could leave his reelection campaign with insufficient funds to respond to an attack by the Republicans and its nominee, the president's advisers decided to raise and spend soft money for the campaign rather than depend on the money that had been or would be contributed to his official reelection committee.

The Clinton fund-raising effort, in which the president, vice president, and first lady participated, raised the ante on soft money contributions. It also embroiled the White House in questionable fund-raising tactics, especially its use of public facilities for the purposes of private solicitation.

The Republicans protested the actions of Clinton and the Democrats, but to no avail. Unable to stop the Democrats from using their position in government to raise money, the Republicans then conducted their own soft money campaign. After the election, the Republican-controlled Senate investigated Democratic fund-raising activities. No new campaign finance legislation was enacted, however.

Sen. John McCain kept the soft money issue alive during his 2000 quest for the Republican presidential nomination. Other principal candidates in that election, notably Democrats Al Gore and Bill Bradley, also said that they favored campaign finance reform to close the soft money loophole. After the election and several high-profile accounting frauds, business failures, and illegalities by corporate executives, Congress, swept up by public indignation over the fraudulent actions of the business and accounting firms, enacted the Bipartisan Campaign Reform Act (BCRA) in 2002.

The 2002 Bipartisan Campaign Reform Act

A principal purpose of the new law was to ban the political parties from raising soft-money money. Another was to prevent them and nonparty groups from using advocacy advertising as a not-so-subtle vehicle for promoting particular candidates. A third objective was to increase the amount that individuals were permitted to give to candidates and their parties.

The BCRA prohibited the national parties from soliciting unregulated contributions. To compensate for their potential loss of revenue, the law raised the individual contribution limits from $1,000 to $2,000 and indexed them to inflation. Party and nonparty groups were not allowed to mention candidates by name in their advocacy ads thirty days or less before a primary and sixty days or less before the general election. Finally, the BCRA allowed federal candidates facing self-financed opponents to raise additional funds to level the playing field—the so called "millionaires amendment."

As with FECA, the BCRA was immediately challenged by those who opposed the law and believed that it violated their First Amendment rights of freedom of speech. In December 2003, in the case of *McConnell v. FEC* (540 U.S. 93), the Supreme Court upheld the major provisions of the law, allowing the legislation to shape the financial aspects of the 2004 election campaign.

Opponents of the law had feared that the political parties would be unable to make up the loss of soft money. The Democrats, most of whom had supported the legislation, were particularly nervous since their party had relied more on these funds to offset the Republicans' traditional fund-raising advantage. Moreover, being in the minority, the Democrats could not use the White House or Congress as they had in previous elections to bolster their fund-raising efforts.

To deal with this potential shortfall, Terry McAuliff, chair of the Democratic National Committee, created a task force of party operatives and supporters to strategize on what could be done. The task force recommended that nonparty, nonprofit groups, which had functioned under two provisions of the Internal Revenue Code, 527 and 501c, be used as vehicles for raising and spending soft money. The spending, however, could not be coordinated with the party or candidates; it had to be done independently.

Beginning in 2003, these groups began to raise money for Democratic candidates. They were aided in their efforts by millions of dollars in "seed money" donated by financier George Soros and insurance magnate Peter Lewis.

Outraged by the ruse, the Republicans appealed to the FEC but unsuccessfully. The commissioners voted four to two not to intervene during the 2004 election campaign. As a consequence, the Republicans belatedly set up their own 527 and 501c organizations to raise and spend soft money. In the end, more than $417 million was raised by these groups and $420 million spent according to Political Moneyline, a public interest group that tracks campaign money.[7]

The parties also took advantage of changes in the law to raise more money than they had in previous election cycles. They were able to do so because of the increase in individual contribution limits, the computerization of their fund-raising databases, and the deep partisan divisions in the country that the policies of the Bush administration, particularly the war in Iraq, fueled.

Thus, the BCRA had a mixed impact on the parties. It did encourage them to improve and broaden their fund-raising base. It did increase the number of small donors, those who contributed $200 or less. In 2000, 25 percent of the total contributions came from small donors; in 2004 that percentage had increased to 34.[8] The provision that limited advocacy advertising in the final thirty days before primaries and sixty days before the general election motivated the parties and groups to spend more money on grassroots efforts with the desired result—a higher voter turnout.

However, soft money, lots of it, continued to find its way into the federal election campaign by virtue of the fund-raising activities and expenditures of party-oriented, nonparty groups. These groups, created to supplement their party's efforts, actually reduced the control the candidates and their parties had over their own campaigns. The prohibition against coordinating party and nonparty activities resulted in the conduct of separate, presumably uncoordi-

BOX 4.1 **Raising the Stakes: The Selling of the Government**

In June 1995, the president's political advisers, notably Dick Morris, recommended to Bill Clinton that a preemptive advertising campaign be launched to reinforce the president's image as a moderate, mainstream Democrat and to help pave the way for his reelection. The campaign was directed at the early caucus and primary states and was meant to discourage anyone from challenging the president. Approximately $2.5 million was devoted to this early advertising effort, which had the additional goal of undercutting public support for the Republicans' balanced-budget proposals in Congress.

The expenditure of so much money so early provoked considerable division within the Clinton White House. Some of the president's advisers believed that the spending put the president in a potentially vulnerable position should a Democratic challenger emerge or should the Republicans unite behind a single candidate and then turn their attention to the president. But Clinton supported Morris's advertising initiative, remembering all too well how the administration's healthcare proposals in 1993–1994 had been defeated by a multimillion-dollar public relations campaign supported by the Health Insurance Association of America.

Where to get the money became the critical issue for the White House. In September 1995, Harold Ickes, deputy chief of staff, came up with an idea: Let the Democratic Party pay for the ads with soft money (which the president could help raise), because the commercials aired were policy oriented and did not directly urge the president's reelection. The White House quickly approved Ickes's plan, which Democratic lawyers believed to be perfectly legal.

What followed was a frantic, no-holds-barred fund-raising effort in which the Democrats raised $124 million in soft money, much of it in sizable donations from wealthy patrons. Working closely with the White House, using the perquisites of the office to great advantage, the Democrats brought in more money than they had ever had before. So fast did the dollars flow in that the party did not take the time to ensure that all the contributions were legal, were voluntarily given, and came from respectable donors. In the end, the Democrats were forced to return millions of dollars to contributors whose legal status to make them could not be established.

nated campaigns. Moreover, the BCRA also allowed the parties to engage in independent spending. As a consequence both major parties spent more money in uncoordinated campaigns than they did in coordinated ones. (For actual party revenue and expenditures, see Table 4.2.)

Thus despite the new law, problems remain. Soft money continues to flow into federal elections; the costs of contemporary campaigns continues to escalate; and the bulk of the contributions come from a relatively small group of wealthy people. Most important, the connection between contributions and expenditures and the special treatment large donors receive continues to raise questions about the democratic character of American elections. The next section examines each of these problems in addressing the principal concern of this chapter—are the unequal resources that people have and use in political campaigns consistent with a democratic electoral process?

The active involvement of the president and vice president also raised questions about whether the effort was really the party's or that of the Clinton-Gore campaign. The specter of taxpayer facilities' being used for political purposes captured the attention of the press, public interest groups, and Republicans. All of them suggested that laws were being violated by donors' being invited to dinners and coffee hours with the president, vice president, and other top administration officials; by sleepovers at the White House and trips on Air Force One; and by the participation of large contributors on U.S. trade missions abroad. The president arranged his travel schedule to participate in as many of these fund-raising activities as possible. The vice president personally solicited contributions from his own White House office. There were even allegations that campaign donors—even donors who represented foreign governments and companies—were directly influencing policy decisions.

To make matters worse, the Democratic National Committee was distributing the money to certain key states designated by the Clinton-Gore campaign. The state parties, in turn, were directed to spend it on advertisements produced by the president's media consultant, Robert Squire. In other words, the national party was circumventing the limit imposed on its spending for presidential campaigns by creating the fiction that these were advertisements bought and aired by state parties.

Meanwhile, the Republicans were also raising soft money—even more than the Democrats. They, too, offered inducements for donors, such as meetings with congressional leaders and access to committee chairs' unlisted telephone numbers. They, too, directed the money to their state and local parties to spend on behalf of their candidates in both the congressional and the presidential campaigns. In other words, they had followed the Democrats' lead.

Pandora's box had been opened.

Source: Stephen J. Wayne, *The Road to the White House 2004* (New York: Wadsworth/Thomson, 2004), 41.

CONTINUING CAMPAIGN FINANCE ISSUES

Are Elections Too Expensive?

Former House majority leader, Tom DeLay, does not think so. In claiming that the campaign finance issue was overblown, DeLay stated, "Americans spend twice as much per year on yogurt than they spend on political campaigns." [9] Does it require billions or millions of dollars to educate the public about the candidates and issues? A subsidiary issue, how well campaigns are educating the public, will be discussed in the next chapter on the mass media.

Elections are much more expensive today, but public participation remains uneven. (Table 4.3 lists the expenditures during the last three presidential election cycles.) Most people do not contribute any money to the candidates or

TABLE 4.2 **Major Party Revenues and Expenditures, 1996–2004 (in millions)**

		1996		2000		2004	
		Revenue	Expenditures	Revenue	Expenditures	Revenue	Expenditures
Democrats	Hard	$221.6	241.3	275.2	265.8	683.8	655.6
	Soft	$123.9	121.8	245.2	244.9	—	—
	Total	$345.5	363.1	520.4	510.7	683.8	655.6
Republicans	Hard	$416.5	408.5	465.8	427.0	784.8	752.6
	Soft	$138.2	149.7	249.9	252.8	—	—
	Total	$554.7	558.2	715.7	679.8	784.8	752.6

Source: Federal Election Commission, "National Party Federal Financial Activity through the 2004 Election Cycle," Press Release, March 2, 2005 (Corrected March 14, 2005), www.fec.gov/press/press2005/20050302party/Party2004final.

their parties. Most do not get personally involved in the campaign and, with the exception of the presidential election held once every four years, most people do not even vote. Clearly, all that soft money presumably being spent on get-out-the-vote activities has not been working terribly well, although if less effort was made and less money spent, even fewer people might vote.

Nor is there any evidence that the contemporary public is any better informed and more attentive to election issues than it was a decade or two ago when campaign expenditures were less. In fact, people may actually be less knowledgeable about the issues than they were when newspapers were the prime source of information. The costs of elections do not seem to be paying off in terms of producing a more educated electorate although spending less money might contribute to an even less informed one.

Does Money Win Elections?

Clearly, many candidates and their managers believe that it does. Having a large war chest is an important advantage that often can dissuade a credible challenger from running. In their quests for reelection, Presidents Clinton and George W. Bush raised millions of dollars to discourage a quality challenger in their own party from running against them for the nomination. They also wanted the money so that they could respond quickly to attacks made by candidates and officials of the other major party.

With the exception of the last Democratic nomination process, the candidate with the most money at the beginning of the election year has won the nomination. Howard Dean was the exception. Had he fared better under the spotlight

TABLE 4.3 **Costs of Federal Elections, 1996–2004 (in millions)**			
Expenditures of the Official Candidate and Party Committees	1996	2000	2004
Congressional candidates	$645.8	$878.0	$945.3
Presidential candidates	$192.2	$239.9	$343.1
Parties	$894.3	$1,236.1	$1,623.7
Total	$1,732.3	$2,354.0	$2,912.1

Source: The Center for Responsive Politics, www.opensecrets.

that the news media usually shine on the front-runner, he too might have won. Campaigns are more costly today because of the revolution in communication technology and the need to hire professional experts in the use of this technology in elections. Polling, media advertising, grassroots organization, even election law and accounting require special skills and knowledge and specially equipped facilities designed to produce the desired product. In the past, political parties provided their nominees with campaign services and the personnel to run them. Today, most of these operations are outsourced to campaign professionals.

Long before their campaigns begin, candidates must retain the consultants who will help connect them to the voters. This connection requires money, lots of it, and much of it up front. Thus donors, particularly those who give the maximum amount and help candidates raise funds from others, exercise considerable clout. Their promise of support can encourage a person to run whereas their lack of enthusiasm can discourage otherwise qualified candidates from seeking their party's nomination.

Having money up front also gives candidates greater flexibility in deciding when and where to campaign. It helps them get press coverage, because the news media view money as an early indication of popularity and electability. Coverage follows the dollar, and that coverage, in turn, can generate more money, which contributes to electoral success. News coverage, in short, takes on the aura of a self-fulfilling prophecy.

In addition to the psychological and public relations advantages that a large war chest, assembled early, can provide, it also increases a candidate's strategic options. For candidates for their party's presidential nomination, accepting federal funds subjects them to state and national spending limits. Candidates who can afford to avoid these limits are advantaged.

Although money buys recognition, hires political professionals, and satisfies other needs, such as fund-raising, staff support, and grassroots organizing, it may not buy much more that. It certainly does not guarantee electoral success, as Ross Perot and Steve Forbes can attest, but it still correlates highly with winning the nomination and the general election.

Not only has the candidate with the largest war chest at the start of the nomination process usually won, but the candidate who spends the most in the general election or has the most spent on his campaign also tends to win. Between 1860 and 1972, the winner outspent the loser twenty-one out of twenty-nine times. Republican candidates have spent more than their Democratic opponents in twenty-five out of twenty-nine elections during this period. The four times they did not, the Democrats won.

The relationship between money and electoral success holds even when independent expenditures, partisan communications, and soft money are considered. In the 1980s, considerably more was spent on behalf of Republican nominees than on their Democratic opponents. In the 1990s, the Democrats narrowed the gap, but still did not eliminate the GOP's fundraising advantage. George W. Bush was the financial as well as electoral victor in 2000, but in 2004, the spending by and for the major party candidates was nearly the same.

In congressional races, however, it was a different story. In 2004, the candidates with the most money won 95.6 percent of the races for the House of Representatives and 91 percent of the Senate contests.[10]

The public perceives that money contributes to electoral success.[11] And it is true that candidates who have larger war chests than their opponents have won more often than they have lost. What is not clear, however, is whether the money was the key to their victory or if the likelihood of their victory encouraged donors to contribute.

Political science research suggests that challengers need more money than incumbents to defeat incumbents; that when incumbents spend a lot of money, it is usually a sign that they are in trouble, not that they are assured of victory; and that money seems to be more of a factor in the election outcome when less is known about the candidates.[12]

Who Pays and What Do They Get for Their Money?

To many, more troubling than the high cost of elections is who pays for them and what do they get for their money. Contributors are unequally distributed among the population. Only a small percentage of people give any money at all to the candidates and the parties.[13] Of those who do, most who give make a contribution of $200 or less. Most of the big bucks come from wealthy donors and well-financed groups.[14]

The Federal Election Commission keeps tabs of contributions and expenditures. Table 4.4 lists the groups that have given and spent the most in recent election cycles.

The concentration of contributors among wealthy individuals and expenditures among corporations, trade associations, and labor unions raises important issues for an electoral democracy. To what extent can and do large contributors influence who runs and wins, and to whom are the winning candidates likely to be more responsive once in office?

TABLE 4.4 **Top PAC Contributors, 2003–2004**

PAC Name*	Total Amount	Dem. %	Rep. %
National Assn of Realtors	$3,787,083	47%	52%
Laborers Union	$2,684,250	86%	14%
National Auto Dealers Assn	$2,603,300	27%	73%
Intl Brotherhood of Electrical Workers	$2,369,500	96%	4%
National Beer Wholesalers Assn	$2,314,000	24%	76%
National Assn of Home Builders	$2,201,500	33%	67%
Assn of Trial Lawyers of America	$2,181,499	93%	6%
United Parcel Service	$2,142,679	28%	72%
SBC Communications	$2,120,616	36%	64%
American Medical Assn	$2,092,425	21%	79%
United Auto Workers	$2,075,700	98%	1%
Carpenters & Joiners Union	$2,074,560	74%	26%
Credit Union National Assn	$2,065,678	42%	58%
Service Employees International Union	$1,985,000	85%	15%
American Bankers Assn	$1,978,013	36%	64%
Machinists/Aerospace Workers Union	$1,942,250	99%	1%
Teamsters Union	$1,917,413	88%	11%
American Hospital Assn	$1,769,326	44%	56%
American Federation of Teachers	$1,717,372	97%	3%
Wal-Mart Stores	$1,677,000	22%	78%

Note: Totals include subsidiaries and affiliated PACs, if any.

*For ease of identification, the names used in this section are those of the organization connected with the PAC, rather than the official PAC name. For example, the "Coca-Cola Company Nonpartisan Committee for Good Government" is simply listed as "Coca-Cola Co."

Source: Based on data released by the FEC on Monday, May 16, 2005. Committee for Responsive Politics, www.opensecrets.org/Pacs/topacs.asp?txt=A&Cycle=2004.

From the public's perspective the answers are clear: the big contributors are most influential, and they are the individuals and groups to whom the winners respond to the most. In a survey conducted by Princeton Survey Research Associates for the Center for Responsive Politics and paid for by the Pew Charitable Trusts, more than half of the respondents expressed the belief that money buys political influence, that members of Congress are more likely to respond to campaign donors outside of their districts than to nondonors within their districts, and that members support policies primarily because these policies are desired by their donors and not because elected officials believe them to be in the best interests of the country.[15] The public is particularly troubled by foreign money in U.S. elections and the implication that the national interest and security could be sacrificed because of it.[16]

Whether or not these public perceptions accord with reality, the fact that most people believe them is significant. A democratic political system is not enhanced if its citizenry believes that government is conducted of, by, and for the special interests rather than the public interest. Such a belief undoubtedly contributes to (and also may be a product of) declining trust in government.[17]

The issue is also one of equity. If the groups that contribute and spend the most money were representative of the population as a whole, the situation would not be as bad than if they represented a particular economic stratum within society. But alas, they do, as Table 4.4 suggests. Business interests spend the most; the expenditures of consumer groups pale in comparison. Organized labor spends less, directs most of it to the Democrats, and represents the interests of blue-collar union workers. Who represents the interests of nonunionized blue-collar workers or white-collar employees? And when is the last time you heard that a group representing the poor had elected or influenced a public official through campaign contributions or expenditures?

As the people see it, politicians are also winners in the money game. Although the public perceives both parties and their candidates as involved in excessive and even questionable fund-raising activities, Republican and Democratic partisans differ over the most egregious campaign finance problems that face the country today. Republicans have directed their outrage at the incipient influence of foreign money and labor unions, whereas the Democrats see special interest money, flowing in large part from business and conservative groups to Republicans, as the issue that most needs rectifying.[18] According to national surveys, the public wants the financial system to be reformed and the abuses ended, but people doubt that politicians in Washington will do so.

Why Has Congress Been So Slow to Deal with These Problems?

The unintended consequences of campaign finance legislation have made members of Congress reluctant to act quickly. Some members are reluctant to act at all because they are philosophically opposed to government regulation in general and campaign finance regulation in particular. Some also object to using taxpayer money to fund national elections partially or wholly.

Besides which, members of Congress are probably the most inappropriate group of public officials to fix a problem from which they have benefited by virtue of their election, and for most of them, reelection. As incumbents, they can raise more money, and they have access to more experienced election consultants, staff, and others needed to run a successful campaign. This built-in advantage naturally makes them hesitant to change the system and level the playing field. Partisanship also plays a role. Republicans have been able to raise more money than the Democrats and thus would stand to lose more if the playing field were leveled by expenditure limits or public funding.

Finally, there has not been much public pressure on Congress to act. Although people say that they desire campaign finance reform, most do not regard it as a top priority.[19] Besides, the public has very limited knowledge of the current finance laws and even less of the proposals to change them.[20]

Why Are Money Problems So Difficult to Fix in a Democracy?

There are serious constitutional issues to rectifying the money problem. As noted at the beginning of this chapter, the First Amendment, as interpreted by the Supreme Court, protects independent spending and campaign advocacy, including the cost of financing that advocacy. Congress has to be careful not to intrude on constitutionally protected rights.

There is also the history of reform to consider when legislating. Despite good intentions, campaign finance laws have produced unanticipated and undesirable consequences, particularly the soft money and issue advocacy provisions. Changes could possibly make things worse. Besides, politicians are known to be particularly creative when it comes to finding ways to circumvent campaign finance regulations.

Although a consensus has not emerged on how to reform the system, certain practices have been subjected to considerable criticism that they undercut the democratic character of American elections: the solicitation of soft money by nonparty groups; the restrictions placed on candidates who accept government funding and PAC contributions; the independent expenditures of individuals, parties, and nonparty groups; and the money and expenditures from foreign sources that finds its way into American election campaigns.

THE CAMPAIGN FINANCE DEBATE TODAY

The issues of high costs, large contributions, and multiple campaign expenditures by candidates, parties, and nonparty groups continue to generate partisan conflict.

Controlling the High Costs of Federal Elections

Each campaign for federal office is more expensive than the previous one. Inflation and population growth contribute to rising costs, as does the increasing use of professional campaign services by candidates, parties, and nonparty groups. Larger contribution limits, reinforced by private wealth, the proliferation and involvement of nonparty groups in election campaigns, and the success of the major parties in maintaining a steady stream of money into their coffers, provide the resources that continue to fuel more and more costly campaigns.

Congress has imposed a few controls: individual and group contribution limits to candidates and parties, public disclosure of all contributions and expenditures of $200 or more, public disclosure of independent spending, personal contribution and expenditure limits for candidates who accept public funds, sale of political advertising at its lowest discounted rate within sixty days of the general election,[21] and a millionaires' amendment that increases the amount of money a candidate can raise from a donor if an opponent's self-financing exceeds a certain amount. With the exception of presidential candidates who accept federal funds, none of these constraints, however, cap campaign revenues or expenditures. They cannot. Doing so would violate the Supreme Court's ruling in the case of *Buckley v. Valeo* (424 U.S. 1, 1976) that the use of private funds for campaigning is protected by the free speech provision of the First Amendment. So long as that decision remains the law of the land, it is unlikely that the costs of campaigning can be subject to federal control.

Regulating Campaign Contributions

Contributions to federal campaigns can and have been regulated, however. Should they be regulated further?

Should Soft Money Be Banned Entirely? When Congress enacted the BCRA in 2002, it prohibited the parties from soliciting and spending soft money. It did so to close a loophole in the law that encouraged parties and politicians to raise unregulated funds for so-called party-building activities. Sponsors of the new law hoped that it also would reduce the amount of time candidates spent raising money and the amount of money that wealthy individuals and groups could funnel to their political friends. They also intended the reform legislation to motivate parties to develop a larger base of smaller donors. Only the last objective has been achieved, however.

The law has encouraged the national parties and their supporters to form sympathetic nonparty groups to raise soft money and mount stealth campaigns. Although these groups are not allowed to coordinate their efforts with the parties or their nominees, they can coordinate efforts amongst themselves. The campaign activities of 527 and 501c groups has reduced the control parties and their candidates have over their own campaigns. This loss of control undercuts the principle of accountability in democratic elections. To whom are elected officials accountable? What are the basic issues that should comprise their policy agenda?

Should new legislation be enacted to ban soft money from nonparty groups? Such a ban may not be constitutional, and even if it were, what would prevent wealthy individuals or groups from using their own resources to establish organizations for the purpose of affecting the outcome of an election? Besides, if information and grassroots activities help inform and involve the electorate in the election process, are these nonparty groups doing a service or disservice to a democratic election process?

Is it undemocratic to have the wealthy pay a larger burden of the election costs? After all, a progressive tax system is based on the notion that people with greater incomes have greater ability and obligations to pay more taxes. Shouldn't the same principle apply to federal elections?

Should PAC Contributions be Eliminated or Reduced? Another reform would be to eliminate or reduce PAC contributions. The law currently restricts the amount donated to $5,000 per candidate, per election. But it sets no overall limit on how much PACs can contribute and spend on their own. One proposal would be to reduce the amount that they could donate. Alternatively, Congress, which created PACs in the legislation that established the campaign finance system, could prohibit them from making individual contributions at all, set an overall cap on the total amount of their contributions in any election cycle, specify a maximum percentage of funds candidates could receive from PACs, or in the most extreme case, eliminate PACs altogether.

Reducing or eliminating PAC contributions would certainly appeal to the general public, who perceives these nonparty groups as a large part of special interest politics in the United States. In reality, however, PAC contributions pale by comparison to the soft money contributions of wealthy individuals and corporate America. Moreover, if PACs were eliminated, it is doubtful that their interests would be eliminated as well. Rather, they would find other ways to affect the political process. PACs are required to report their contributions and expenditures to the FEC. Whether and to what extent other entities that replaced them would be required to do so is unclear. Finally, the elimination of PACs could result in less information and control of election activities than currently exists.[22]

Should Contributions and Expenditures from Foreign Sources Be Prohibited? Another source of public concern are foreign contributions. Under the existing law, contributions are restricted to U.S. citizens or noncitizens who are permanent residents. American subsidiaries of foreign-owned companies also may create PACs or make contributions, provided they do so with money earned in the United States. A foreign company cannot give its American subsidiary money to spend in U.S. elections.

Congress could prohibit any individual contribution from a person who is not a U.S. citizen. It also could prevent foreign-owned companies from making contributions. It probably could not, however, prevent American employees of these companies from forming PACs and making contributions. Nor would Congress want to do so because this could potentially discriminate against American workers.[23]

In today's interdependent, international economic environment, Congress must be very careful how it treats foreign companies for fear of hurting American interests abroad. Although the problem is perceived as foreign influence, as often as not the beneficiaries are American companies who do business abroad. Take the case of Loral Space and Communications, whose chief executive officer, Bernard Schwartz, gave $100,000 to the Democratic National

Committee during the 1995–1996 election cycle. Loral wished to sell satellite technology to the Chinese government to help it launch commercial satellites. Fearing that this technology could be used for military purposes, the state and defense departments opposed the sale, but the commerce department and the White House supported it. The president, Bill Clinton, ultimately approved the sale. Did Schwartz's $100,000 have anything to do with the president's decision?

Increasing the Amount of Public Funds?

The flip side of constricting contributions is expanding government grants. One of the original aims of the FECA was to enlarge the field of potential candidates and level the contest. Providing matching funds gives lesser-known candidates a chance that they might otherwise not have to demonstrate their qualifications and establish their electability.

A task force commissioned by the Campaign Finance Institute, a nonprofit, public interest organization devoted to campaign finance disclosure and reform, has proposed increasing the amount of money candidates who are seeking their party's presidential nomination would receive by upping the size of the match on the first $100 contributed. The task force also recommended that candidates receive public funding the year before the election. To do so would require that the treasury fund from which these grants are made be enlarged.

Providing the grant earlier would give candidates funds when they need it most—at the beginning of the process. Increasing the size of the initial match would encourage candidates to seek small contributions rather than focus their efforts on those who give the maximum amount. Finally, enlarging the treasury fund would be necessary if more candidates sought their party's presidential nomination and accepted government grants. The task force has proposed a $2 increase in the income tax check-off from $3 to $5 per taxpayer.

Another objective of the task force's recommendations is to reduce the need for and the amount of generic advertising that the national parties have to air during the period that follows the contested phase of the nomination process and before their national nominating conventions. The task force's proposals, however, would not impede fund-raising and independent spending by party and nonparty groups.

The grant for the federal election also could be increased. Candidate expenditures have risen at a greater rate than inflation during the more than thirty-year period since the initial campaign finance legislation has gone into effect. Yet, the amount that the major party candidates receive is still tied to the $10 million figure established in 1974, adjusted by the rate of inflation. Giving the candidates more money or allowing them to supplement their federal funds with private contributions would make them less dependent on their parties and nonparty groups, both of which regularly spend more than the presidential candidates do on the presidential candidates' campaigns.

However, it is unlikely that Congress and the general public would support an increase in tax check-offs that would be necessary to enlarge the pool of election funds. Only about 11 percent of taxpayers are currently checking the box to put $3 of their taxes into the fund for presidential candidates. However, studies of public opinion suggest unhappiness with campaign finance today. When pollsters' questions include reference to the role of money and/or special interest groups, support for public funding increases. When taxes are mentioned as a source of revenue for the fund, public support decreases. [24]

Equalizing Campaign Expenditures

The revenue side is only one half of the campaign finance equation; spending is the other. Can campaign expenditures be equalized without denying candidates, their parties, and the groups that support them freedom of speech? Some reformers say that they can if spending limits were eased or eliminated or if independent expenditures were subject to some controls.

Should the Federal Campaign Spending Limits Be Modified? For the first time since the enactment of FECA, the BCRA has tied individual contribution limits to inflation. However, the law did not do the same to the state and overall spending limits or to the matching funds. As a consequence, federal funds have become much less attractive, because of the increasing costs of campaigns and the increasing number of candidates who have, or have the potential to raise, large sums of money without accepting matching funds. In 2004, the spending limits for the nomination were $49 million overall, including money for fund-raising, legal, accounting, and compliance costs. State limits ranged from $746,200 for the least populous states to $15.56 million for the most populated (California), and for the general election, the candidates received $74.6 million, plus money for legal and accounting expenses that could be raised from private sources.

Increasing the expenditure limits would make federal funds a more viable option for candidates faced with the dilemma of not being able to raise or spend as much as their primary and general election opponents. It would help extend the contested phase of the nomination and make that phase more equal. Easing or eliminating the contribution and spending limits after the nomination was effectively decided also would equalize the pre-election campaign between the prospective nominees in the period after the primaries and before the national nominating conventions.[25]

Raising the spending limits, however, would also force the candidates back into the fund-raising game, creating competition between their solicitation campaigns and those of their party's, allied groups, and congressional candidates. Cohesion between the party and its nominee might be loosened. In addition, it might put pressure on Congress to once again increase the amounts that individuals and groups can contribute. On the other hand, it might save public funding, which will become increasingly irrelevant if the spending limits are not increased.

Can Independent Spending by Individuals and Groups Be Reduced or Eliminated? Limiting spending in a campaign would obviously cut down on the costs of elections and make candidates less dependent on outside sources of revenue. But the limits would have to be voluntary, because the Supreme Court stated that involuntary restrictions on campaign spending violate freedom of speech. Several countries, such as the United Kingdom and Canada, impose spending limits on candidates for national office although they do not limit party spending.

One proposal that has received considerable attention would set a voluntary ceiling for House and Senate elections, such as $600,000 for House races (about one dollar per person in the district) and $950,000 to $5.5 million for the Senate, depending on the population of the state. Candidates who abide by these ceilings would receive free and reduced-cost time on television and cheaper mailing rates.

Voluntary limits with inducements for compliance would equalize spending and keep costs from getting out of hand. Incumbents who can raise more money might seem disadvantaged by this arrangement, but most will not be. Challengers usually need more money to balance the incumbent's advantages of recognition, constituency service, and record of accomplishments in office. But voluntary spending limits also could give greater advantage to wealthy candidates who do not have to abide by them.

Providing free or low-cost communications also might be a problem. The television industry strongly opposes doing so because they would lose revenue. Lower mail rates would have to be subsidized either directly by the taxpayers or by the postal industry by raising other postal rates higher. Countries such as Germany, Mexico, and the United Kingdom do require their television broadcasters to provide free time to political parties but not to individual candidates. The United States could do the same as a condition for renewal of television licenses, but what about minority parties and independent candidates? What about stations that do not use the airwaves but operate via cable or satellite?

SUMMARY: CAMPAIGN FINANCE DILEMMAS IN A NUTSHELL

American elections are getting more and more expensive. For some candidates it seems almost as if the sky is the limit when it comes to campaign spending. And there is no end in sight. Each election has become more costly than the previous one.

The need for money has become an obsession for candidates and has encouraged them to spend increasing amounts of time, energy, and money raising it. Their drive to fill their own campaign coffers has created (at least in the public's mind) a political system in which the wealthy exercise the most influence, thereby undermining the equity principle in a democracy.

For the last thirty-five years, Congress and the president have had to contend with campaign finance issues and the scandals, allegations, and demoralization that have resulted from them. Initially, the solution was thought to lie in requirements that limited contributions to candidates for federal office, established voluntary spending limits for presidential candidates who accepted government subsidies and grants, and established comprehensive reporting requirements monitored by an election commission.

The legislation enacted in the 1970s achieved some of these objectives. It broadened the base of public participation; for a time, it decreased the influence of the wealthy on the election process and brought campaign finance into full public view. But many of these achievements were subsequently dissipated by the soft money loophole created in 1979, exploited most fully in 1996 and 2000, and only partially closed in 2002. The soft money problem persists as a consequence of partisans finding a way to circumvent the law, and the Federal Election Commission's inability and unwillingness to rule against this practice.

The restrictions placed on issue advocacy advertising in the closing thirty days before a primary and sixty days before a general election have limited stealth advertising for the presidential candidates by advocacy groups. They have, however, encouraged the parties and their group allies to place greater emphasis on grassroots activities in the closing days of the campaign. The increase in turnout in 2004 and 2006 in part may have resulted from these turnout-the-vote activities.

The problems of high costs, large contributions, and increasingly unlimited expenditures remain, however, buttressed in large part by the Supreme Court's interpretation of independent spending as free speech protected by the First Amendment to the Constitution. It is this dose of liberty that makes equality so hard to achieve in the American electoral process and creates the dilemmas that confront those who try to do so.

Can campaign spending be equalized without impinging on constitutionally protected freedoms? Can candidates be assured that they will have sufficient money to get their message across without increasing the burden on taxpayers, forcing the news media to provide free time, or maintaining a situation in which those who have access to money are advantaged? And finally, can incumbents who have profited from the current system be induced to change it in a manner that reduces their advantage?

In addition to the free speech–equal influence quandary, fixing the problem of federal funding is difficult because of the ideological opposition to any federal subsidies by some elected officials and the lack of public support for public funding of all election activities.

The inability to overcome these difficulties has contributed to public cynicism in the electoral system. The general perception today is that government is for sale to the highest bidder. Money, once seen as the mother's milk of politics, is now perceived as the root of all evil, a poison pill.

Now It's Your Turn

Discussion Questions

1. Is money really as corrupting an influence on politics and government as people believe?
2. Do the wealthy exercise disproportionate influence on the conduct of elections and, through that influence, on the operation of government?
3. Are American elections really too expensive? What would be a reasonable criterion by which to evaluate whether the costs of elections are excessive?
4. Can money in elections be regulated without violating First Amendment protections of freedom of speech? If so, how? If not, why not?
5. Does money buy electoral success?

Topics for Debate

Challenge or defend the following statements:

1. All laws regulating campaign finance, except for the reporting requirements, should be abolished.
2. All federal elections should be publicly funded.
3. Congress should increase the matching funds and decrease the spending limits that accepting those funds impose on candidates seeking their party's presidential nomination.
4. The required political composition of the Federal Election Commission should be abolished and replaced by the appointment of independent, nonpartisan commissioners.
5. The Bipartisan Campaign Reform Act is fatally flawed and should be repealed.
6. The Constitution should be amended to specifically exclude campaign spending from the free speech protection of the First Amendment.

Exercise

This exercise has two parts. The first is to design a nonpartisan, public relations campaign on the need for campaign finance reform in the United States today. In your campaign indicate why the system must be reformed and what those reforms should be. Make sure that you try to anticipate the objections that different groups may raise.

For the second part of your exercise, assume that your campaign has worked, that you have generated enough of a public outcry to move Congress into action. At this point, assume the role of a Democratic or Republican member of a committee (your choice depending on your own political persuasion) charged with investigating the issue and proposing a legislative solution.

1. Outline the major points of a bill that addresses the problems you have cited in your public relations campaign. (Remember you are now a partisan, so

your bill should not adversely affect the interests of your party. However, if it is to be enacted into law it must not adversely affect the interests of the other party.) In your statement anticipate the criticisms that members of the other party on the committee are likely to make and respond to them.

2. With your class as the full committee, have a vote at the end to see whether or not your proposals should be sent forward to the floor of Congress.

INTERNET RESOURCES

- Center for Responsive Politics: www.opensecrets.org
  A public interest group that focuses on money and elections; publishes alerts, news releases, and major studies on campaign finance issues.
- Campaign Finance Institute: www.campaignfinanceinstitute.org
  The Institute, associated with George Washington University, collects and analyzes detailed finance information from the most recent federal elections and makes recommendations on how to improve the electoral system.
- Common Cause: www.commoncause.org
  An organization that considers itself a citizens' lobbying group; for years, it has been at the forefront of campaign finance reform.
- Public Citizen: www.publiccitizen.org
  A public interest group that provides information about problematic relationships among money, elections to office, and governance.
- Political Money Line: www.politicalmoneyline.org
  A Web site that provides an up-to-date financial data on candidates, campaigns, and public officials.
- Federal Election Commission: www.fec.gov
  The official source of campaign revenues and expenditures for federal elections; puts candidate finance reports on its Web sites as well as analyzes data from these reports and makes it available to the public.

SELECTED READINGS

Corrado, Anthony. *Paying for Presidents: Public Financing in National Elections.* New York: Twentieth Century Fund Press, 1993.

Magleby, David B., Anthony Corrado, and Kelly D. Patterson, eds. *Financing the 2004 Election.* Washington, D.C.: Brookings Institution, 2006.

Malbin, Michael, ed. *The Election After Reform: Money, Politics, and the Bipartisan Campaign Reform Act.* Lanham, Md.: Rowman and Littlefield, 2006.

Mann, Thomas E. "The U.S. Campaign Finance System Under Strain: Problems and Prospects," in Robert D. Reischauer and Henry J. Aaron, eds. *Setting National Priorities: 1999*. Washington, D.C.: Brookings Institution, 1999.

Ornstein, Norman J., et. al., "Reforming Campaign Finance," in Anthony Corrado, Thomas E. Mann, Daniel R. Ortiz, Trevor Potter, and Frank J. Sorauf, eds. *Campaign Finance Reform: A Sourcebook*. Washington, D.C.: Brookings Institution, 1977.

Princeton Survey Research Associates. "Money and Politics: A National Survey of the Public's Views on How Money Impacts on the Political System," commissioned by the Center for Responsive Politics, Washington, D.C., March 1977.

Sabato, Larry J. *PAC Power*. New York: Norton, 1985.

Sorauf, Frank J. *Money in American Elections*. Glenview, Ill.: Scott Foresman, 1988.

NOTES

1. A survey conducted by the Pew Research Center for the People and the Press found that three out of four Americans are concerned about the influence of lobbyists and special interest groups in Washington. Almost half said that they were very concerned about the issue. "Public Disillusionment with Congress at Record Levels," Pew Research Center for the People and the Press, April 20, 2006, http://people-press.org/reports/display.php3?ReportID=275.

2. See the 1998 Pew survey on public trust in government, *Deconstructing Distrust* (Washington, D.C.: Pew Research Center for People and the Press, 1998). Another report on a national survey was conducted for the Center on Policy Attitudes in January 1999. *Expecting More Say: The American Public on Its Role in Government Decisionmaking* also found a majority of the populace believing government is run by special interests not for the benefit of all the people, question 12, 36.

3. Joseph Carroll, "Most Important Problem: Government Dissatisfaction as the Nation's Most Important Problem," Gallup Poll, January 10, 2006, http://poll.gallup.com/content/default.aspx?ci=14338.

4. Center for Responsive Politics, "The Big Picture-1996, 2000, 2004," www.crp.org/pubs/big-picture/overview.

5. In an effort to control spiraling media expenses, the law limited the amount that could be spent on advertising. This provision later was eliminated after new legislation was drafted in 1976 following the Supreme Court's *Buckley v. Valeo* decision that voided several provisions of the recently enacted legislation.

6. Initially, the names of the contributors and the amounts they gave did not even have to be reported. Congress subsequently imposed a reporting requirement similar to the one that existed for all other contributions.

7. Political Moneyline.com, "Money in Politics Databases," www.politicalmoneyline.com.

8. Michale J. Malbin, "A Public Funding System in Jeopardy: Lessons from the Presidential Nomination Contest of 2004," in Michael J. Malbin ed., *The Election after Reform: Money,*

Politics and the Bipartisan Campaign Reform Act (Lanham, Md.: Rowman and Littlefield, 2006), 226–232.

9. Tom DeLay, "Statement on Shays-Meehan Bill," August 3, 1998, www.majoritywhip.house.gov/Reform/080398/cfrkillshaysmeehan.asp.

10. Calculated by author from data from the Committee for Responsive Politics' Web site for the 2003–2004 election cycle, "Winning vs. Spending," www.opensecrets.org/bigpicture/bigspendersasp?Display=A&Memb=s&sort=D.

11. According to a survey conducted by Princeton Survey Research Associates for the Center for Responsive Politics, 52 percent of the respondents believe that the use of money in elections determine whether a political candidate wins or loses an election "often," 38 percent "sometimes," and only 7 percent, "hardly ever." Center for Responsive Politics, "Money and Politics: A National Survey of the Public's Views on How Money Impacts on the Political System," 1997, Question 20B.

12. Gary C. Jacobson, *The Politics of Congressional Elections* (Boston: Little, Brown, 1983), 42.

13. In 2004, 13 percent of those surveyed by the National Election Studies said that they contributed money to a candidate running for office. Found at the American National Election Studies, Table 6B, www.umich.edu/~nes/nesguide/toptable/tab.5b_5.htm.

14. Center for Responsive Politics, "Money and Politics," Part II, 1–2.

15. According to the 1992 "Money and Politics" survey conducted by Princeton Survey Research Associates for the Center for Responsive Politics, the following percentages of the respondents say that the use of money to buy political influence occurs "often":

    • Leads elected officials to support policies they don't think are best for the country: 45%
    • Leads elected officials to spend too much time fund-raising: 63%
    • Leads elected officials to vote against constituent interests: 44%
    • Keeps important legislation from being passed: 48%
    • Gets someone appointed to office who would not otherwise be considered: 50%
    • Gives one group more influence by keeping another from having its fair say: 55%

    Found at www.opensecrets.org/pubs/survey/s2.htm.

16. A poll of 1,347 adults conducted April 2–5, 1997, by the *New York Times*/CBS News asked "Whose attempts to buy influence bother you the most?"

    The responses were as follows:

Wealthy People	21%
Foreign Governments	45%
American Special Interest Groups	25%
Don't Know	8%

    Found in "Financing Campaigns: Skepticism, and a Need for Change," *New York Times*, April 8, 1997, A14.

17. Less than one third of the American people in 2006 believed "they could trust the government to do what was right just about always or most of the time." Gallup Brain, "Trust in Government," www.brain.gallup.com/content/?ci=5392. "Money and Politics" survey conducted by the Princeton Survey Research Associates for the Center for Responsive Politics, 3–4, www.opensecrets.org/pubs/survey/s2.

18. Ibid.

19. In the "Money and Politics" survey only 15 percent of respondents rated campaign finance as the nation's top priority; 45 percent saw it as a high priority, Question 25.

20. Even though people say the system is broken and needs fixing, they have very limited knowledge of the current law, how it works, who has benefited, and what changes may be necessary. The survey conducted for the Center for Responsive Politics in April 1997 asked

respondents to answer five multiple choice questions about the current law and its impact. Fewer than 1 percent of respondents got them all right; 4 percent got 4 correct, and 8 percent three correct. Even more disheartening, 30 to 40 percent did not even try to guess the right answer for each question.

Here are the questions asked and the percentage that got each correct. An asterisk indicates the right answer.

Do you happen to know which political party's national committee raised more money during the 1996 election cycle: Was it the Democrats or the Republicans, or did the two parties raise about the same amount of money?

Democrats	24%
Republicans*	21%
About the same	12%
Don't Know	43%

As far as you know, how much money does current law allow CORPORATIONS to give: (1) as much as they want, (2) only a limited amount, or (3) are they not allowed to contribute any money? Don't Know (4)

	1	2	3	4
DIRECTLY to campaigns of candidates for president and Congress	17	43	4	36
to national parties for party building activities, such as get-out-the-vote efforts	24	32	2	42

As far as you know, how much money does current law allow PRIVATE CITIZENS to give: (1) as much as they want, (2) only a limited amount, or (3) are they not allowed to contribute any money? Don't know (4)

	1	2	3	4
DIRECTLY to campaigns of candidates for president and Congress	27	41	2	30
To national parties, for party building activities, such as get-out-the-vote efforts	32	27	1	40

Ibid., questions 22–24.

21. However, ads bought at the lowest rate can be preempted by advertisements bought at a higher rate. To avoid preemption, candidates must buy at a fixed rate that is higher than the lowest rate category.

22. A related concern is the practice of bundling. Pioneered by Emily's List, a PAC that supports women candidates, the bundling procedure solicits individual contributions for candidates, collects them, bundles the checks for individual candidates together, and sends them to the candidates. In this way, the PAC's activities can result in much more money for a candidate than the $5,000 maximum a PAC can contribute. By prohibiting this practice, Congress could reduce the influence of PACs that have perfected this procedure, but would not decrease the dependence of congressional candidates on special interest money or the desires of these groups to find ways to help the candidates of their choice. And as discovered with the politics of campaign finance, where there is a will, there is a way.

23. Congress would probably not want to prevent what has become a widespread practice in the United States, that of having foreign corporations and even governments hire American firms to represent their interests in the United States.

24. Stephen R. Weissman and Ruth A. Hassan, "Public Opinion Polls Concerning Public Financing of Federal Elections, 1972–2000: A Critical Analysis and Proposed Future Directions," Campaign Finance Institute, 2005.
25. Related to spending limits are loan limits. Candidates often are forced to borrow huge sums of money to finance their campaign. If they win, they may spend several years raising the money to pay back these; if they lose the loans may not be repaid. Sometimes as a condition for support, the winning candidate in a nomination contest will help the losers pay back their loans. Sometimes they won't.

chapter 5

News Media

Watchdog or Pit Bull?

Did you know that. . .
- there are more free and accessible sources of campaign information than in the past, yet public knowledge remains abysmally low?
- although Americans say they believe in freedom of the press, almost half the people believe that the media have too much freedom?
- the more education people have, the less they trust the media?
- a majority of the population wants to prevent the broadcast media from projecting a winner in presidential elections while people are still voting?
- the voting-age group least informed about campaigns is the youngest: those between eighteen and twenty-nine?
- television is the primary source of election news in almost every advanced democratic nation?
- television news covers campaigns and elections as if they were sporting events?
- when the public has been asked to evaluate news media coverage of recent national campaigns, the average grade they have given has been between a C and a C+?
- the "spin" put on campaign coverage today is more negative than positive?
- television anchors and correspondents received six times more airtime than the candidates on the evening news shows of the major networks during the most recent presidential campaigns?
- the only professional groups that rate lower than television and newspaper correspondents on Gallup's honesty and moral character scale are members of Congress and people who sell used cars?
- 1996 was the first presidential election in which all the major candidates for president and Congress had Web sites?
- the Internet is the fastest growing communications vehicle for the major news organizations?
- John Kerry had much more favorable press during the 2004 presidential campaign than did George W. Bush?
- only one in four people between the ages of eighteen and twenty-nine reports paying close attention to the news?

Is this any way to run a democratic election?

A free and fair press is essential to a democratic electoral process. In theory, the news media expand the information available and reach more people than would a campaign conducted by word of mouth, printed literature distributed by parties, or an event-driven campaign. The press provides a more objective presentation and analysis of that information than could be expected from self-interested candidates and parties. Reporters facilitate comparisons among those running for office and puts the campaign debate within a historical and contemporary context, which makes for a more informed judgment. For all these reasons, media coverage of election campaigns is important, more so as the electorate has expanded and the number of elections has increased.

Weak grassroots party organizations and new communications technology, however, have placed additional burdens on the media, burdens that the press has had difficulty handling. The news media have become fair game for criticism from candidates, elected officials, parties, and the general public.

Why is the news media's role in the electoral process so crucial? How well are the various news media playing that role? To answer these questions, the discussion turns first to the reasons why elections have become so media driven. Then it explores the changes in communications technology that have thrust the news media front and center. Next, it looks at the ways contemporary campaigns are communicated to voters and the impact of that communication on the electorate and the electoral process. The final part of the chapter discusses various proposals for improving the scope and content of campaign communications with the goal being a more informed and involved public.

MEDIA-DRIVEN DEMOCRATIC ELECTIONS: "THAT'S THE WAY IT IS"

With the words "That's the way it is," long-time television news anchor Walter Cronkite used to end each broadcast of the CBS *Evening News*. It was as if there could be no other news than what Walter and the network's correspondents reported, nor any other way to present it than in the pictures and words that came into living rooms across the country every weekday evening for half an hour.

Seeing is believing, and the three major networks made Americans believers. They also made the candidates into television personalities and their campaigns into made-for-TV productions. Radio and television became the principal vehicles through which campaigns were conducted and the electorate informed. And that's the way it still is today. The mass media and their news outlets form the major link between the candidates, their parties, and the electorate; it is the screen on which the vast majority of people view the elections and make a judgment.

Not only do the news media report election campaigns in living color, they also interpret them. They "spin" the news by what they choose to present and how they choose to present it. Moreover, they explain the meaning of the elections, help define the agenda for newly elected officials, and then become the watchdogs of those officials and assessors of their performance in office. These functions give the news media enormous power.

To the extent that the information presented is accurate, comprehensive, relevant, and impartial, the electorate is well served. To the extent that the information is incomplete, inaccurate, incomprehensible, truncated, skewed, biased, or in any other way unfair, the electorate is shortchanged, and the democratic electoral process suffers. In short, the scope, content, and spin of the news can enhance or warp the public's vision, facilitate or impede its electoral decisions, energize or turn off voters, and provide realistic or unrealistic policy expectations of the newly elected government. All of this can and does affect attitudes toward politicians and government.

New Technology and the News: More Sources, More Speed, but Less Reliable

Technology has driven some of these changes. It has speeded up and expanded communication links, shortening the time frame in which news reaches people and making it easier, cheaper, and in some ways even better (in the sense of getting the big picture) to stay at home to watch a campaign unfold and to listen to the candidates than to attend campaign events.

For better or worse, the press has moved or been thrust into the roles that parties used to play when communicating with the voters. And, according to Thomas E. Patterson, in his very influential book *Out of Order*, the news media are not suited for this task:

> The job of parties is to aggregate society's interests and offer voters a choice between coherent competing alternatives. . . . The press is not equipped to play a comparable role. The media's incentive lies in attracting and holding the audience's attention, and thus it endeavors to deliver the news in a form that will do so. . . . The press is necessarily guided by its own conventions and organizational imperatives, and these are certain to dominate its decisions. Hence, it cannot be expected to organize political choice in a coherent way.[1]

Pack Journalism

If members of the press were subject to the same type of scrutiny they give to the candidates and their campaigns, this enlarged role might not be so dangerous or dysfunctional for contemporary electoral politics. But, alas, they are not. The First Amendment guarantees a free press, and the news media are quick to bridle at any restrictions on their freedom to cover an election, report it as they see it, and protect their confidential sources.

Part of the problem stems from what they report and how they report it. Another part stems from their "pack" tendencies, which magnify the coverage they emphasize and minimize other less reported or unreported news about the election. Yet another part of it stems from the candidates' reaction to the coverage they expect. Candidates orchestrate and compartmentalize their newsworthy activities and statements into morsels that they hope the press will devour and then regurgitate. Moreover, candidates also try to reinforce their good news and their opponents' bad news through paid advertising, which is *not* subject to the same standards for truthfulness and accuracy as is commercial advertising. To make matters worse, the media bombardment precedes and follows the campaign, drawing the news out over many months and, in the case of a presidential election, even years, thereby numbing voters.

It's almost as if three interrelated campaigns are going on at once. In one, the candidates are appealing directly to the electorate for votes. In another, they're attempting to win the media campaign by controlling the agenda, spinning their news, leaking unfavorable stories about their opponents, and reacting quickly to controversies about themselves and their supporters highlighted in the press. The third campaign is the one the media report to the electorate. It consists of entertaining news that commands the attention of their consumers, rather than news intended to educate the polity in the exercise of its civic responsibilities.

How did we get to this state of affairs?

THE EVOLUTION OF ELECTION NEWS

The American press has always been politicized. From the onset of the Revolutionary War, to the debate on ratification of the Constitution, to the evaluation of the nation's new government, the press had a discernible political perspective that shaped what was reported as news. Early newspapers were opinionated and argumentative, but they weren't aimed at the general population. They were intended for the educated and business classes.

The audience for and content of newspapers began to change during the 1830s, as the parties expanded their popular base. Technological improvements, a growth in literacy, and the movement toward greater public involvement in political affairs all contributed to the rise of the "penny press"—newspapers that sold for a penny and were profitable by virtue of their advertising and mass circulation. To sell more papers, news stories had to be entertaining and exciting. Electoral campaigns fit this mold better than most other news about politics, government, and public policy. As a consequence, campaigns have received extensive coverage through the years.

Technology has played its part. The invention of the telegraph helped make it possible for an emerging Washington press corps to communicate information about national political issues to the entire country. The first radio station began operating in 1920, and radio remained the principal electronic news medium from the 1920s to the 1950s. The 1924 presidential election was the first to be reported on radio; the conventions, major speeches, and election

TABLE 5.1 Changing Sources of Campaign News, 1992–2004 (percentages)

Question: How Did You Get Most of Your Election News?

November	1992	1996	2000	2004
Television	82	72	70	76
Newspapers	57	60	39	46
Radio	12	19	15	22
Magazines	9	11	4	6
Internet	n/a	3	11	21

Note: Numbers add to more than 100 percent because voters could list up to two primary sources.

Source: Trends 2005 (Washington, D.C.: Pew Research Center for the People and the Press), 47.

returns were broadcast to a national listening audience. During the 1928 election, both major presidential candidates (Herbert Hoover and Alfred E. Smith) spent campaign funds on radio advertising.

Television and the Broadcast News Networks

Television came into its own in the 1950s, and the number of television sets and the hours that people watched quickly grew. TV soon became the primary source of fast-breaking news events and the primary communication vehicle for people to acquire their knowledge of the candidates and issues. In contrast, newspaper readership declined, particularly among the younger generations. Table 5.1 indicates the primary sources on which people in the United States depend for their campaign news.

The primary source for televised news used to be the half-hour news broadcast on the three major networks: ABC, NBC, and CBS. With the growth of cable, however, the public's news sources have become more fragmented. There also has been a tendency for people to rely on that source that most closely reflects their ideological and partisan orientation: Republicans turn to Fox News, Democrats to CNN, and young people to the *Daily Show with Jon Stewart.*[2]

The effect of television was felt as early as 1952, when Republican vice presidential candidate Richard Nixon denied allegations that he had obtained and used campaign gifts for himself and his family. The speech in which Nixon also vowed not to give up the family dog, Checkers, who had been given to the Nixons by political supporters, generated favorable public reaction and testified to the power of television if used effectively by candidates. Forty years later, Bill Clinton turned to television first to deny accusations of extramarital affairs that threatened to derail his presidential campaign. He later used the medium to repackage himself as a mainstream moderate, the protector of the people's popular health, education, and environmental programs, which, he claimed, the Republicans were threatening. Finally, his administration created an event-based environment to portray the president as hard working and much traveled, doing the nation's business as the Republican Congress unleashed its personal vendetta against him that culminated in his impeachment by the House of Representatives.

The marketing of candidates on television, through paid political advertising and newsworthy speeches and events, has revolutionized the electoral process, particularly the strategy and tactics of campaigning. It has enabled candidates to craft their own images and to challenge those of their opponents. Another example of the power of television came during the four debates held in 1960 between the two major presidential candidates, Sen. John F. Kennedy and Vice President Richard M. Nixon. In their first debate, the vice president's pallid appearance, darting eyes, and unrehearsed responses damaged his image and probably contributed to Kennedy's narrow victory.

The growing importance of television affected the print media as well. Because television reported events at or close to the time they happened, newspapers and magazines had to supplement their coverage and commentary in order to provide an additional dimension and thereby maintain a product that people would want to buy. One way they did so was to "find" news by investigating activities that on the surface might not have appeared newsworthy.

The Impact of Cable

The development and expansion of twenty-four-hour cable news left the major broadcast networks in a similar situation. Because they aren't usually the first to report fast-breaking events, they've had to find news and make it as interesting as possible. To do this, the broadcast networks have become more investigative and adversarial in their reporting of election news. Their news stories have become shorter and more action oriented to placate the short attention spans of viewers who sit with remote controls at their fingertips.

News from the broadcast networks also has become *softer,* "more sensational, more personality-centered, less time-bound, more practical, and more incident-based than other news." [3] Soft news is less concerned with policy matters, less concerned with political leadership, less concerned with major events and their consequences, and much less complex than traditional hard news. It also is consuming an increasing proportion of the content of network and cable news. [4]

To make matters worse, the major networks cut back on their news staff in the 1990s. They reduced the size of their foreign news bureaus and the coverage they devoted to foreign affairs, at least until the terrorist attacks of September 11, 2001, and the U.S. response in Afghanistan and Iraq. They even decreased their coverage of electoral politics from 1988 to 2000. (See Table 5.2.)

When declining coverage of campaigns is combined with increasing amount of soft news on news shows, the result is less detailed information

TABLE 5.2 **Election News Coverage, 1988–2004**

	1988	1992	1996	2000	2004
Amount of Coverage					
Number of stories	589	728	483	462	504
Minutes per day	1,116	1,400	788	805	1,007
Average number of stories per day	10.5	11.5	7.7	7.3	9
Average sound bite (seconds)	9.8	8.4	8.2	7.8	7.8
Focus of Coverage (percent of stories)					
Horse race	58%	58%	48%	71%	48%
Policy issues	39%	32%	37%	40%	49%
Tone of Coverage (percent good press)					
Dem. nominee	31%	52%	50%	40%	59%
GOP nominee	38%	29%	33%	37%	37%

Note: Based on evaluations by nonpartisan sources in election stories on ABC, CBS, and NBC evening newscasts.

Source: From "Campaign 2004 Final: How TV News Covered the General Election," *Media Monitor* (November/December 2004): p 5. Used by permission of the Center for Media & Public Affairs.

readily available to the general viewing public by the major television networks. However, there has been an increase in national election coverage by local news organizations. One study of eleven regional markets during the 2004 presidential election found that almost two out of three local news shows contained at least one election story, half of which concerned the presidential race.[5]

Moreover, because the major news networks now have to compete with hundreds of cable and satellite entertainment channels, the information they provide has to be captivating, current, and concise. In short, there is more information, although it is not necessarily more newsworthy.

There is another problem. Not only has the diversity of programs available to the general population by cable and satellite increased, but so has the speed at which information travels. Rumors move so fast these days that the establishment press has had to relax its two-source verification rule, often giving allegations as much attention in the news as verifiable items. Coverage of a rumor or allegation lends credibility to it, clouding the line between fact and fiction.

To make matters worse from the candidates' perspective, a credibility gap has emerged: the news media no longer give politicians and public officials the benefit of doubt. The press regularly imputes political motives of the candidates when they make statements and take policy positions. In turn, candidates see the press as hostile and overly negative. In fact, they often point to that negativism when justifying their own attempts to put a favorable spin on the news. And they've taken to talk or entertainment radio and television to circumvent the national press corps and get their messages across.

Internet News

Finally, the broadcast and cable news networks, major magazines, and newspapers have all established Web sites on which they regularly post information on fast-breaking events, present their regular news reports and commentaries, and archive past news stories. There also has been a growth of public interest Web sites on which more detailed policy discussions and candidate evaluations are provided. Were members of the public to access these sites, they could gain a substantial resource for learning about the campaign.

And people increasingly are going online for campaign news. About 11 percent of the population reported that the Internet was their main source of campaign news in 2000, and that number almost doubled to 21 percent for 2004.[6] People who use the Internet in this manner tend to access the popular news Web sites: CNN, America Online, and Yahoo.[7] They do so primarily because those sites offer a quick and convenient way to stay informed.[8]

If the most informed individuals stay informed by regularly going on the Internet, then the availability of more sites and more information may not be expanding the informed public as much as it is keeping these people up-to-date and reinforcing the political predilections they bring to a campaign. Because Internet users can bookmark their favorite sites, they are more likely to choose sites that reflect rather than challenge their beliefs and attitudes. The bottom line seems to be that there is more information out there but most of the general public is not using it to become more knowledgeable about campaigns and elections.

THE ADEQUACY OF CONTEMPORARY CAMPAIGN COVERAGE

To what extent do the news media present information about elections fairly and accurately? To what extent do they skew the news toward the desires of their mass audience, presenting what they believe people want to know, not necessarily what they need to know to make an informed, enlightened judgment on election day? To what extent do they fulfill the informational needs of a democratic electoral process?

Journalistic Bias: Ideological or Professional?

In deciding what to report, the news media impose their bias. Some believe that it's an ideological bias. Conservatives and Republicans in particular see the national press as liberal, Democratic, and likely to favor candidates who share

TABLE 5.3 **Perceptions of News Media Accuracy, 1985–2005 (percentages)**

Question: In general, do you think news organizations get the facts straight or do you think news organizations' stories and reports are often inaccurate?

	Facts Straight	Often Inaccurate	No Opinion
2005 (May)	45	48	7
2003 (May)	36	62	2
2000 (December)	32	65	3
1998 (July)	50	45	5
1989 (August)	54	44	2
1988 (January)	44	48	8
1985 (June)	55	34	11

Source: Gallup Poll, "Poll Topics: Media Use and Evaluation," 1985–2003, www.gallup.com/content/default.aspx?ci=16638&pg=1. The 2005 data is from Princeton Survey Research Associates in a poll conducted for the Annenberg Public Policy Center, "Public and Press Differ about Partisan Bias, Accuracy and Press Freedom," May 24, 2005.

this political perspective. To support their contentions, these conservative critics often point to studies about the media that show the overwhelming number of national news reporters and correspondents to be Democratic, liberal, and urban oriented and to content analyses that show more favorable treatment of Democratic presidential candidates than Republican candidates.[9] (See Table 5.2.)

Others, however, point to the influence of the conservative corporate executives who oversee the communications empires of newspapers, radio stations, and television networks; to the corporate interests that advertise on these media and contribute to their profits; and to the editorials that reflect the conservative views of the owners, the publishers, and corporate advertisers.[10] They also note that news spin rarely coincides with electoral outcomes, suggesting that if the news media are biased, it is toward the underdog rather than the expected winner.

Although most people see some political bias in the news, a majority in the last four presidential elections judged news coverage of the principal candidates to be fair.[11] Nonetheless, there are persistent evaluative differences among partisans, with Republicans being more critical of the news media than independents, who are more critical than Democrats.[12]

Whereas politicians and partisans perceive an ideological bias, academic observers believe that there is a more pronounced professional bias, one reflected in the definition of what is newsworthy. All events, activities, and statements during elections are not equally newsworthy. The criterion of audience interest is the principal one the press uses to determine the newsworthiness of an item or event. From the perspective of the press, if an item is new, surprising, exciting, different, dramatic, or involving conflict, then it is more newsworthy than one that does not share any of these characteristics. The first utterance is more newsworthy than the second one, the unexpected development more newsworthy than the predicted outcome, the misstatement more newsworthy than the standard speech, and the contest more newsworthy than the substance of the issues, and controversy is usually deemed more newsworthy than consensus.

The media's orientation also extends to the format in which news is reported. It must be direct and, above all, simple. Positions are presented and contrasted as black or white; gray areas get less attention. The story usually has a single focus. There is a punch line or bottom line toward which the report is directed.

A Sound Bite Mentality

The concepts of what is news and how news is reported creates incentives for candidates to come up with new angles, new policies, and new events to galvanize public attention. It also encourages them to play it safe, not think out loud, and not take chances. Words, expressions, and ideas are pretested in focus groups to gauge the likely response before candidates express them in public. To combat a press eager to highlight critical and unexpected reactions, candidates stage their events, recruit their audiences, and try to engineer a "spontaneous" response from them. They speak in sound bites designed to capture public attention and do so in an environment tailored to reinforce them. The size of the "bite" serves an additional need of the news media, particularly radio and television. It facilitates the compartmentalization of news, compressing it into proportions that the press believes the public can digest.

To the extent that the public gains its information about the campaign from these short, simple statements, the amount of knowledge and especially the depth of it suffers. Newspapers, particularly national ones, such as the *New York Times, Christian Science Monitor,* and *Wall Street Journal,* and comprehensive metropolitan dailies, such as the *Chicago Tribune, Los Angeles Times,* and *Washington Post,* provide more extensive coverage. But only a small portion of the electorate regularly reads these papers, much less focuses on election news in them. As a result, what the bulk of the electorate receives is a snapshot, a partial and truncated piece of the campaign. Is it any wonder that people are poorly informed, that they retain so little of the news they see on television?

Interpretive Reporting

There's another problem with contemporary campaign coverage in the mass media: it is highly mediated. People today see and hear more from the correspondents reporting the news than from the candidates making it. S. Robert Lichter and his associates reported that the average campaign story on network evening news had correspondents and anchors on six times longer than the candidates.[13] In fact, the candidates are seen and heard only briefly. The average length of a quotation from a candidate on the evening news since the 1988 presidential election has been less than ten seconds! (See Table 5.2.) Compare this to 42.3 seconds in 1968. To communicate their message themselves, candidates seek alternative channels today such as talk radio, entertainment television, and the Internet.[14]

A major part of the media's interpretation of campaign news is the story line into which most campaign events are fitted. According to Thomas Patterson, a dominant story emerges and events within the campaign are explained in terms of it. In 1992 the story was the vulnerability of President Bush, first revealed by Pat Buchanan's surprising showing against him in the early caucuses and primaries, then by the "conservative takeover" of the Republican National Convention, and finally, by the president's weak showing in the general election. The character issues that Bush raised about his opponents, and his own plans for future policies, weren't nearly as newsworthy in that election. Patterson describes this particular story line as the "likely-loser scenario." [15] It plagued George Bush in 1992 and Robert Dole in 1996.[16]

For Clinton, the story line, especially in 1996, was just the opposite. It was that of the "front-runner" who had a large lead and skillfully maneuvered to keep it. In this particular story, the press attributed Clinton's lead and inevitable success to a beneficial economic environment, superior resources, the perquisites of the presidency, and an extremely well-organized and well-run campaign. The news media's depiction of Ronald Reagan's 1984 presidential campaign had been presented in a similar manner, providing yet another illustration of the media's use of the front-runner script.[17]

Many people believe that members of the news media often let their preferences influence the way they report the news. Interpretive reporting contributes to the perception of media bias. It has made voters more wary and less trusting of television correspondents. According to a Gallup poll conducted in 2006, only 31 percent of respondents expressed a great deal or quite a lot of confidence in television news, and only 30 percent felt the same about newspapers. Congress, big business, and organized labor were rated even lower.[18]

Part of the problem has been declining perceptions of the accuracy of the press in reporting, as indicated in Table 5.3. These perceptions have been fueled in recent years by the news media's revelations of their own errors. One of the most glaring of these admissions was the acknowledgment by CBS that the documents its evening news presented during the 2004 presidential campaign as evidence of George W. Bush's questionable service in the Alabama National Guard were not authentic.

The Election Game

The story about the election is almost always reported as if it were a sporting event. The candidates are the players, and their moves (words, activities, and images) are usually described as strategic and tactical devices to achieve the principal goal of winning the election. Even their policy positions are evaluated within this game schema and are often described as calculated attempts to appeal to certain political constituencies.

The metaphor most frequently used in the election game is that of a horse race. A race—especially if it is close and if the result isn't readily predictable—generates excitement. Excitement holds interest, which sells newspapers and magazines and increases the size of radio and television audiences. Surprise, drama, and human interest stories do the same. When these elements are present, elections get more coverage than when they are absent.

In addition to conveying excitement and stimulating public interest, there is another reason why the media use the game format. It lends an aura of objectivity to reporting. It encourages the press to present quantitative data on the public's reaction to the campaign. Public opinion surveys, reported as news, are usually the dominant news item during the primaries and caucuses, often at the expense of substantive policy issues, and they share the spotlight with other campaign-related events during the general election.

Emphasizing the horse race is not a new phenomenon, but it often occurs at the expense of the policy debate. Table 5.2 indicates the amount of time given on the evening news to horse race, policy, and other campaign issues in the last five presidential elections. With the war in Iraq as the principal focus of the 2004 presidential campaign, policy issues received barely more attention than did the horse race.

What's the consequence of this type of coverage on the electorate? Simply put, it results in people's remembering less about the policy issues and about the candidates' programs for dealing with them. Although the candidates' positions get attention in the news media, the costs and consequences of their proposed solutions don't get nearly as much. A few national newspapers and magazines do provide this type of coverage, and occasionally the major broadcast networks have a special program on a particularly vexing economic or social issue, but for most people it is the horse race, the candidates themselves, and their strategies and tactics that get the most attention.

The Bad News Campaign

Campaign news coverage also tends to be highly critical. Of course, criticism per se isn't harmful to a democratic electoral process; in fact, it's a necessary part of that process. But an overemphasis on the negative, particularly on negative personal and character issues, can disillusion voters, decrease turnout, and render the election a contest among lesser evils.[19]

Why all the negativism? Are the candidates less qualified now than they were in the past? Most scholarly observers don't think so. They offer three principal reasons for the contemporary press's negativism: underlying skepticism about the motives and interests of politicians and elected officials; increasing emphasis on character issues, combined with scrutiny of private behavior; and increased competition with tabloid journalism in the news and entertainment marketplace.

The Vietnam War and the Watergate scandal ushered in an era of investigative journalism in which the media adopted an attitude of distrust and disbelief in their coverage of politics and government. Public officials and candidates for office were no longer taken at their word, no longer given the benefit of doubt. The press assumed that the statements and actions of those in power or vying for office were self-interested and not necessarily in the public interest, and that it was the job of the media to reveal hidden motives, strategies, and goals. In other words, it was their responsibility to present the other side.

As mentioned, campaign coverage became more candidate centered as investigative journalism began to focus more on the people seeking office than on their partisan connection. Pretty soon the line between public and private was obliterated, with the press trumpeting the importance of character as its rationale for reporting what used to be considered private (and therefore not pertinent) behavior.

With the tabloid press eager to highlight the personal foibles and relationships of prominent people, even if only rumored, the mainstream press found itself pressured by competition to follow suit. It often uses a report in the tabloid media, a news conference, or an unsubstantiated investigative report as the pretext for presenting this type of information as news. Thus the allegations of Gennifer Flowers that she was Bill Clinton's lover for eleven years became front-page news during the 1992 Democratic nomination, as did facsimiles of memos questioning George W. Bush's service in the Alabama National Guard and ads disputing John Kerry's heroism in the Vietnam War in 2004.

Opposition research by campaigns regularly stimulates and supplements this type of media coverage. Leaks have become a common and accepted way to alert the press to negative facts and rumors about one's opponents. Because the negative often is surprising and unexpected, this type of news feeds into the media's addiction to information that grabs their audience.

From the candidates' perspective, the bad news is magnified by the fact that they don't get the opportunity to respond in kind, to explain their side of events in anywhere near the detail as the charges made against them. Moreover, if the charges prove to be inaccurate, any corrections made by the press don't get nearly the amount of coverage as the events that prompted them.

As a result, candidates are left with little alternative but to defend themselves against even the most reckless charges, thereby giving even more attention to the charges at the expense of substantive policy issues. Not only must candidates respond quickly to allegations against them, so as not to allow an unfavorable image to become part of the public's perception, but they have an incentive to get "dirt" on their opponents. To make matters worse, candidates also have an incentive to reinforce negative personal news by running negative personal advertising against their opponents.

A number of unfortunate consequences for a democratic electoral process follow from this type of campaign behavior and media coverage. The electorate gets a jaundiced view of the campaign. It becomes more of a personal contest between two or more gladiators than an issue-oriented policy debate or a campaign between two parties with opposing philosophies and goals. It's presented by television anchors, correspondents, and star newspaper reporters, not by the candidates. It emphasizes the bad over the good.

PUBLIC CYNICISM ABOUT THE MEDIA

Not only does the news media's coverage of campaigns focus on the contest and the contestants rather than on the consequences of their policy, not only does it lessen respect for the candidates of all parties, not only does it impute their motives, but it also contributes to cynicism about the press itself.

In theory, there is broad support for a free press. Although many people may not understand the protections that the First Amendment provides media in the United States today, they do believe that newspapers, radio, television, and news magazines are necessary for a democratic society to hold the government in check.[20] However, according to a survey conducted by the Annenberg Public Policy Center, most people also believe that a government may restrict the right of the press to report a story, a position to which most journalists do not subscribe.[21] The belief that a free press is essential to a democratic society is shared by people in other democracies, as is the value placed on keeping up with national affairs.[22]

Despite the support for a free press, the desire to keep up with events, and the dependence on the media for election news, criticism of how the media do their job has been growing. Surveys conducted by the Pew Research Center for the People and the Press found a drop of 16 percent in respondents who expressed a great deal or some confidence in the press between 1990 (74 percent) and 2000 (58 percent).[23] Put simply, people today find the press less believable, less accurate, and more biased than they did in the past.

Yet despite the criticism of the press for what it reports and how it reports it, for its invasiveness, its inaccuracies, and its "gotcha" type of journalism, people are attracted to tabloid-like news and retain information from it. They evidence greater knowledge of celebrities in the news than they do of public officials.[24]

The public's ambivalence toward the news media; the people's desire for gossip, scandal, and conflict; and their criticism of the press for providing and emphasizing this type of information, create a situation in which the marketplace dictates the outcome. The mass media give their audience what they believe their audience wants. In this sense they are responding to their consumers' demands.

The interests of the public and the orientation of a profit-oriented media toward satisfying these often conflicting needs pose a real dilemma for a democratic society. How do we achieve an informed citizenry, involved in public affairs, in a free market economy, *if that citizenry doesn't want to be informed and involved in public affairs?* Before addressing this vexing dilemma, it is necessary to explore two subsidiary issues. Is today's citizenry less informed by the news media than were citizens two or three decades ago? And, equally important, how much public information is necessary for people to make informed voting decisions?

The Dumbing of the Electorate: Does It Matter?

The time frame for the first question about the level of information that the general public possesses is relatively short if answered with survey data. National polls of public knowledge, attitudes, and opinions were not conducted with any regularity until after World War II. Moreover, to make comparisons, responses to similar questions have to be analyzed. Finally, the vast majority of public affairs surveys ask attitude and opinion questions rather than informational ones. In fact, information is frequently provided in the question or statement so that people can respond intelligently.

The anecdotal evidence is not encouraging. Americans retain little information about specific issues and people. Many are hard-pressed to name their congressional representatives, much less assess their performance in office—unless, of course, they have been involved in a scandal or abused their position. National surveys reveal limited recognition of public officials until they regularly appear in the news. At the outset of the 2004 presidential election campaign (December 19, 2003, to January 4, 2004), 59 percent indicated they had never heard of Democratic candidate Howard Dean's comment about wanting to win the votes of guys with Confederate flags in their pickup trucks, 63 percent did not know that Wesley Clark had been a U.S. Army general, and 67 percent did not know which Democratic candidate had served as the majority leader in the House of Representatives.[25] (It was Richard Gephardt.)

The purpose of the campaign is to inform, and it does, at least to some extent. Surveys conducted by the Annenberg Center for Public Policy indicate that political learning does occur over the course of a national campaign. Campaign news coverage, political advertising, and coverage of such events as conventions and debates contribute to the learning process.[26] But do people learn enough? Can they make an enlightened judgment on election day? Most people believe that they can, as indicated in Table 5.4.

Information and Democracy: Three Views

How much public knowledge and activity are necessary to maintain the health and vitality of a democratic society? There are several schools of thought.

Those who subscribe to the **elitist model** of democracy believe that as long as the leadership is informed, involved, and responsible to the people through the electoral process, the political system can function properly. This minimalist theory of public involvement maintains that democratic criteria are satisfied if the citizenry has the opportunity to participate in elections and enough basic information to do so. Citizens need to be able to differentiate the

TABLE 5.4 **Voters' Perceptions of Information Adequacy, 1988–2004 (percentages)**					
Perception			Year		
	1988	1992	1996	2000	2004
Learned enough to make an informed choice	59	77	75	83	86
Did not learn enough from the campaign	39	20	23	15	13
Don't know/refused	2	3	2	2	2

Source: Pew Research Center For The People & The Press, "Voters Like Campaign 2004, but Too Much 'Mud-Slinging'," November 11, 2004.

candidates and their principal policy positions, factor in their own perceptions of reality, and make voting decisions. But not everyone has to be informed and participate in civic affairs for the system to work.

The **pluralist model** sees the system as democratic if it permits people to pursue their interests within the political arena. Elections are one of the political processes in which they can do so, but not the only one. Public demonstrations, letter-writing campaigns, and personal contacts are other means by which those outside of government can influence those in it. Again, the burden of being informed and involved rests primarily on the group leadership, on those in and out of power; the requirement for the populace is that its interests can be discerned, expressed, and pursued.

In both the elitist and the pluralistic models, the process by which people express their views is the main criterion for claiming that the system is democratic. The **popular**, or **plebiscitary, model** demands more. It requires a higher level of public involvement in politics and government. Within the electoral arena, this translates into more public debate, more interaction between the candidates and the electorate, and more people voting.

Those who adopt this perspective see the decline in public trust and confidence in politics and government as dangerous because it can lead to a concentration of power in the hands of a few. It also can reduce support for governmental decisions and for the people who make them and weaken the legitimacy of the rules and processes of the political system itself. One sign of alienation would be the growth of organized, armed vigilantes or militias, those who see it as their mission to take the law into their own hands. Another would be an increase in civil disobedience. A third might be the failure of a significant portion of the population to participate in elections and to vote.

It is difficult to answer the question of how informed and involved a citizenry must be to maintain a democratic political system. But there is little doubt that the more information, involvement, and active support the general population gives to the candidates who run for office, to the party platforms on which they run, and to their qualifications for office and performance in it, the more likely it is that people can make enlightened judgments when they vote.

Of course, people don't get all their information about campaigns from the news media. Candidate advertisements are another source of information, as are personal contacts and experience, particularly when those experiences reinforce or refute the claims candidates make. However, news coverage is still a very important component of the process of gathering sufficient information to make an informed voting decision—hence the issue addressed in the last part of this chapter: how to facilitate an attentive and involved public through the mass media.

WHAT CAN BE DONE?

Criticizing contemporary press coverage of elections is much easier than making constructive suggestions for changing it. The electorate may be getting what it wants but not necessarily what it needs. It is all well and good to berate the news media for not presenting a detailed discussion of the issues. But what good is it to present such a discussion if the public is not interested in it, does not follow it, or is turned off by it? Besides, as already noted, there is plenty of detailed and easily accessible information about the candidates and their campaigns, the parties and their platforms, and the voters and their interests and desires. It is readily available in national newspapers and magazines, on public radio and television, and on the Web sites of the participants, as well as in interest group publications received by members.

We can wring our hands and bemoan the fact that most people don't regularly consult these sources. We can say that they should, but we certainly aren't ready to reinstitute literacy tests as a condition for voting. We can blame this state of affairs on the failure of civic education in the schools, a claim that probably has some merit, but shaking our heads sadly about underinformed, uninvolved, generally apathetic citizens won't change the situation, although it might enable some to rationalize it more satisfactorily.

We can blame the problem on the news media. Thomas Patterson believes that those who determine media markets have made a wrong-headed assumption that people interested in news want an endless diet of soft, tabloid-oriented pabulum to consume. Not so, he says. In a study of the news preferences of television audiences, he found hard news to be more appealing to more people than soft news. Moreover, he also discovered that consumers of hard news were less tolerant of soft news than consumers of soft news were of hard news.[27] Patterson concludes that in their effort to compete with the increasing variety and number of news/entertainment shows, the national news networks have done themselves and our democracy a disservice by increasing their emphasis on soft news.[28] So the question becomes, what can be done to change contemporary media coverage of elections?

Redefine Election News

One suggestion is to induce those who control the scope and methods of electoral coverage to change their definition of news, their standards for reporting it, and their game-oriented emphasis. A task force on campaign reform has urged such an approach. It suggests that the press "use the campaign controversies as spring boards for reporting on the real substance of politics and political careers, rather than treating them as self-contained episodes." [29] Similarly, instead of entertaining horse race stories reporting polls of who is ahead and by how much, the task force recommends more analysis of *why* different groups seem to be supporting different candidates; more in-depth reporting, be it on character or substantive policy concerns; and more emphasis on the big issues that transcend day-to-day events. The task force report also makes the observation that election news could be more repetitive, that news does not always have to be new, and that the test for including information should be the level of public knowledge on a subject, not the level of the press's knowledge about it.[30] Too often the catalyst for a story is the desire to scoop other journalists for something new and different rather than the salience of the issue to the voters and the country.

Thomas Patterson reaches much the same conclusion when he argues that the hard news component must be strengthened if people are to have the information they need to make an informed judgment on election day. "What is good for democracy is also good for the press," he writes.[31]

These are excellent suggestions, but they require the news media to change their journalistic orientation. Such changes tend to come slowly, if at all, and they are usually dictated by the marketplace. Citizens could vote for these reforms with their television remotes and radio dials by tuning in to news programs that provide more in-depth, policy-oriented coverage, such as public radio and television, two media outlets whose audiences have increased over the last two decades.[32] But that opportunity currently exists, and we see the results. Without a massive, negative reaction to contemporary election coverage or a massive public relations campaign like those for eating healthy foods, refraining from smoking, or not drinking and driving, people are unlikely to change their reading, listening, and viewing habits quickly or easily.

Shorten the Campaign

A different type of suggestion was proposed by Thomas Patterson several years ago. In *Out of Order,* Patterson recommends shortening election campaigns, particularly the long and arduous nomination contests that now consume more time than the general election.[33] A more compact campaign, he believes, would of necessity focus the mass media on the more important issues, cut down their interpretations and negativity, and force the political parties to play a greater role in communicating with the voters.[34] But it also would provide less time for an inattentive public to learn about the candidates and issues.

Moreover, national legislation would probably be required to impose the time period in which campaigning could occur, thereby increasing even more the regulatory role of the federal government in elections and possibly conflicting with the free speech protections of the First Amendment. Unless campaign finance laws were changed, candidates would still have to raise considerable sums of money and do so *before* the official campaign began. How would they obtain money without campaigning? If candidates were forbidden to raise early money, and if the current laws remained in place, incumbents and wealthy candidates would be even more advantaged than they are today. Besides, what guarantee would there be that the news media would become any less interpretive and negative?

Communicate More Directly

Another recommendation, made in some of the campaign finance proposals as well as by several bipartisan groups and commissions, is to conduct more of the campaign spontaneously and directly though the mass media. This would be done by extending the number of debates among the candidates, as well as by providing them with free broadcast time. Most European democracies feature debates among the principal candidates or party leaders, and some require on-air time to be provided to the parties. But most of these countries also operate government-controlled networks on which to provide such time; the United States does not.

If these suggestions were implemented in the United States, they might reduce but not eliminate the press's role as mediator between the candidates and the electorate. Depending on the format of the debates and the amount of free time to which candidates were entitled, these changes would give those running for office greater opportunity to address the issues in their own words. Candidates and parties also would exercise more control over the agenda of the campaign.

Require More Debates

Debates are useful for several reasons. They enable the public to see, compare, and evaluate candidates in the same setting, at the same time, and on the basis of the same criteria: their knowledge of the problems, their priorities and issue positions, and their communicative skills. Debates attract relatively large audiences, larger than most other political events during the election cycle. They allow candidates to speak in their own words uninterrupted for a specified time to which the participants have agreed. Coincidentally, certain debate formats reduce the press's role as intermediary.[35]

But not all candidates benefit equally from debates. Front-runners, particularly incumbents, see little advantage in debating their challengers; when they do, they are usually able to dictate the timing and format of the debate to their perceived advantage. Most candidates play it safe, anticipating their opponents' arguments and rehearsing lines in advance. Spontaneity is minimized. The candidates sound like their ads.

TABLE 5.5 **Presidential Debates: Combined Total Viewers, 1976–2004**			
Year	Networks	Dates	Total Viewers (millions)
1976 (Carter-Ford)	ABC, CBS, NBC	10/22 10/6 9/23	62.7 63.9 69.7
1980 (Carter-Reagan)	ABC, CBS, NBC	10/28	80.6
1984 (Mondale-Reagan)	ABC, CBS, NBC	10/21 10/7	67.3 65.1
1988 (Dukakis-Bush)	ABC, CBS, NBC	10/13 9/25	67.3 65.1
1992 (Clinton-Bush-Perot)	ABC, CBS, NBC, CNN	10/19 10/15 10/11	66.9 69.9 62.4
1996 (Clinton-Dole)	ABC, CBS, FOX, NBC, CNN	10/16 10/6	36.3 36.1
2000 (Gore-Bush)	ABC, CBS, FOX, NBC, CNN FOX NEWS, MSNBC	10/17 10/11 10/3	37.7 37.6 46.6
2004 (Bush-Kerry)	ABC, CBS, FOX, NBC, CNN FOX NEWS, MSNBC	10/13 10/8 9/30	51.2 46.7 62.5

Source: Nielsen Media Research.

Nor do the parties gain much from debates held during the nomination phase. Candidates usually try to distinguish themselves from one another rather than indicate what good partisans they are and with what party policy positions they concur. Moreover, nomination debates are rarely carried on the major broadcast networks, although they may be aired on local affiliates in the region or state in which the primary election occurs. The cable networks may cover some of them, and C-SPAN usually does, but its audience is quite small. The greater the number of debates, the smaller the television audience tends to be.

At the presidential level in the general election, the audience is larger. (See Table 5.5.) But the availability of many other entertainment shows, including competition with the baseball playoffs and World Series, reduces the size of the viewing audience and the duration of time people watch.[36] Thus, even if the debates were more easily available on television, it is likely that once their aura wore off, the principal audience would probably be composed of strong partisans who root for their candidate and inadvertent viewers who watch for a few minutes and then move on to other channels.

Until 2004, there was a decline in the proportion of the viewing audience who watched the presidential election debates since they started being held on a regular basis in 1976. Political polarization and the war in Iraq renewed interest in the debates in 2004. Table 5.5 shows the estimated debate audience in terms of numbers of voters.

There are other problems with having debates as the principal vehicle through which the candidates communicate with voters. Debates reward performance skills. They benefit telegenic candidates who are well prepared, well coached, and comfortable with television, essentially those who can give quick and catchy responses to the questions of moderators or the comments of their opponents. Those who take longer to make a point, who agonize over the complexities of issues, who don't communicate easily or quickly in sound bites, may be disadvantaged. Are debate skills important for elected officials? Should they be a major factor potentially affecting the election outcome?[37]

If the networks did not voluntarily air debates or provide free airtime, could they be forced to do so as a condition for obtaining their broadcast licenses? Would they be compensated for lost advertising revenue? If so, by whom— the taxpayers, the parties, the candidates, or perhaps commercial debate sponsors? Maybe the candidates could eat Ball Park hot dogs, drink Bud Light, wear Nike athletic shoes, or freshen themselves with a particular deodorant.

Then there are the issues of how many debates should be held, for what offices, and which candidates should be invited to them: all who are running or just those of the major parties? The longer the invitation list, the more candidates who would be encouraged to run. In the nomination phase, a plethora of candidates would factionalize the parties even further and trivialize the debates. In contrast, having only the major party candidates debate in the general election would reinforce their built-in advantage under the current system, unleveling the playing field even more for third-party and independent candidates.

Take the case of H. Ross Perot. In 1992 he was invited by the commission sponsoring the presidential debates to participate in them. The members of the commission believed that Perot was a viable candidate and could win the election or at least deny one of the major party candidates an Electoral College victory. Perot was not invited in 1996 nor was Ralph Nader or Pat Buchanan in 2000 or Nader again in 2004 because the same commission believed they couldn't carry a single state, let alone win the national election. Thus, in the commission's view, these third-party candidacies would not preclude a Democratic or Republican Electoral College majority from occurring

The commission's decision became a self-fulfilling prophecy. Without the debate podium, with less public funding, none of these candidates could overcome the impression, reinforced by the media, that they weren't viable.

A shorter campaign combined with a required debate format could reduce the news media's role, although, if the past is any indication, the press would still analyze the debates, solicit and report public reactions, and declare winners and losers. Would voters benefit from this arrangement? Would they gain and retain more objective information about the candidates, their positions, and their intellectual, communicative, and political skills? Would they be better able to make considered judgments on election day?

Give Candidates Free Airtime

Whatever your answer to these questions, it's clear that the candidates and their handlers would not be satisfied if debates were the only way they could use the mass media to reach voters.[38] Candidates want to communicate on their own, in their own setting. And the Constitution protects their right to do so, much as it protects the reporters' right to cover the election as they see fit.

Occasionally some candidates have been given a little free time by a major network, as in the 1996 and 2000 presidential elections. The networks provided an average of sixty-four seconds of free time per night in the month before the elections; local stations offered up only forty-five seconds per night for the same period.[39] Only a small percentage of voters report that they had seen the candidates during one of these brief periods. Such a small amount of air time is unlikely to have a discernible impact on public knowledge and voter decision making or discourse, which may explain why the impact of free television time thus far has been negligible.[40]

Various free-time proposals have been advanced. One would simply depend on voluntary time made available by the networks and independent stations. Another would *require* the networks to provide a certain amount of time to meet their public interest obligations and as a condition for getting and renewing their broadcast licenses. Congress also has granted the major networks free access to digital technology. Free time could be regarded as a partial payback.

Naturally, the major corporations that control the communications industry oppose a free-time requirement imposed on them by government, particularly one that obligates them to provide such air time during prime time. They fear that they would lose money. They point to the large number of candidates for national office who would want to take advantage of such time. Could minor party candidates be excluded? Who would decide? And how could the free time be monitored?

Although most candidates would probably use free time were it made available to them, it is unlikely that when doing so they would forgo other forms of communication, such as political advertising, or even deviate very much from the message of their ads. So would more free time really be more of the same political "propaganda," little more than advertising in another form?

SUMMARY: NEWS MEDIA DILEMMAS IN A NUTSHELL

The press is a critical link between the candidates and the electorate. Since the 1830s, the mass media—first newspapers, then radio and television, and now the Internet—have brought campaigns to the voters. That function has become even more important in the last four decades with the weakening of political parties' grassroots organizations and advances in communications technology.

Moreover, the news media themselves have changed. From a few major news networks to many media outlets, from radio to television to the Internet, from once-a-day reporting to constant and instantaneous news, the media have become both diverse and, at the same time, omnipresent. If these changes had contributed to a more attentive, informed, and involved electorate, then the democracy would have been well served, but alas, they have not.

Part of the reason is the scope, content, and format of the election news that is reported; part is the spin and the public's reaction to it. A journalistic orientation toward making the election news as interesting and captivating as possible (in light of greater competition) has resulted in media coverage that lacks substance. The emphasis is on newness, controversy, and drama, rather than on partisan and policy debates. The coverage has become more compartmentalized, more interpretive, and, with the advent of investigative reporting, more negative. The candidates are presented as players in an unfolding drama. The campaign story is told with sports metaphors and analogies, is strewn with juicy personality tidbits, and features the contending forces, each trying to manipulate the electorate to its advantage.

Coverage affects the campaign. It forces the candidates to orchestrate their activities for television with irresistible sound bites in their speeches, captivating pictures and personalities at their events, and well-known talking heads to spin their messages.

The public is informed primarily by this coverage. From the media's perspective, it is what their audience desires, although Patterson's research indicates that the news media may be wrong about this marketing judgment. From the perspective of democratic theory, it isn't enough of what an informed, intelligent electorate needs in order to make meaningful decisions on election day. The public, too, is critical of this coverage, yet continues to consume it and claim that it has sufficient knowledge to make intelligent voting decisions. Herein lays one dilemma: What good would it do to present more of the substantive policy debate if people were turned off by it and tuned it out? A second dilemma is how to energize the electorate and make people more positive about the electoral process without government regulating the form and content of news coverage. Is this the media's role?

Suggestions have been made to shorten the campaign and facilitate more direct communication between the candidates and voters with more debates and free airtime. Whether these could or should be imposed on profit-making media and, if so, whether they would provide more of the substantive debate that is presently lacking, is unclear.

Now It's Your Turn

Discussion Questions

1. What is the connection between public interest in politics and news about politics?
2. How does journalistic bias affect the scope and content of information that people learn about elections?
3. Is sufficient information available for the electorate to make informed judgments on election day? If not, who's at fault? If so, what's the problem? Does it lie with the news media or the electorate? How can it be fixed?
4. Should government exercise more control over the scope and content of campaign coverage?
5. What inducements might encourage the news media to provide more substantive policy information about contemporary election issues and more in-depth studies of the qualifications of those who seek elective office?
6. Can campaigns for federal office be made less dependent on media coverage? Should they be?
7. Do you think that the press exercises too much influence on election outcomes?

Topics for Debate

Challenge or defend the following statements:

1. A free press cannot be a fair and objective press.
2. If voters lack the information they need to make an informed voting decision today, it's their own fault.
3. A democratic electoral process requires the electorate to be opinionated but not necessarily informed.
4. Government should require the principal broadcast and cable news networks to give all candidates for federal office free and adequate airtime.
5. The private behavior of candidates is relevant to their public performance in office and should continue to be reported as election news.
6. The news media have a liberal ideological bias.
7. The news media have an obligation to report substantive policy debate in depth, whether or not the people are interested in that debate.

Exercises

1. A major television network asks for your advice on how to improve its campaign coverage of the next election. It would like you to prepare a memo with three goals in mind: meeting the network's public responsibility to inform voters, satisfying the interests of the viewing audience,

and gaining audience ratings higher than the competition's. Draft the memo. In your analysis, indicate the following:

   a. the aspects of the campaign that you would cover and the proportion of coverage you would give to each,

   b. the attention to be given to third-party and independent candidates versus major party candidates, to national versus local coverage, and to primaries versus the general election.

In addition, the network would like to know whether it should:

- relax its two-source verification rule in the interest of competition,
- air rumors and allegations about personal behavior if they appear credible,
- include in the candidates' personality profiles information about their physical and mental health, and
- give attention to candidate misstatements, inconsistencies, and off-color remarks?

2. Critique the news coverage of a current election campaign on one of the twenty-four-hour news networks, on public television, and on one of the broadcast networks on the basis of its adequacy, fairness, and information quality. In your critique, indicate the following:

   a. what you consider to be the most important issues of the campaign and the scope and emphasis given to each,

   b. whether the reporting was objective and the analysis fair and helpful,

   c. whether the candidates and parties were treated equally, and

   d. which medium provided the best coverage from the perspective of a democratic electoral process.

On the basis of the individual coverage provided, do you think voters would have enough accurate information to make informed decisions on election day?

INTERNET RESOURCES

- Annenberg Public Policy Center: www.appcpenn.org
  Part of the Annenberg School of Communications of the University of Pennsylvania, this public policy center conducts studies on the media, which it makes available on this Web site.
- Center for Media and Public Affairs: www.cmpa.com
  A organization that evaluates the amount and spin of the major broadcast networks' coverage of the news.
- The Freedom Forum: www.freedomforum.org
  An organization sponsored by the Gannett Foundation that provides information on media issues, particularly as they relate to the First Amendment; links to other Gannett groups, Newseum, and Press Watch, that also contain useful information on coverage of elections.

- Newspaperlinks.com: www.newspaperlinks.com
  Provides links to the online editions of local newspapers across the country.
- Politics Online, www.politicsonline.com
  A good source for presidential campaigning on the Internet.
- Other media sources with campaign Web sites:
  ABC News Politics: http://abcnews.go.com
  Associated Press: http://wire.ap.org
  CBS News: www.cbsnews.com
  CNN: http://cnn.com
  C-SPAN: www.cspan.org
  Fox News: http://foxnews.com
  Los Angeles Times: http://latimes.com
  NBC News: www.msnbc.com
  New York Times: www.nytimes.com
  USA Today: www.usatoday.com
  Washington Post: http://washingtonpost.com

SELECTED READINGS

Ansolabehere, Stephen, and Shanto Iyengar. *Going Negative: How Political Advertisements Shrink and Polarize the Electorate*. New York: Free Press, 1995.

Baum, Matthew A., and Samuel Kernell. "Has Cable Ended the Golden Age of Presidential Television," *American Political Science Review* 93 (1999): 99–111.

Cappella, Joseph N., and Kathleen Hall Jamieson. *Spiral of Cynicism: The Press and the Public Good*. New York: Oxford University Press, 1997.

Davis, Richard, and Diana Owen. *New Media and American Politics*. New York: Oxford University Press, 1998.

Downie, Leonard, Jr., and Robert G. Kaiser. *The News about the News: American Journalism in Peril*. New York: Alfred Knopf, 2002.

Druckman, James N. "The Power of Television Images: The First Kennedy-Nixon Debate Revisited," *Journal of Politics* 65 (2003): 559–571.

Farnsworth, Stephen J., and S. Robert Lichter. *The Nightly News Nightmare: Network News Coverage of U.S. Presidential Elections, 1988–2000*. Lanham, Md.: Rowman and Littlefield, 2003.

Graber, Doris A. *Mass Media and American Politics*, 7th ed. Washington, D.C.: CQ Press, 2005.

Hershey, Marjorie Randon. "The Campaign and the Media," in *The Election of 2000*. Gerald M. Pomper, ed. New York: Chatham House, 2001.

Iyengar, Shanto, Helmut Norpoth, and Kyu S. Hahn. "Consumer Demand for Election News: the Horserace Sells," *Journal of Politics* 66 (2004): 157–175.

Iyengar, Shanto, and Donald Kinder. *News That Matters: Television and American Opinion.* Chicago: University of Chicago Press, 1987.

Jamieson, Kathleen Hall. *Everything You Think You Know About Politics and Why You're Wrong.* New York: Free Press, 2000.

Just, Marion, et al. *Crosstalk: Citizens, Candidates, and the Media in a Presidential Election.* Chicago: University of Chicago Press, 1996.

Kerbel, Matthew R. "The Media: The Challenge and Promise of Internet Politics," in Michael Nelson, ed. *The Elections of 2004.* Washington, D.C.: CQ Press, 2005, 88–107.

———. *If It Bleeds It Leads.* Boulder, Colo.: Westview, 2000.

Lichter, S. Robert, Stanley Rothman, and Linda Lichter. *The Media Elite.* Bethesda, Md.: Adler and Adler, 1986.

Patterson, Thomas E. *Out of Order.* New York: Knopf, 1993.

Sabato, Larry J. *Feeding Frenzy: Attack Journalism and American Politics.* Baltimore, Md.: Lanham Publishers, 2000.

NOTES

1. Thomas E. Patterson, *Out of Order* (New York: Knopf, 1993), 209.
2. "Media: More Voices, Less Credibility" in *Trends 2005* (Washington, D.C.: Pew Research Center for the People and the Press, 2005), 42 and 47.
3. Thomas E. Patterson, *Doing Well and Doing Good: How Soft News and Critical Journalism Are Shrinking the New Audience and Weakening Democracy—And What News Outlets Can Do About It* (Cambridge, Mass.: Harvard University Press, 2000), 4.
4. Ibid., 4–5.
5. Martin Kaplan, Ken Goldstein, and Matthew Hale, "Local New Coverage of the 2004 Campaigns: An Analysis of Nightly Broadcasts in 11 Markets," University of Southern California, Annenberg School for Communication, www.localnewsarchive.org.
6. Pew Research Center for the People and the Press, *Trends 2005,* 47.
7. "Cable and Internet Loom Large in Fragmented Political News Universe," Pew Research Center for the People and the Press, January 11, 2004, http://people-press.org/reports/display.php3?ReportID=200.
8. Ibid.
9. The study most often cited is S. Robert Lichter, Stanley Rothman, and Linda Lichter, *The Media Elite* (Bethesda, Md.: Adler and Adler, 1986).
10. Republican candidates have traditionally enjoyed the backing of more newspaper editorials on the election than have Democratic candidates. Doris A. Graber, *Mass Media and American Politics,* 5th ed. (Washington, D.C.: CQ Press, 1997), 250.
11. Prior to the last three presidential elections the Pew Research Center for the People and the Press asked people, "To what extent do you see political bias in news coverage? The responses received were:

	Aug. 1989	Jan. 2000	Jan. 2004
A great deal	25	32	30
A fair amount	51	37	35
Not too much	19	20	24
Not at all	3	6	9
Don't Know/ Refused to Answer	5	2	2

Pew Research Center for the People and the Press, "Cable and Internet Loom Large in Fragmented Political News Universe," January 11, 2004, question 37, http://people-press.org/reports/display.php.3?ReportID=200.

12. Pew Research Center for the People and the Press, "The Tough Job of Communicating," 10–11, and "Media Seen as Fair, but Tilting toward Gore," October 15, 2000, 1, http://people-press.org/reports/display.php3?ReportID=29.

13. "Take This Campaign—Please," *Media Monitor* (September/October 1996): 2, and "Campaign 2000 Final," *Media Monitor* (November/December 2000): 2.

   Why do reporters and correspondents dominate election coverage? From the producers' perspective, interpretive news is more interesting, more focused, more likely to hold an audience, and more likely to present the big picture than are one-sided extended remarks by candidates. From the reporters' perspective, explaining the story makes it more understandable to more people and at the same time contributes to individual professional careers, salaries, lucrative speaking invitations, book contracts, and future opportunities for fame and fortune. From a candidate's perspective, reporters and producers are interpreting the news for their own benefit rather than reporting what the candidates actually say. In their view and that of their handlers, the news media present an incomplete, often inaccurate, and warped perspective of the campaign.

14. The use of the talk/entertainment format has several advantages for candidates. They are treated more like celebrities than like politicians. Hosts tend to be more cordial and less adversarial than news commentators and reporters. Moreover, the audience is different. Those who watch these shows tend to be less oriented toward partisan politics and thus may be more amenable to influence by the candidates who appear on them.

15. Patterson, *Out of Order,* 119–120.

16. Senator Dole was portrayed as a weak candidate hopelessly trailing the popular incumbent president. Moreover, his low rating in the polls, compared with President Clinton's ratings, was used as a basis for evaluating and assessing the status of his campaign and how his strategy and tactics were not working. The news media repeatedly referred to Dole's struggling campaign and to his attempts to "jump-start" it.

17. Two other narratives are about a "bandwagon" that attracts supporters and allows candidates to build a lead and about "losing ground." In the first scenario, the image of strong and decisive leadership generates support; in the second, the image of weak and vacillating leadership contributes to erosion. Jimmy Carter's primary spurt in 1976 provides an illustration of the bandwagon; his decline in the general election exemplifies the losing-ground story. Patterson, *Out of Order,* 118–119.

18. Gallup Poll, "Poll Topics: Confidence in Institutions," June 2006, www.gallup.com/conents/default.aspx?ci=1597.

19. Negativism has been particularly evident at the presidential level and has been directed against incumbents. In 1980 Jimmy Carter was treated more harshly than Ronald Reagan, and in 1984 Reagan was treated more harshly than Walter Mondale. Vice President George Bush, running for president in 1988, fared poorly as well, but so did his Democratic oppo-

nent, Michael Dukakis. Much the same pattern emerged in 1992. S. Robert Lichter and his associates at the Center for Media and Public Affairs found that 69 percent of the evaluations of Bush—his campaign, his positions, his performance, his general desirability—were negative, compared with 63 percent for Clinton and 54 percent for Perot. Bill Clinton did better in 1996, but Robert Dole did not. Only half of Clinton's coverage on the evening news was negative; two out of three comments about Dole were negative. "Campaign 2004 Final: How TV News Covered the General Election," *Media Monitor* (November/December 2004): 5. Bush got more negative coverage than Kerry in 2004, as indicated in Table 5.3.

20. In a survey conducted by the Center for Survey Research and Analysis at the University of Connecticut in the spring of 2001, 82 percent of the respondents said that a free press is necessary to hold the government in check. "American Attitudes about the First Amendment, 2001," 4.

21. "Public and Press Differ about Partisan Bias, Accuracy and Press Freedom," Annenberg Public Policy Center of the University of Pennsylvania, May 24, 2005, www.annenberg publicpolicycenter.org.

22. Surveys conducted in Canada, France, Germany, Italy, Mexico, Spain, and the United Kingdom in 1994 reveal broad support for a free press. Times Mirror Center for the People and the Press, "Mixed Message about Press Freedom on Both Sides of Atlantic," March 16, 1994.

23. Pew Research Center for the People and the Press, *Trends 2005*, 50.

24. Pew Research Center for the People and the Press, "Press 'Unfair, Inaccurate and Pushy': Fewer Favor Media Scrutiny of Political Leaders," March 21, 1997, 1.

25. Pew Research Center for the People and the Press, "Cable and Internet Loom Large in Fragmented Political News Universe," January 11, 2004.

26. See for example, "Voters Learned Positions on Issues since Presidential Debates; Kerry Improves Slightly on Traits, Annenberg Data Show," National Annenberg Election Survey, October 23, 2004, www.annenbergpublicpolicycenter.org/naes/2004_03_%20Voters-and-the-issues_10–23_pr.pdf.

27. Patterson, *Doing Well and Doing Good*, 5–15.

28. Ibid., 7–9.

29. "Campaign Reform: Insights and Evidence," *Report of the Task Force on Campaign Reform*, Woodrow Wilson School of Public and International Affairs, Princeton University, September 1998, 23.

30. Ibid., 21–26.

31. Patterson, *Doing Well and Doing Good*, 15.

32. Ibid., 8.

33. Patterson, *Out of Order*, 207–242.

34. Ibid., 210.

35. A less intrusive format for the press could include a single moderator to start the debate and regulate time allotted the candidates or a single moderator to serve as a master of ceremonies, who would preside over a town meeting at which the audience, not journalists, asked the questions.

36. In 2004, the third debate between Bush and Kerry drew an estimated 51.2 million viewers, compared to 15.2 million who watched the baseball playoffs.

37. There are also important procedural questions that could have a major impact on the electorate. When would debates occur? Who would set the dates? Who would be invited? Would candidates have to participate? What would the format be? Which institution would set the rules, choose the moderators, and oversee the debate? Would instant commentary by news

media representatives be permitted? Such commentary may color public perceptions, as it did of the second Ford-Carter debate in 1976. That debate concerned foreign policy. Initial public reaction was favorable to President Ford. However, Ford made a misstatement in the debate, leading some to conclude that he was unaware of the Soviet Union's domination of countries in Eastern Europe. The media pointed out Ford's error in their commentary. The president's failure to correct himself for three days, combined with the media's emphasis on his mistake, changed public perceptions about the debate and its winner, and about Ford's competence in foreign affairs.

38. In the 2000 Democratic nomination process, Vice President Al Gore challenged his rival Bill Bradley to forgo ads and just debate. Bradley refused, claiming that he needed to advertise because he was not as well known as Gore and did not have the vice presidential podium.

39. Alliance for Better Campaigns, "Gouging Democracy: How the Television Industry Profiteered on Campaign 2000," www.bettercampaigns.org/Doldisc/gouging.htm.

40. Christopher Adasiewicz, Douglas Rivlin, and Jeffrey Stronger, "Free Television for Presidential Candidates: The 1996 Experiment," Annenberg Public Policy Center, University of Pennsylvania, March 1997.

Are American Parties Still Representative?

Did you know that. . .

- the Democratic Party of the United States is the oldest political party anywhere?
- in this age of telegenic candidates and carefully scripted candidate appeals, partisanship still remains the most important influence on voting behavior?
- more people claim to be independent today than vote consistently in an independent manner?
- the least and most educated voters tend to vote Democratic in presidential elections?
- although changes in the nomination process were designed to improve the representative character of the parties, more people think the parties are less representative today than they were in the past?
- a key factor that has led to a resurgence of party influence during electoral campaigns is money and lots of it?
- no third-party or independent candidate has ever won the presidency?
- only two independent or third-party individuals have been elected as independents to the House of Representatives since the end of World War II?
- people who usually are most supportive of third-party candidates are those between the ages of eighteen and twenty-nine?
- the more cohesive the parties, the more divisive the government is apt to be, particularly if one party controls the White House and the other controls one or both houses of Congress?
- the United States is one of the few democratic countries with a two-party system?

Is this any way to run a democratic election?

PARTIES AND AMERICAN DEMOCRACY

Why Political Parties Are Important

Political parties are considered an important part of a democratic electoral system. In fact, some scholars consider them absolutely essential.[1] They provide critical links among the electorate, the candidates, and the government. Parties help orient, organize, and energize voters. They tie candidates to one another and allow them to make both generic and specific appeals replete with partisan imagery. And they provide people with a basis for evaluating the performance of elected officials and holding them collectively responsible for their actions or inaction in office. Responsiveness and accountability are two critical components of a representative democracy.

In a heterogeneous society like that of the United States, interests are many, varied, and often conflicting. Political parties provide a structure for aggregating these interests, for packaging them and presenting them to voters. Parties articulate interests in their platform, their campaign communications, and the collective campaigns of their candidates. Finally, parties provide a mechanism for governing, for bringing together elected officials on the basis of their shared values, interests, and policy goals and holding them accountable for their performance in office.

In elections, as in government, parties are likely to be the most effective coalition builders. They can unite diverse elements of the electorate, as well as overcome the institutional separation of powers to facilitate the operation of government. But parties also can have the opposite effect. Divided partisan control of government reinforces the separation of powers and impedes consensus building across institutional bodies.

Each of these functions—interest aggregation, articulation, and electoral accountability—is critical to a viable democratic political system.[2] That is why parties are important.

What Parties Do in Elections

Within the electorate, parties organize and orient voters. They create alliances among groups and allegiances among individuals. They inform people about the issues, get them involved in the campaign, and encourage them to vote.

Parties also structure electoral choices. They enable voters to transcend the many individual decisions they must make and allow them to superimpose a collective judgment that both guides and justifies their micro-level decisions. For the vast majority of voters, a major party label conveys legitimacy, whereas a minor party label does not. The candidates' partisan association gives the electorate a means to evaluate their policy direction and political impact if they are elected.

Parties anchor policy preferences. Parties have an organizational history and a policy record that enable the electorate to learn what they have stood for,

BOX 6.1 Multiparty Politics: Pros and Cons

There are those who believe that two parties can never satisfactorily represent a country as large and diverse as the United States. Instead of having two major parties reflecting, even exaggerating, the views of their most active and ideological partisans, wouldn't representation be enhanced if a range of narrow-based parties existed and competed across the entire political spectrum?[1]

Smaller and less diverse countries than the United States, such as France, Germany, and Spain, have such a system and have been able to maintain stable and effective government for relatively long periods of time. Others, however, such as Italy and, to a lesser extent, Israel, have not been as successful in maintaining stability and continuity. Italy has had more than forty governments since the end of World War II. And the major governing party in Israel has to depend on the support of minor parties to gain and sustain a parliamentary majority. The types of party systems in major democratic countries are listed here.

Types of Party Systems

	STRICTLY BY NUMBER OF PARTIES			
TAKING ACCOUNT OF RELATIVE SIZE OF PARTIES	Predominant Party Systems	Two-Party Systems	Party Systems with Three to Five Parties	Party Systems with More Than Five Parties
Predominant Party Systems	Japan			
Two-Party Systems		Great Britain New Zealand United States		
Two-and-a-Half Party Systems			Australia Austria Canada Germany Ireland	
Systems with More than Two-and-a-Half Parties				
One Large Party			Norway Sweden	
Two Large Parties				Israel Italy Belgium
Even-Party Systems			France Denmark Israel Netherlands	Finland Iceland Luxemburg Switzerland

1. Theodore J. Lowi, *The Personal President* (Ithaca, N.Y.: Cornell University Press, 1985), 195–208.

(continued on next page)

evaluate how successful they have been, and anticipate how successful they may be in the future.

For the candidates, parties provide a collective presence and perspective, an organizational base, and the potential for enhancing their individual influence if elected. The collective entity is the party organization and its perspective, shared values, beliefs, and opinions. The organization has the resources, money, media expertise, and grassroots mobilization to aid candidates in their campaigns and extend their influence in government.

Partisanship provides candidates with a core of faithful supporters; it also gives them the opportunity to reinforce some of the ideas, beliefs, and interests they have in common with fellow partisans. These benefits that parties give to candidates have led one astute observer, John H. Aldrich, to theorize that parties exist because office-seekers and officeholders find them useful. They contribute to the outcomes that these ambitious politicians desire.[3]

Parties also provide a framework for evaluating election results, organizing the government, and subsequently assessing its performance. In doing so, they convert individual victories into a collective effort, help define priorities for newly elected officials, and provide a continuing incentive—reelection—for keeping public officials sensitive to the interests and opinions of those who elected them.

But how many parties are necessary to represent the diverse views of a heterogeneous society, such as the United States? There is no right answer. Many countries less diverse than the United States have multiparty systems, as indicated in Box 6.1. The United States does not have one, nor has it had one throughout most of its history. Thus the first question that should be considered is: How has the United States has managed to maintain a two-party system even as the country has become more diverse?

BOX 6.1 **Multiparty Politics: Pros and Cons** *(continued)*

In a multiparty system, the parties themselves combine to form governing coalitions, and compromise occurs among them. In the United States, if there is a majority party, as there was between 1932 and the late 1960s, compromise occurs within it, among the various groups competing for influence. If the major parties share power as they have for much of the time since 1968, then they must compromise within and between themselves.

Whether a two-party or a multiparty system is best may depend on the priorities placed on representation, accountability, and effective governance. But the question also may be academic, given the long and dominant two-party tradition in America, to which both major parties are committed and from which both derive benefit.

Source: Alan Ware, *Political Parties and the Party System.* Copyright © 1998, Oxford University Press. Reprinted by permission of Oxford University Press.

The Two-Party Tradition in the United States

The persistence of two major parties relates in part to their flexibility, and to a willingness to adjust and survive in the light of the changes that have affected American society. The major parties have successfully weathered these changes because, until recently, they have been more pragmatic than ideological, more inclusive than exclusive, and more decentralized than centralized.

They also have not attempted to impose their beliefs and issue positions on their supporters, their candidates for office, or even their elected officials as a condition of party affiliation or electoral acceptability, although obviously they try to persuade them to toe the party line.[4]

Moreover, the major parties have advantages in the political system, advantages that they jealously guard. The major parties are well recognized and have standing. They have organizations in all the states, a leadership structure, and core supporters and financial benefactors. Independent candidates and especially third parties generally lack these resources.

The major parties have systemic advantages as well. They are automatically on the ballot in all fifty states as long as they win a certain percentage of the vote. Third parties are much less likely to have won that percentage. Their candidates, and those running independently, usually have to collect a certain number of signatures of registered voters just to get on the state ballots. Besides, as noted in chapter 3, the single-member district system in which the person with the most votes wins also benefits major party candidates at the expense of minor party candidates.

The presidential election system confers the same advantage on the major parties. The winner-take-all method of Electoral College voting used by forty-eight of the fifty states disadvantages third-party candidates whose support is widely distributed across the country, as Ross Perot's was in 1992 and 1996. If the election moves into the House, the major parties also are advantaged. Campaign finance laws that benefit the major parties reinforce these structural features, as does the more extensive media coverage they receive.

Despite public opinion, which periodically looks to third parties and independent candidates when the people are dissatisfied with the major parties, third parties have had difficulty gaining acceptance and maintaining public support. The argument that they cannot win contributes to their difficulty in winning. Figure 6.1 indicates how Americans evaluate the major parties today.

If third parties and independent candidacies were the only ways minority viewpoints could be heard and minority groups represented, then the bias of the system would be a serious failing in a democratic political process. But, as already presented, there are many other ways minorities can and do get representation and exercise influence on elections and government. In fact, many believe that demographic and ideological minorities are overrepresented within the major parties and exercise disproportionate influence on them, much to the dismay of moderate, mainstream, rank-and-file voters. And outside of the parties, interest groups have proliferated in the form of political action com-

FIGURE 6.1 **Evaluations of the Major Parties, 1992–2006***

Question: Would you say your overall opinion of the Republican/Democratic Party is very favorable, mostly favorable, mostly unfavorable, or very unfavorable?

■ Favorable
☐ Unfavorable

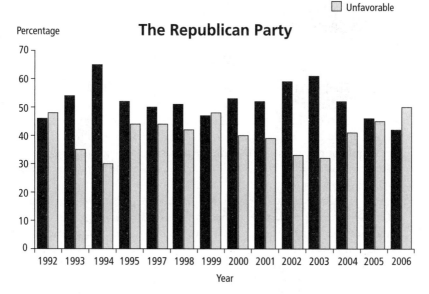

The Republican Party

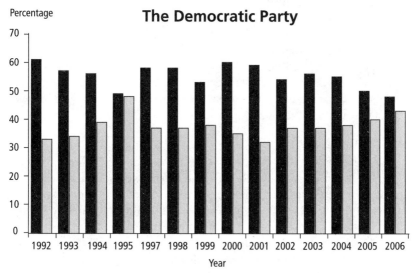

The Democratic Party

*Yearly average; rounded to nearest whole number.

Source: Pew Research Center for the People and the Press, "News Interest Index," April 2006.

mittees (PACs) within the electoral arena and lobbying groups within the governing arena.

The rest of this chapter examines each of the ways parties help electoral democracy. It looks at parties and the electorate, parties and electoral choice, and parties and electoral accountability. First, however, it presents a brief overview of the evolution of American political parties to provide a historical context for evaluating how well parties are serving the needs of electoral democracy today.

THE EVOLUTION OF U.S. POLITICAL PARTIES

Parties are not mentioned in the Constitution, nor did the framers anticipate them when they created the electoral system. They did anticipate that groups would be active within the political arena, however. Fearing domination by any one of these groups, they divided institutional spheres of authority and created separate but overlapping constituencies as a hedge against any one group, including a majority, disproportionately influencing the formulation of national policy.

Implicit in this constitutional design, however, was the assumption that a lot of public policy would not be necessary at the national level. With an ocean for protection, a huge frontier, and seemingly unlimited natural resources, this nation composed largely of self-sufficient farmers was not thought to need or desire a very active national government. Although economic and social needs have changed, and government has grown and become more involved in many aspects of life, its constitutional structure has essentially remained the same—hence the dilemma of how to bridge the institutional divide and facilitate the operation of government. By providing common perspectives, policy goals, and political structures, parties can unify what the Constitution separates, if they control the institutions of government. However, if institutional control is divided, partisanship can reinforce the constitutional division, thereby impeding the functioning of government. Over the course of American history, parties have done both.

Birth and Infancy

The creation of parties at the end of the eighteenth and beginning of the nineteenth centuries presented the political system with both a challenge and an opportunity. The challenge was to prevent a major party from dominating the system in such a way as to deny the minority its rights and disregard its interests. The opportunity was to utilize common beliefs, goals, and interests as a consensus-building mechanism within and among the institutions of government.

Thomas Jefferson's Democratic-Republican Party, which emerged as the first broad-based political party in the United States, controlled national politics and government for more than twenty-five years, from 1800 to 1828. It was the majority faction that the framers feared, but it also bridged the gap that was developing between an expanding and more diverse electorate and the national elites who had controlled the government since its founding. By the 1820s, the Federalist Party, which supported the policies of the Washington and Adams administrations, had faded from the scene, and the Democratic-Republicans, the only viable party remaining, divided into factions along regional lines. Two of these factions eventually evolved into broad-based parties: the Democrats, who backed Andrew Jackson, and the Whigs, who opposed him.

Adolescence: A Growth Spurt

Between 1828 and 1844, state party organizations loosely affiliated with the two major parties developed and subsequently changed the character of the two-party system by federalizing it.[5] The parties increasingly began to reflect America's federal structure. The national parties became little more than collectivities of state parties, and the state parties began to aggressively build a mass base.

Beginning in the 1840s, both parties used their presidential campaigns to mobilize voters. During nonelectoral periods, they used their resources and exercised their political influence to provide their supporters with tangible economic and social benefits (see chapter 2, page 26.) By energizing the electorate, the parties not only extended their political influence but also began to address the economic and social needs of the society.

In the 1850s, sectional rivalries inflamed by the passions of slavery and westward expansion splintered the parties and eventually led to the demise of the Whigs and the division of the Democrats into northern and southern factions. The Republican Party emerged out of this political chaos. Organized in 1854, the Republicans appealed to former Whigs and to northern Democrats, who supported the abolition of slavery; to white laborers and small farmers who objected to its expansion; and to industrial workers who feared that the influx of new immigrants would lower their wages or cost them their jobs.

Out of the turmoil created by the Civil War and Reconstruction, new partisan coalitions emerged. Big-business tycoons who had profited from the industrial revolution gained control of the Republican Party and dominated it for more than fifty years. The Democrats remained divided into a rural southern faction, controlled by the socially conservative white elite, and a more industrialized northern one that was influenced by banking and commercial interests.

The popular bases of both parties shrank in the second half of the nineteenth century;[6] voter turnout declined; and the partisan political environment became less competitive. Poorer farmers, blue-collar workers, and newly arrived immigrants increasingly found themselves alienated from both major parties.[7]

Adulthood: The Eras of Partisan Majorities

The Republican Era, 1896–1928. A recession in 1893 during the administration of Democrat Grover Cleveland, combined with the Populist movement in the West that further splintered the Democratic Party into "free silver" supporters and opponents, resulted in the emergence of a new Republican majority. Strong in the North, popular among Protestants and older immigrant groups, buoyed by the support of business and also increasingly by labor, and benefiting from the country's economic prosperity, the Grand Old Party (GOP), as it had come to be called, dominated American politics for the next three decades. Although the Democrats were still a major party, ruling the South and even managing to gain control of both the White House and Congress from 1912 to 1918, the Republicans held onto their numerical advantage with voters until the Great Depression.[8]

The Democratic Era, 1932–1968. A major realignment of the parties occurred in the 1930s. The Democrats, riding on the coattails of Franklin Roosevelt and his New Deal policies, broadened their base by appealing to those at the lower end of the socioeconomic scale, whereas the Republicans held onto the allegiances of the business community and the well-to-do members of society. The principal exception to this economically based division of the electorate was in the South, where, regardless of socioeconomic status, voters retained their Democratic loyalties.

The economic division between the parties became evident in their policy perspectives as well. The Democrats looked to government to take the lead in solving the nation's economic and social policies, whereas the Republicans viewed government involvement in the economy as a threat to the free enterprise system. The Democrats supported Roosevelt's efforts to redistribute resources on the basis of individual need; the Republicans did not. They continued to believe that a capitalistic system, free from government control, would provide the greatest benefit to the society as a whole.

The Democrats maintained the allegiances of a majority of voters until the end of the 1960s. However, changes in the economic environment following World War II, growing prosperity nationwide, an expanding middle class, and gains for organized labor all weakened the economic foundation on which the party had built its electoral and governing coalitions. New social and international issues—the civil rights movement; the Korean and Vietnam Wars and the public's reaction to them; violent demonstrations on college and university campuses; deteriorating conditions in the cities, with associated increases in crime, drug trafficking, and racial unrest—all divided the Democrats and helped unify the more socially conservative Republicans. By the 1970s, the Democrats had lost their status as the majority party; by the 1980s, they had lost their electoral plurality; by the 1990s, the parties were operating at rough parity with each other and continue to do so today.[9]

Although the Republicans benefited from the fraying of the Democrats' electoral coalition, they didn't become the new majority, except in the South and the Rocky Mountain areas. Rather, the electorate entered into a period of partisan transition, with neither party able to gain a permanent electoral advantage.

Transitional Politics: The Volatile '60s and '70s

The dealignment of the American electorate began in the late 1960s. During this period, voters became more independent, more candidate-centered, and more volatile in their voting behavior. Party leaders lost control of the nomination process to party activists (see chapter 7); the party organizations no longer ran their candidates' campaigns. Television became the principal means of electioneering, and candidates hired campaign professionals to raise money, poll, design media, and identify and mobilize supporters. Outside groups became more active, raising money, airing commercials, and organizing their members and sympathizers for the candidates who supported their issue positions. In the short run, these changes weakened the major parties and their role as the major intermediary between candidates and voters.

Moreover, the growing parity between the Republicans and Democrats, combined with more split-ticket voting, ushered in a period of divided government, with control of the White House and Congress shifting between the parties.

Decline in Partisanship. The weakening of partisan allegiances beginning in the late 1960s and continuing into the mid-1980s decreased turnout and contributed to a more candidate-centered electoral process. It did so because partisanship acts as a lens through which political activity is viewed, a conceptual framework that helps people sort out the candidates and the issues, tell the "good guys" of one party from the "bad guys" of the other. Partisan attitudes reduce the burdens of voting for those who identify with a political party by providing an easy guide to follow when casting ballots. These attitudes also provide an incentive to become more involved, to get more information, to be more active, and to vote.[10] Any change in the direction and strength of these attitudes is bound to have an impact on the electorate's voting behavior.

As partisan loyalties weakened, people looked to other factors when deciding how to vote. They focused on the candidates themselves and their positions on salient issues. Television encouraged this focus as candidates depended more and more on the mass media to create a favorable image and communicate it to voters along with their specific policy appeals. The more independent behavior of candidates for office also contributed to the personification of electoral politics; most candidates tapped themselves to run, organized their own campaigns, and took their own policy positions on salient issues within their constituencies. In fact, their independence was often a selling point in their campaigns; these candidates argued that they were beholden to no one but their constituents. The news media also began to emphasize personal characteristics, blurring the distinction between private and public behavior.

To counter the image-making of their opponents, candidates and their handlers placed more and more emphasis on the negative, why people should *not* vote for their opponent rather than simply trumpeting their own achievements and qualifications for office.[11] News coverage became more negative as well.[12] (See chapter 5). This negativity left a bad taste in the mouths of many voters.

It makes a difference in the attitudes toward parties and the candidates who run on their label if people feel they are voting for the least bad candidate or for the best one. Excessive negativism can dampen public enthusiasm, contribute to lower turnout, and undermine confidence in elections, candidates, and elected officials.

In an effort to overcome their own negative portrayal in the news and by their opponents, candidates began to turn to professional imagemakers, public relations experts, and pollsters to design personas and policy appeals that resonated with voters. Sometimes, in their desire to win, they made promises and created expectations that they could not possibly fulfill, particularly in a political system that shares responsibilities and checks and balances powers.

Finally, the emphasis on individuals rather than on parties undermined accountability in government. It is one thing to hold a party responsible if that party controls the White House or is a majority in one or both houses of Congress. But how can an individual within a system based on separation of powers be held accountable for anything other than his or her own personal behavior? Table 6.1 indicates the partisan identity of contemporary American voters.

TABLE 6.1 **Partisan Identification of the American Electorate, 1960–2004 (percentages)**

Year	Democrats		Independents	Republicans		Other
	Strong	Weak		Strong	Weak	
1960	20	25	16	14	23	2
1964	27	25	11	14	23	1
1968	20	25	10	15	30	2
1972	15	26	10	13	34	1
1976	15	25	9	14	37	1
1980	18	23	9	14	34	2
1984	17	20	12	15	34	2
1988	17	18	14	14	36	2
1992	18	18	11	14	38	1
1996	18	19	12	15	35	1
2000	19	15	12	12	40	1
2004	17	16	16	12	39	0

Source: The American National Election Studies, "The ANES Guide to Public Opinion," Table 2A.1, www.umich.edu/~nes/nesguide/toptable/tab2a_1.htm.

The Division of Government. The personalization of politics produced another effect; it increased the probability of a divided government. By voting for the person and not the party, the electorate ended up with a mixed government composed of individuals who did not share as many common unifying priorities as did loyal partisans who were recruited by party officials, funded by local and state party committees, and beholden to the organization of the party for guiding and financing their campaigns. Instead, elected officials increasingly thought of themselves as free agents, more oriented to their constituents who had elected them than to their party. Nor did many of them develop the close-knit personal relationships that facilitated compromise, so essential to policymaking in a large and diverse democratic society.

Under such circumstances, consensus building became harder to achieve, policy coalitions shifted from issue to issue, and legislative output decreased. Table 6.2 indicates the decline in the number of laws during this period. Individually and collectively these factors contributed to public disillusionment, disengagement, and when conditions merited it, discontent.

TABLE 6.2 **Legislation, 1987–2004**

Congress	Public Laws	Private Laws
100th (1987–1988)	713	48
101st (1989–1990)	404	7
102nd (1991–1992)	589	14
103rd (1993–1994)	465	8
104th (1995–1996)	234	2
105th (1997–1998)	394	10
106th (1999–2000)	580	24
107th (2001–2002)	377	6
108th (2003–2004)	498	6

Source: Harold W. Stanley and Richard G. Niemi, *Vital Statistics on American Politics, 2005–2006* (Washington, D.C.: CQ Press, 2006), 213.

The Reemergence of Partisanship

The changes in electoral behavior were short-lived, however. Beginning in the 1980s, the parties began to regain strength. Partisan voting patterns reemerged, and the policy differences between the major parties became clearer.

The resurgence of the Republican and Democratic Parties was generated by the national parties' improved fund-raising prowess; their acquisition of the skills and technologies of the new communications age; their increasing involvement in the recruitment, training, and funding of candidates for national office; and the partisan gerrymandering of congressional legislative districts.

The strengthening of partisan attitudes is a bit more difficult to explain. Part of it may have been a reaction and readjustment to the turbulent '60s and '70s, to the policies that generated this turbulence, and to the government that exercised its power to effect social change through programs that promised to end racial discrimination, poverty, and crime.

The attractiveness of an alternative conservative philosophy, championed by Ronald Reagan, to those who criticized the liberal policies of previous Democratic presidents and Congresses encouraged a realignment of partisan attitudes along ideological lines. Democrats remained liberal and Republicans conservative, and the two major parties became more internally cohesive and externally distinct. Partisan allegiances strengthened, while partisan cleavages within government became more pronounced. Eventually, partisanship unified what the constitutional system divided. A model of responsible party government was emerging. (See Box 6.2.)

The Contemporary Parties

Today, the electoral coalitions that comprise the Democratic and Republican Parties are distinct economically, socially, and culturally. The Democrats continue to attract the allegiances of those at the lower end of the socioeconomic scale: people with lower incomes, less formal education, and fewer professional job skills and opportunities. These core supporters want and need more social services from government, including better public schools, more public housing, and a variety of healthcare and welfare services. They tend to favor government policies that redistribute resources and provide help to those less able to help themselves.

The disproportionate concentration of certain minority groups, such as African Americans and Hispanics, among this economic sector of the population adds a racial and ethnic dimension to the Democrats' base of support and further distinguishes the party's policies on affirmative action and immigration from those of the Republicans.

In contrast, the GOP attracts most of its supporters from the majority group in the population, from people in the upper-middle and higher income brackets who have had and benefited from more education and the job skills and personal contacts that provides. This Republican support group is less enamored with a large government role within the economic sphere and programs that provide extensive social services. However, Republicans support and emphasize government efforts to protect the security of the citizenry and the nation.

Such cultural factors as religion, language, and traditional community values also distinguish the major parties and their electoral bases from one another. People who hold traditional religious beliefs and regularly attend religious

BOX 6.2 **The Responsible Party Model**

The doctrine of having more responsible parties was first proposed by Professor Woodrow Wilson in his book *Congressional Government*.[1] Wilson lamented the fact that American parties were not as cohesive as those in the British parliamentary system; he urged the adoption of practices designed to make them more responsible, such as each party proposing a national program, campaigning for it, and carrying it out if its candidates were elected.

But no matter how good the idea sounded in theory, it would have been difficult to implement in practice. U.S. parties are more heterogeneous than their British counterparts in large part because the United States is a larger, more diverse country than the United Kingdom. Moreover, power is more dispersed within the American governmental system. In Britain, control of the House of Commons amounts to control of the government; in the United States, control of the House of Representatives, the people's house, is a far cry from control of the government. So is control of Congress, for that matter, if the president is of the opposite party from Congress. Besides, even when parties constitute a legislative majority, they usually aren't able to dictate their public policy outcomes. The committee and subcommittee systems in both houses, the unlimited debate rule in the Senate, and the strong constituency orientation of most members have made it difficult for the parties' legislative leaders to impose discipline on their members, much less take collective responsibility for the policies and practices of government.[2]

Nonetheless, the idea of having more responsible parties has surfaced from time to time. It appealed to political scientists as their discipline developed after the Second World War. E. E. Schattschneider, a proponent of this view, headed a committee of the American Political Science Association that called for the Democrats and Republicans to offer clear-cut alternatives to the voters, pursue them if elected, and be held accountable for their success or failure.

The period during which this idea gained currency, however, was not one in which the major parties strove to be different. After World War II both accepted the need for a strong national government, both were strongly anticommunist, and both were divided internally over social issues, particularly civil rights. The Republican Party, still in the minority, did not try to reverse New Deal policies as much as improve their administration and moderate their effects. In 1968 when George Wallace said, "There's not a dime's worth of difference" between the major parties, he was probably more right than wrong.

Contemporary parties are more consistent with the responsible party model than were the Democrats and Republicans in the mid-twentieth century. They have become more internally cohesive and externally distinctive. They are more divisive along ideological lines. They also have become more unified in government. Whether these changes make elections more democratic and government more effective remains a hotly debated issue, however. Critics still complain about the parties—that they are not representative of their own rank and file, much less the country; that they do not reflect the popular will in elections; and that they have not produced a more effective and efficient government.

---

1. Woodrow Wilson, *Congressional Government* (1885; reprint, New York: Meridan Books, 1960).
2. Morris P. Fiorina, "The Decline of Collective Responsibility in American Politics," *Daedalus* 109 (Summer 1980): 25–45.

services tend to be Republican; those who hold more secular views and do not attend religious services regularly are more likely to consider themselves Democrats. Each partisan group naturally favors policies that coincide with its basic values and beliefs. Republicans are more opposed to abortion, same-sex marriage, and government-sponsored stem-cell research than are Democrats. They are more likely to back government policies and action to make English the nation's official language, to allow voluntary prayer in school, to increase the government's policing powers, and to make desecration of the American flag a criminal offense. Democrats place a higher value on the exercise of political freedoms, particularly as that exercise relates to First Amendment rights. They are more supportive of social and cultural diversity and the policies that promote such diversity.

The other partisan distinction within the electorate is based on gender. Women, particularly younger, single women are more likely to be Democrats; men, especially white men with a European ancestry, lean toward being Republican. This demographic division manifests in foreign policy differences, with men more likely to support more aggressive government action based on strong security forces than are women. Within the domestic healthcare and economic spheres, however, women favor a stronger government role than do men.

Today, the parties have become quite ideologically consistent and clearly differentiated from one another, although this internal consistency has produced some backlash from partisans who do not share the strong ideological convictions and policy positions of party leaders and elected officials.

PARTIES, ELECTORAL REPRESENTATION, AND DEMOCRATIC GOVERNANCE

Has the reemergence of partisan voting patterns, the strengthening of party organizations as campaign entities and governing coalitions, and the reappearance in 2002 of unified government strengthened or weakened the democratic character of the American electoral process? Have these changes helped or hurt democratic governance?

Proponents of these developments say that they have contributed to a more responsible party system and a more accountable government. They cite the criticism of American parties during much of their existence: their ambiguous and sometimes inconsistent policy stands, their sacrifice of principle for pragmatism, and their "big tent" philosophy that welcomes all comers. For those who adhere to well-defined belief systems, value policy over politics, claim that they would rather be right and lose than wrong and win, these very same qualities are viewed as detriments, not attributes.

Third-party candidates, such as George Wallace and H. Ross Perot, have voiced similar criticisms of the major parties, as have Ralph Nader and Pat Buchanan. Ideological and issue group leaders also complain that the parties are unresponsive to their views and interests, despite research that found consistent differences between the major parties over the years on the most salient policy issues.[13]

Critics of the contemporary parties cite the rise of cynicism, decrease in trust, and downward spiral in election turnout (until 2004) as evidence that something is wrong and that the major parties should shoulder much of the responsibility for the current unhappy state of political affairs. They point to the lack of representation for moderate views and voters, the ideological rhetoric that divides and inflames governmental policymaking, and the extreme political positions used to create wedge issues.

Do Contemporary Political Parties Facilitate or Inhibit Democratic Elections?

The answer to this question depends on how satisfied people are with the candidates running and with the views they express. To the extent that the candidates are more extreme in their beliefs than the electorate as a whole, the choices they provide are less satisfactory. So why would parties nominate candidates like these? This question is answered in chapter 7, where the discussion focuses on reforms in the nomination process that have shifted power from party leaders to rank-and-file partisans—particularly to those activists who feel more strongly about issues and exercise disproportionate influence in the selection of party nominees.

The reemergence of partisanship has increased turnout and that, of course, is good from a democratic perspective. Partisanship has encouraged the parties to concentrate on their base, devoting more time, effort, and money to developing grassroots operations. Correspondingly, independents in a highly polarized electorate have become less numerous and less important targets for the parties, which have less incentive to modify their policy appeals and more to remain ideologically consistent. In addition, parties and their nominees also are encouraged to use negative stereotypes to demonize their opponents. Negative campaigning energizes and mobilizes the base.

Increasing turnout, creating distinct choices, providing information on the candidates and their proposals, advocating a governing agenda, and if elected, converting that agenda into public policy is certainly consistent with a democratic electoral process. So is soliciting contributions, hiring campaign professional, mobilizing volunteers, and engaging in get-out-the-vote activities—all functions that parties perform during elections. What is more problematic are activities that depress turnout by providing false and negative information, redistricting that creates more noncompetitive legislative districts, and policy positions that do not reflect the more moderate views of mainstream America.

Do Contemporary Parties Facilitate or Inhibit Democratic Governance?

The transitional period in American politics created by the weakening of partisan attitudes, the rise of split-ticket voting, and the growing advantages of incumbents produced a Congress of individualists more intent on furthering their own constituency needs and personal goals than their party's. Partisan unity suffered as a consequence.

Congress also decentralized power to accommodate more members of both the majority and minority parties. A standing subcommittee system was established in the mid-1970s, and the seniority rule for picking committee chairs was abolished. Shared power, combined with many more veto points in the legislative process, made agenda setting and coalition building more difficult. Divided government created even more hurdles. Legislative output declined.

Although party leaders were able to forge legislative majorities on specific issues, they were not able to maintain those majorities across different issue areas. President Reagan was successful in building bipartisan support for his economic program (with the help of conservative southern Democrats) and maintaining that support for his national security plan, but by the end of his term, his party had lost control of the Senate and Reagan's support declined in the Democratic-controlled House. And the number of southern Democrats and moderate Republicans to whom presidents could appeal across party lines diminished. Ideology reinforced the partisan divide.

Beginning in the 1980s, increasing ideological consensus within the major parties resulted in greater party unity in Congress. When government is divided, that unity, enhanced by ideology, discourages compromise and can result in a political and institutional stalemate; when government is unified, however, it can result in the majority party achieving its legislative agenda. Such conditions occurred in 2002 and were augmented by President Bush's focus on national security issues in the aftermath of the September 11, 2001, attacks.

With majority rule comes significant costs for those in the minority. They lose influence, particularly in the House of Representatives, in which the rules adopted by its members facilitate plurality voting decisions. In the Senate, rules that permit any senator to put a hold on a nomination and require the support of sixty senators for most authorization bills give the minority leverage to achieve compromises or prevent the Senate from acting, leverage that the minority does not have in the House of Representatives.

Another consequence of majority rule in unified government is that the minority has to shout to be heard. Rhetoric becomes shrill, heightened by the ideological character of contemporary partisan debate. Civility and comity in Congress suffer as a result.

In short, congressional parties began to demonstrate more unity beginning in the 1990s than they had in the two preceding decades. The more ideological orientation of members of Congress, the more visible public arena in which decisions were made and votes cast—all covered by C-SPAN and the twenty-four-hour television news networks—as well as the decline of the civility and informality that facilitated compromise in the past, contributed to the warring camps atmosphere prevalent in Congress during the last decade of the twentieth century.

Partisan bickering has been highlighted by national press coverage, with the consequence being that the public approval of Congress has declined. Prior to the 2006 midterm elections, only 24 percent approved of the way Congress was handling its job; 68 percent disapproved. Since the mid-1970s, more people have expressed disapproval on how Congress has been performing its job than have approved of its work.[14]

Individual members still tend to get more positive assessments from their constituents than does Congress as a whole. The discrepancy between these two evaluations creates a significant and persistent ambiguity in public assessments of Congress.

The lack of competition in most legislative elections, either because an incumbent is so advantaged or because the district is dominated by the partisans of one of the major parties, also makes it difficult to read much into the vote for Congress. For a collective judgment to be made, a partisan victory would have to occur, as it did in the congressional elections of 1946, 1994, and 2006 after which legislative control switched from one party to the other.

Is Collective Accountability Possible?

Throughout this book the argument has been that elected officials must be held accountable for their decisions and actions. Since the 1970s it has become easier to hold individual government officials accountable because of the increasingly public arena in which policy decisions are made, the multitude of information sources on government that are available, the investigative bent of the news media, and the continuous scrutiny of policymaking by interested outside groups. Personal accountability has been enhanced during elections by the amount of research that parties and candidates conduct about their opponents, as well as by the campaigns themselves, which highlight the candidates, their qualifications, achievements and failures, and their responsiveness to their constituents.

What about *collective* responsibility? Do contemporary parties contribute to that as well? The answer is that they may. Cohesive parties within a unified government provide an opportunity for the electorate to nationalize a midterm election and make a collective judgment on those in power. A negative judgment can result in a new congressional majority.

Every decade or so, the conditions for such a judgment occur. In the elections of 1946 and 1952, a Democratic majority was repudiated by the voters. Republicans gained power only to lose it two years later in each instance. In the 1974 election, following President Nixon's resignation, the opposite situation occurred. The Democrats substantially increased their congressional representation at a time when their proportion in the electorate was declining. Democrats lost control of the Senate in the Reagan landslide of 1980, but won it back six years later. In 1994, an electorate upset with the internal dissent and scandalous behavior of some Democrats voted that party out of power in the political revolution that brought Republican control of the Senate and a new, more conservative leadership to the House under the direction of Newt Gingrich. In 2006, the public rebuked the Republicans for supporting the president's policy in Iraq, for their ideological rigidity, and for the scandals that beset members of their party in the 109th Congress—bribery, ethical lapses, immoral and illegal actions, and the attempted cover-up of these activities by those in leadership positions.

Naturally, the ability to make a collective judgment enhances democratic government. However, when control of Congress shifts, particularly in an age of highly polarized parties, the consequence may be significant shifts in policy when government is unified and political stalemate when it is divided.

SUMMARY: PARTISAN DILEMMAS IN A NUTSHELL

Parties are important to a democratic selection process. They provide a critical link between candidates and voters and among elected officials and the people who elected them. Without such a link, it would be more difficult to hold elected officials collectively responsible for their actions and thereby to hold government accountable to those who elected them.

Parties organize ideas, people, and institutions. The allegiances they engender, the attitudes they shape, and the electoral behavior they influence provide the electorate with a framework for a campaign, a motivation for participating in it, and an orientation that can be used to arrive at a voting decision.

The major parties have gone through cycles in which they have gained and lost adherents; their electoral coalitions have shifted over the years. The late 1960s ushered in an era in which partisan allegiances weakened, the number of self-declared independents grew, and voters began to split their tickets, voting more for the person or issue.

During this period, the candidates also became more independent in deciding whether to seek office and how to do so. They depended less on their party's organization and more on the campaign professionals they hired, experts skilled in the new computer-based technology, survey research, grassroots organizing, and media-oriented research and communications.

By the mid-1980s, the transition in politics had begun to run its course. Partisan ties strengthened, and partisan voting behavior increased. There was more partisan unity in government, and the parties began to rebuild their financial and grassroots bases. They also became more ideological, nominating and electing candidates with more consistent policy views. These changes divided the country and polarized the government. They led to long periods of divided government in the years from 1968 to 2002, during which domestic policy making became more difficult. Trust and confidence in government declined.

Today, the parties are more internally cohesive and externally distinctive than they have been in some time. Civility in political discourse has declined, as has comity within Congress as well as between it and the White House.

Warring partisan coalitions contest policy publicly rather than deliberate quietly behind closed doors. Reaching compromise has become more arduous, and serving constituency interests remains the key to reelection.

Is the current state of political affairs beneficial or harmful to a democratic electoral process? The nomination process is more open and decentralized, but party activists exercise the most influence over the outcome. They are also a factor in the general election. Candidates self-select themselves, but are dependent on political professionals for getting elected. Incumbents continue to be advantaged as the number of safe seats has increased. As a consequence, it becomes more difficult for elections to reflect the popular mood of the moment. Democratic tendencies are undermined by a noncompetitive election structure.

Is the voice of the people being heard more clearly? Is that voice being effectively and efficiently translated into public policy? Experts are divided. Some see a responsible party system emerging and collective accountability increasing; others see a decrease in the representation of people with moderate views and a continuing distinction between the influence of those in the majority and racial and ethnic minorities. They perceive government as being increasingly responsive to its core supporters rather than to the general public. They see it as making politically expedient decisions at the expense of longer-term policy solutions.

What should be done to enhance partisan representation and to make the parties more responsive and the government more effective? Imposing reforms on the parties is neither wise nor feasible. The parties need to reform themselves. They need to better reflect the diverse character of American society. But if they do so, can they still be cohesive and collectively responsible? These are some of the critical party-related issues that America's electoral democracy must address.

Now It's Your Turn

Discussion Questions

1. Why did partisan loyalties decline in intensity during the transitional period, beginning in the late 1960s and continuing into the 1980s? Why have these loyalties gotten stronger today?
2. Has the realignment of the major parties along ideological lines strengthened or weakened their capacity to represent the American public? Has it improved or reduced their capacity to govern effectively?
3. Is it better in a democracy to vote for the best candidate regardless of that candidate's party or to vote for the candidate of the party that best represents a voter's political beliefs?

4. Are political parties the key to collective responsibility in government? If not, how can government be held accountable for its public policy decisions?

5. Does having only two major parties facilitate or impede the representation of American voters, the conduct of elections, and the operation of government?

6. Does having two major parties make it more or less likely that public policy reflects the views and interests of the majority of people in the United States?

7. What type of electoral system most effectively represents the views of all the people? What type of electoral system results in the most effective government?

Topics for Debate

Challenge or defend the following statements:

1. All candidates who run on a party label should be required to promise that they will support the principal tenets of their party as stated in the last party platform or be removed from the party line on the ballot.

2. Partisanship is undesirable; thus all candidates for office should run in nonpartisan elections.

3. Political parties are unnecessary and undesirable for a democratic government.

4. A two-party system is more efficient but may be less effective in representing the views of society.

5. A new third party should be created that speaks for the average American voter.

6. American political parties can represent public opinion or they can govern effectively, but they cannot do both simultaneously.

Exercises

1. Design a strategic memorandum for a new political party that addresses the needs and desires of your generation. In your memorandum, indicate the following:
   a. the key issues and the new party's position on them,
   b. the campaign appeals that your party should make, not only to your generation but also to others,
   c. likely sources of income for the party and its nominees, and the methods you would use to raise the money,
   d. other nonparty or party groups to which you might appeal for funds and votes in an election, and
   e. what your first order of business would be if your party were to win control of a legislative or executive branch.

2. The major parties in the United States have been criticized for being too ideological by catering to the views of their most active partisans. Do you

think this criticism is valid? Answer this question by comparing the major parties today on the basis of the following:
  a. their demographic and regional composition,
  b. their positions on the major issues before Congress and the president today, and
  c. their political philosophies.

INTERNET RESOURCES

- Democratic National Committee: www.democrats.org
  This is the main Web site of the national Democratic Party, with links to other Democratic organizations, as well as to state Democratic parties.
- Democratic Congressional Campaign Committee: www.dccc.org
  This committee raises money and identifies Democratic candidates for elections to the House of Representatives.
- Democratic Senatorial Campaign Committee: www.dscc.org
  This committee raises money and identifies Democratic candidates for elections to the Senate.
- Republican National Committee: www.rnc.org
  This is the main Web site of the national Republican Party, with links to other Republican organizations, as well as to Republican state parties.
- National Republican Congressional Committee: www.nrcc.org
  This committee raises money and identifies Republican candidates for elections to the House of Representatives.
- National Republican Senatorial Committee: www.nrsc.org
  This committee raises money and identifies Republican candidates for elections to the Senate.
- Other political parties:
  Communist Party of the United States: www.cpusa.org
  Democratic Socialists of America: www.dsausa.org
  The Green Party: www.gp.org
  Libertarian Party: www.lp.org
  Reform Party: www.reformparty.org
  Socialist Party: www.sp-usa.org
  Socialist Labor Party: www.slp.org

SELECTED READINGS

Aldrich, John H. *Why Parties? The Origin and Transformation of Political Parties in America.* Chicago: University of Chicago Press, 1995.

Bibby, John F., and L. Sandy Maisel. *Two Parties—or More?* Boulder, Colo.: Westview, 1998.

Black, Earl, and Merle Black. *The Rise of the Southern Republicans.* Cambridge, Mass.: Harvard University Press, 2002.

Bond, Jon R., and Richard Fleisher, eds. *Polarized Politics: Congress and the President in a Partisan Era.* Washington, D.C.: CQ Press, 2000.

Fiorina, Morris P., with Samuel J. Abrams and Jeremy C. Pope. *Culture War? The Myth of a Polarized America.* New York: Pearson/Longman, 2005.

Gerring, John. *Party Ideologies in America: 1828–1996.* New York: Cambridge University Press, 1998.

Green, Donald P., Bradley Palmquist, and Eric Schickler. *Partisan Hearts and Minds: Political Parties and the Social Identities of Voters.* New Haven, Conn.: Yale University Press, 2002.

Hetherington, Marc J. "Resurgent Mass Partisanship: The Role of Elite Polarization," *American Political Science Review* 95 (September 2001): 619–632.

MacKuen, Michael B., and George Rabinowitz, eds. *Electoral Democracy.* Ann Arbor: University of Michigan Press, 2003.

Schattschneider, E. E. *Party Government.* New York: Rinehart, 1942.

Stonecash, Jeffrey M. *Political Parties Matter: Realignment and the Return of Partisan Voting.* Boulder, Colo.: Lynne Rienner, 2006.

Wattenberg, Martin P. *The Decline of American Political Parties: 1952–1992.* Cambridge, Mass.: Harvard University Press, 1994.

White, John K. *The Values Divide: American Politics and Culture in Transition.* New York: Chatham House, 2003.

NOTES

1. E. E. Schattschneider, *Party Government* (New York: Rinehart, 1942), 1.
2. These party functions are presented and discussed in Samuel J. Eldersfeld, *Political Parties: A Behavioral Analysis* (Chicago: Rand McNally, 1964).
3. John H. Aldrich, *Why Parties? The Origin and Transformation of Political Parties in America* (Chicago: University of Chicago Press, 1995), 18–27, 277–296.
4. When David Duke, a former Nazi sympathizer and member of the Ku Klux Klan, announced that he would run for governor of Louisiana as a Republican, the party denounced his candidacy, although it could not prevent him from running or claiming he was a Republican. The Democrats have had similar problems with Lyndon LaRouche, who has run for the Democratic nomination for president—the last time, from his jail cell.
5. Aldrich, *Why Parties?* 118–135.
6. They did so as a consequence of new laws designed to improve the honesty and integrity of federal elections. The laws, which were enacted by the states, required citizens to register in order to vote. Some also imposed a poll tax to pay for the conduct of elections and a literacy test to ensure that voters could read and had a basic understanding of the Constitution. Unfortunately, many of these laws were imposed in a discriminatory manner, particularly in the South, so as to prevent African Americans and some poor whites from voting.

7. Frances Fox Piven and Richard A. Cloward, *Why Americans Don't Vote* (New York: Pantheon, 1988), 64–95.

8. The Democrats' success in the second decade of the twentieth century came as a result of a split within the Republican Party at the national level between those supporting William Howard Taft and those backing Theodore Roosevelt's candidacy for the presidency in 1912.

9. Gallup Poll, "Major Political Parties in Competitive Situation," December 3, 1999, www.gallup.com/poll/releases/pr991203.asp. Updated with data from the Gallup Poll, "Poll Topics: Party Affiliation," www.gallup.com/default/aspx?ci=15370.

10. Angus Campbell et al., *The American Voter* (New York: Wiley, 1960), 133–136.

11. See Lynda Lee Kaid and Anne Johnston, "Negative versus Positive Television Advertising in U.S. Presidential Campaigns, 1960–1988," *Journal of Communication* 41 (Summer 1991): 53–64, and John G. Geer, *In Defense of Negativity: Attack Ads in Presidential Campaigns* (Chicago: University of Chicago Press, 2006).

12. Thomas E. Patterson, *Out of Order* (New York: Knopf, 1993).

13. Gerald Pomper's analysis of Republican and Democratic platforms from 1944 to 1976 revealed that they were more distinctive than duplicative and more policy oriented than simply rhetorical. Pomper found that many of the differences centered on issues that one party addressed and the other did not. He argued that such differences were important because they meant that the parties were trying to keep their promises. See Gerald M. Pomper with Susan S. Lederman, *Elections in America* (New York: Longman, 1980), 161; Gerald M. Pomper, "From Confusion to Clarity: Issues and American Voters, 1956–1968," *American Political Science Review* 66 (June 1972): 415–428; and Michael Margolis, "From Confusion to Confusion: Issues and the American Voter," *American Political Science Review* 71 (March 1977): 31–43. Jeff Fishel also found that presidential candidates tried to fulfill their campaign promises and were reasonably successful in doing so. See Jeff Fishel, *Presidents and Promises* (Washington, D.C.: Congressional Quarterly Books, 1985), 38–43.

14. Gallup Poll, "Poll Topics and Trends: Congress and Public Approval," www.gallup.com/content/default.aspx?ci=1600&+.

The Nomination Process

Whose Is It Anyway?

Did you know that. . .

- party reforms to increase rank-and-file influence over the presidential nomination have essentially shifted power from one party elite to another, from state leaders to ideological activists?
- the goal of improving representation at the national nominating conventions has resulted in the selection of delegates who are more representative demographically but may be less ideologically representative of mainstream partisans?
- the changes in party rules to open the nomination process to a variety of candidates continue to advantage those who are nationally known and well funded?
- despite the length of the nomination campaign and the extensive coverage of it by local and national news media, voter turnout has remained about one third that of the general election, or about 15 percent of the voting-age population?
- aspirants to a party's presidential nomination usually take more extreme policy positions in their quest for the nomination than they do in their general election campaign?
- the last time a presidential nominee did not personally select his running mate was in 1956, when the Democratic convention—not nominee Adlai Stevenson—chose Estes Kefauver over John F. Kennedy as Stevenson's vice-presidential candidate?
- the amount of broadcast network television coverage of the national nominating conventions has decreased as the parties' attempts to orchestrate them for television have increased?
- the incumbency advantage is greater in the nomination process than in the general election?
- the increasing front-loading of presidential primaries works to benefit front-running candidates?
- the race for money has become in effect the first presidential primary?

Is this any way to run a democratic election?

No aspect of the electoral process has changed more fundamentally and more quickly since the 1970s than has the way in which the major political parties choose their candidates for office. In the past, when party organizations were stronger, the leaders of those organizations shaped the process by which nominees were selected. Although the actual mechanisms varied from state to state, most nominations were controlled by party organizations whose leadership dictated the results.

In exercising that control, the leadership had three goals in mind in addition to its primary objective of winning the election. First, party leaders wanted to reward the faithful who had worked for their candidates in previous elections. Next, they sought to choose experienced people who had worked their way up the ladder of elective office, who understood the rules and practices, and who, above all, were willing to abide by them. Finally, party leaders wanted to select partisans whose primary loyalty was to the party, its positions, its programs, and especially its leadership.

The merit of such a nomination system was that it fostered and maintained strong party organizations and loyalties. The organizations in turn provided continuity in programs, policies, and personnel. The loyalties gave a party a cadre of workers and voters on whom it could depend.

The main disadvantage of such a system was that it was a top-down rather than a bottom-up system. It was less participatory, less democratic. It kept party bosses, even corrupt ones, in power. It facilitated an old-boys' network. People had to play by the rules to get ahead. Rank-and-file partisans had little influence on the nominees and their policy positions.

THE MOVEMENT FROM AN ELITE TO A MORE POPULAR SYSTEM

The Progressive movement began in the early years of the twentieth century as a reaction to the closed and seemingly elitist character of American political parties. Progressives wanted to reform the political system to encourage greater public participation in the nomination and election processes. Conducting primary elections in which partisans could select the candidates they preferred for public office was one of their most touted political reforms.

The movement prospered for almost three decades. From 1900 to 1916, twenty-five states enacted laws to permit or require primary elections. After World War I, however, low turnout, higher election costs, and unhappy party leaders persuaded state officials to return to the older ways of selecting nominees.

Not until after World War II did democratizing tendencies begin to reemerge, along with a communication technology in the form of television that could bring candidates into full public view in American living rooms. The rapid expansion of television programming, the purchase of television sets, and people's addiction to this new entertainment/news medium provided incentives for candidates, particularly for those unable or unwilling to obtain positions of power within the traditional party hierarchy, to take to the airwaves to gain public support. Thus commenced a new era in democratic political activity.

The catalyst behind the shift from a party leadership-dominated nomination system to a more publicly based one was the rule changes that first occurred in the Democratic Party after its raucous 1968 presidential nominating convention. At that time, the successful nominee, Vice President Hubert H. Humphrey, won without campaigning in any of the party's primary elections. As a unifying gesture to those who had participated in the primaries and were frustrated by their failure to affect the choice of nominees, the Democratic convention approved the establishment of a commission to review and suggest changes in its presidential nominating procedures.

In making its recommendations, the commission had one primary charge: to make the selection process more open to rank-and-file partisans and in this way more democratic. A set of rules designed to facilitate rank-and-file involvement in the nomination process and greater diversity in the composition of convention delegates was enacted. The rules established selection criteria that state parties had to meet to ensure that their delegates would be certified as official delegates to the national convention. Delegates not chosen in conformity with party rules could be challenged and even prevented from representing their state parties at the convention.[1]

The Democratic Party in the 1970s and early 1980s was in a strong position to impose its new rules on the states. As the plurality party, the Democrats controlled about three quarters of the state legislatures, and they were able to convince elected officials in the states that had Democratic legislators to enact laws that put them in compliance with the new party rules.

The changes affected the Republican Party's selection process as well. Although the GOP did not initially mandate rule changes for its state parties in the presidential nomination process as the Democrats did, the new laws enacted by the states were applicable to them as well, forcing or giving their state affiliates the option of conducting primary elections.[2] Most of them did so, not wanting to be seen as opposing popular reforms.[3]

The new system rapidly took hold. Today, all states conduct primaries for nominations for federal and state offices. More than half use them exclusively; others employ a combination of primaries, state caucuses, and conventions.[4]

In effect, the parties opened up their nomination process. They further decentralized power that already had been decentralized by virtue of the federal system of government. Power flowed to those who participated. The parties hoped that increased participation would broaden their base of support, energize their electorate, enhance the representative character of the parties, and make them more responsive to the interests of their partisans. It seemed like a win-win situation for the party organization and its partisans. In practice, however, it was not.

THE DEMOCRATIZATION OF NOMINATIONS: REPRESENTATIVE OR UNREPRESENTATIVE?

The Good News

The rule changes have contributed to the democratization of the nomination processes in both parties. By opening up the nomination process, the parties have involved more people in the selection of nominees. Table 7.1 indicates the number of primaries and voters and the percentage of delegates selected in primaries from 1912 to the present.

A second consequence of more open nominations has been broader representation of the party's electoral coalition at its national conventions. Delegates who attend these conventions are demographically more representative of rank-and-file party voters than they were prior to the rule changes. There are more women, more minorities, and more young people.

A third result, which also has improved the democratic character of the system, has been to tie candidates closer to the desires and interests of their electoral supporters. To gain the nomination, candidates have to take positions on salient issues, and keep them if elected, because their renomination is always open to challenge.

A fourth consequence has been to increase the pool of potential candidates. The number of people vying for their party's nomination at all levels of government has increased, especially when incumbents decide not to run for reelection.[5] The range of challengers is also greater. Anyone with access to the mass media, by virtue of his or her own career or financial base, can mount a campaign and, in some cases, even win. George McGovern, Jimmy Carter, Michael Dukakis, and Bill Clinton would not have been likely presidential nominees under the old system in which state party leaders chose the candidate. Al Gore, George W. Bush, and John Kerry might have been, however.

Another more democratic aspect of the new nomination process is that it enlarges the arena of debate by allowing candidates to use the process as a vehicle to promote their ideas—be they the liberal economic and social programs that Jesse Jackson trumpeted in his quest for the 1984 and 1988 Democratic presidential nomination; the traditional, more conservative Christian values that Pat Robertson (1988), Pat Buchanan (1992 and 2000), and Alan Keyes and Gary Bauer (1996 and 2000) advocated when they ran for the Republican presidential nomination; or the anti-war views of Democrats Howard Dean, Dennis Kucinich, and Al Sharpton in 2004. Millionaire Steve Forbes's campaign for the 1996 and 2000 Republican nominations on the promise of a flat income tax and socially conservative policy positions is but another example. Needless to add, in the process of running for the nomination, the candidates also promote themselves, thereby fostering their own political ambitions and satisfying their own psychological needs.

| TABLE 7.1 **Number of Presidential Primaries and the Percentage of Convention Delegates from Primary States, , 1912–2004** |

Year	Democratic		Republican	
	Number of State Primaries	Percentage of Delegates from Primary States	Number of State Primaries	Percentage of Delegates from Primary States
1912	12	32.9	13	41.7
1916	20	53.5	20	58.9
1920	16	44.6	20	57.8
1924	14	35.5	17	45.3
1928	16	42.2	15	44.9
1932	16	40.0	14	37.7
1936	14	36.5	12	37.5
1940	13	35.8	13	38.8
1944	14	36.7	13	38.7
1948	14	36.3	12	36.0
1952	16	38.7	13	39.0
1956	19	42.7	19	44.8
1960	16	38.3	15	38.6
1964	16	45.7	16	45.6
1968	15	40.2	15	38.1
1972	21	65.3	20	56.8
1976	27	76.0	26	71.0
1980	34	71.8	34	76.0
1984	29	52.4	25	71.0
1988	36	66.6	36	76.9
1992	39	66.9	38	83.9
1996	35	65.3	42	84.6
2000	40	64.6	43	83.8
2004	38	83.2	27*	56.9

* Five Republican primaries, with a total of 309 delegates, were cancelled because only George W. Bush qualified as a candidate.

Source: Harold W. Stanley and Richard G. Niemi, *Vital Statistics on American Politics, 2005–2006* (Washington D.C.: CQ Press, 2006), Table 1-23, 66.

The number of candidates seeking their party's nomination, the range of issues, and the diversity of their public appeals all have sensitized the parties to their heterogeneous base. Lauding their diversity, the parties have given economic and social groups within them a chance to be heard, to pursue their interests, and even to put forth candidates who can win nominations. All of this has put the parties more in touch with themselves. That's the good news.

The Bad News

The bad news is that the reforms and changes in the nomination process have given states that hold their contests at the beginning of the process more influence; candidates able to mobilize the rank-and-file partisans more effectively by virtue of their national standing, financial resources, and organizational support are advantaged. Cohesive groups within the party and partisans who participate more as a consequence of their more intense feelings and beliefs have benefited from this arrangement.

Uneven Representation of Partisans. Although the presidential nomination process is open to all partisans, participation is uneven. It is higher at the beginning of the process and lower at the end, especially after the nominee has effectively been determined. Partisans in states that hold their contests early receive more attention. Candidates are encouraged to concentrate their efforts in the early states, spending their resources and addressing the issues of these states. Media attention follows.

As a consequence of these perceived benefits, states have been moving their nomination contests earlier and earlier, thereby front-loading the schedule. In 1972, 17 percent of the delegates had been chosen by mid-April; by 1976 that percentage had increased to 33. In the 1980s and 1990s front-loading continued unabated. By 1992, 40 percent of the delegates had been selected by the end of the first week when states were permitted to hold their nomination contests. That percentage increased to 54 in 1996, 67 in 2000, and 71 in 2004.

Front-loading has very serious and undemocratic consequences for the parties and their partisans, for the candidates, and for the public at large. For the parties, it gives greater benefit to the states that hold their contests first. To the extent that partisans in these states are not representative of the party's rank and file, their electoral choices can skew the outcome. The winning candidate may not be the first choice of most party voters or even the most acceptable compromise candidate.

Take Iowa and New Hampshire, for example. Both have legislation that requires them to go first—Iowa with a caucus selection process and New Hampshire with a primary. These states are certainly not representative of their respective party's electoral coalition. Together they account for less than 1.5 percent of the country's total population. Moreover, they lack ethnic and racial diversity. African Americans constitute only 2.2 percent of Iowa's population and .8 percent of New Hampshire's, compared to about 13 percent of the country as a whole and between 20 to 25 percent of the total Democratic vote in recent elections; similarly, Hispanics comprise only 3.7 percent of Iowa's population and 2.1 percent of New Hampshire's yet about 14.5 percent of the country and a growing proportion of the Democratic Party's electoral coalition.[6] How fair is that?

Moreover, a front-loaded contest is decided before all the election issues become evident, before all relevant background information on the candidates becomes public, and before events that may influence the electorate's determination of the most relevant qualifications of the candidates may occur.

From a democratic perspective, the most serious consequence of having early caucuses and primaries determine the outcome is that the nomination is decided before most people are paying attention to it. By the time the party's electorate tunes in, many of the candidates may have dropped out. Six of the twelve Republican contenders for the 2000 nomination withdrew even before the first state voted; two of the ten Democratic candidates did so as well in 2004, with others leaving the campaign as their war chests emptied and their support dwindled.

Unequal Opportunities for Candidates. For the candidates, front-loading moves their campaign forward into the year preceding the election, lengthening the nomination period but shortening its competitive phase. In 2000 and 2004, both nominations were settled in the six weeks from the first caucus in January through Super Tuesday in early March.

A compressed, front-loaded schedule leaves little time for candidates who have fewer funds initially to parlay a strong showing in Iowa, New Hampshire, or one of the other early contests into a successful fund-raising campaign, as Jimmy Carter was able to do in 1976.[7] For them, fund-raising must begin earlier, in the year or two prior to the election. But even here, front-runners are advantaged. Lesser-known candidates need to demonstrate their electability to raise sufficient funds, yet they cannot do so until the nomination process is under way.

Nor do matching government grants provide the same opportunities that they did in the past. A front-loaded schedule provides greater incentive for front-runners to raise more money than would be allowed if federal grants were accepted. Once candidates decline government funds, other candidates are disadvantaged by accepting them because of the spending limits those funds impose.

Giving advantage to nationally recognized candidates is not necessarily undesirable or undemocratic. Political experience normally is considered a valuable prerequisite for higher office. However, when national recognition and political experience combine to create unequal campaign resources, then outsiders without these resources are penalized. Even personal wealth does not suffice. Ross Perot and Steve Forbes could buy the recognition they needed in 1992, 1996, and 2000 by spending millions of their own money on advertisements, but they couldn't buy experience or obtain the votes required to win.

Finally, front-loading creates a down period of three to four months after a winner has emerged but before the conventions are held. Naturally, public interest declines during this period, forcing the parties and candidates to engage in expensive advertising to remain in the public spotlight and to keep their base energized.

Unequal Representation of the Electorate. A front-load schedule is not the only problem. The people who participate in the nomination process are not representative of the average Republican and Democratic voters, much less the electorate as a whole. Primary voters and caucus participants overrepresent those in higher income and education groups. Older people who have more information, time, and incentive also tend to be more involved than the under-thirty age cohort.

The open system also has given party activists—people who tend to be more ideologically and issue-oriented than the average partisan and much more so than the average voter—more influence because of their activism, their organizational skills, and the resources available to them. The more extreme the activists' beliefs, the more likely they are to find candidates who do not share their beliefs, which in turn provides these activists with greater motivation to get involved to make sure that these candidates do not receive their party's nomination. If activists are successful in winning the nomination for their candidate, they are likely to encourage those with the most strongly held opposing views to get involved as well in their party's primary or in the general election. Ideological zeal begets ideological zeal.[8] The growth of media advertising, specifically issue advocacy, during the nomination phase of the electoral cycle also has contributed to the mobilization of more ideologically driven partisans (for a discussion of issue advocacy in the 2004 election, see chapter 8).

The need to mobilize increasingly apathetic partisans has given groups within the parties that have and are willing to commit resources to educating the public and to mobilizing their supporters on behalf of particular candidates much greater impact on the primary elections. This impact often is reinforced by the activities of these groups during and after elections, lobbying that keeps party candidates and elected officials tied to their core supporters. By emphasizing the policy positions that these groups advocate, the candidates have become more ideologically and issue-oriented themselves. They believe they have to be so to get nominated, elected, and reelected.

This trend toward the parties' ideological core is seen in the presidential selection process, particularly at the beginning of the nomination quest. Aspirants for the Republican nomination move to the ideological right of their party, Democrats to the ideological left of theirs. Later on, they may find that these early positions alienate mainstream voters whose perspectives are more moderate and whose policy orientation is more pragmatic. This ideological trend also is seen in the delegates selected to attend the national party conventions. They, too, tend to be more ideological in their thinking and beliefs than do rank-and-file party identifiers.[9]

What an irony! Parties have reformed their nomination processes to better reflect the attitudes, opinions, and candidate choices of their rank-and-file supporters. They've adopted rules to tie the eventual selection of nominees more closely to the party's electorate. However, that electorate has been disproportionately influenced by activists who tend to hold (and are probably motivated by) more strongly held and ideologically consistent beliefs than are typical voters or even typical partisan voters. Thus, as a consequence of opening the process to achieve better representation, the parties may not represent the moderate, mainstream electorate nearly as well as they did when their leaders picked the nominees. A democratic process has led to undemocratic consequences.

And that's not all. Not only have the parties' elected officials become less representative of their rank and file, they also may be less capable of governing. Ideologues are not good compromisers.

THE IMPACT OF NOMINATIONS ON GOVERNMENT

Taking more consistent ideological stands is just the first step toward pursuing these policy positions if elected. The growing ideologicalization of American parties has resulted in sharper partisan divisions within Congress and, parenthetically, less civility among its members. The old-boys' club that operated according to informal folkways and mores has given way to the new activist politics replete with ideologically laced rhetoric and partisan confrontation. This is what closed down the government in the winter of 1995–1996 for almost a month; two years later it led to a presidential impeachment, and at the very least, it has impeded the enactment of legislation, particularly during periods of divided government.

The ideological gap between the two major parties has filtered down to the grassroots level. The partisan electorate is highly polarized and evenly divided, creating an explosive political environment in which deliberation gives way to strident oratory, compromise is impeded, and the public is more cynical and less trusting of those who represent them than they were two or three decades ago.

Obviously, all of the factors that have contributed to the deterioration of America's political culture and to its governing problems cannot be blamed on the nomination process alone. The causes are deep-seated and varied. They have taken place over a longer period of time than have nomination reforms. Moreover, they have been exacerbated by social, technological, and political change. Nonetheless, the democratization of the nomination process has had a discernible impact that many evaluate as negative.

IMPROVING THE NOMINATION SYSTEM

What can be done about this representational problem and its impact on government? A return to the good old days, when party bosses controlled the selection of party candidates and influenced the policy positions they took, seems both unlikely and undesirable. There would be little public support for making the selection process more elitist and for reducing the input of rank-and-file voters, despite the fact that so many party identifiers choose not to take part in the nomination process.

Nor would there be much support for taking a party's internal politics out of the public arena or limiting media access to it. Some might desire the press to exercise more self-control, particularly when reporting and assessing the personal traits and private behavior of candidates, but there is far from unanimity on this point.

Can and Should Nominations Be Made More Democratic?

If going back to the old system isn't a viable option, then what is? Perhaps the parties could level the playing field by getting a greater cross-section of their partisans to participate. Because activists gain disproportionate influence from their political involvement, getting more people aware, interested, and involved in primaries could lessen this influence. Presumably, if a broader cross-section of a party participated in nomination politics, the candidates would have more incentive to appeal to a wider range of interests and views. But how can more people be encouraged to get involved, particularly given the cynicism and apathy so apparent at the end of the twentieth and beginning of the twenty-first century?

The average turnout in primaries remains at only about 15 percent of the voting-age population, although in highly competitive, early primaries the turnout tends to be higher.[10] Presumably, candidates seeking their party's nomination are doing all they can to bring out as many of their supporters as possible.

Even if it were possible to motivate more people to participate, there's another danger. Energizing more partisans could polarize the party, making a divisive nomination struggle difficult to overcome in the general election campaign.

From the perspective of party leaders, divisive nominations are a problem. The more candidates and the longer they campaign the more likely that the party will remain divided and as a consequence, the higher the odds against winning the general election, because the nominee's image has been damaged by his or her opponents in the primaries and some supporters of the losing candidates remain on the sidelines.[11] As a consequence, party leaders would like to reduce the negative effects that bitter internecine warfare produces, not exacerbate them.

Can Divisive Nominations within Parties Be Avoided in a Democratic Nomination Process?

Reducing divisive primaries and their impact, however, is not achieved by leveling the playing field. It is accomplished by "unleveling" it even more, by giving advantage to the advantaged—to well-known, well-financed candidates and, frequently, to incumbents. In short, the parties are faced with a situation in which they can encourage more candidates and voters to participate, possibly factionalizing themselves even further in the process and hurting their chances for electoral victory, or they can discourage participation, possibly making the nominees less representative of those with strong views. But they can't seem to do both simultaneously.

The Democrats adjusted some of the rules in their presidential nominating process to give their national leaders with national reputations an advantage. They made two adjustments. First, they created the position of unpledged superdelegate, which they bestow on state and national party leaders and elected officials. Theoretically, superdelegates can exercise the dominant influence at a divided convention by voting in favor of the most electable candidate. In practice, however, nominations have been decided well before the conventions, leaving the superdelegates with little more to do than try to enhance their own visibility and image by speaking before live television cameras.

Second, they tried to tighten the nomination schedule to decrease the odds that outside candidates could parlay early caucus and primary victories into a bandwagon for the nomination. They did this by creating a window of time during which caucuses and primaries can be held, from the first Tuesday in February to the second Tuesday in June. But as already seen, that schedule has not prevented inequalities in representation, nor has it provided equal opportunities for candidates seeking their party's nomination. Moreover, imposing these rules on recalcitrant states that move their nominating selection process earlier than allowed by the official schedule has proved difficult for the Democrats, even though the Supreme Court has held that parties can enforce rules for the selection of delegates to their national nominating conventions. The Republicans have not imposed a schedule on their state parties.

Inequitable state representation, reduced rank-and-file participation, and the need to raise more money to keep their preemptive nominee on television has encouraged both major parties to reexamine their nomination processes and their impact. The Republicans established an advisory committee in 2000 that proposed a series of regional primaries and an incentive system to give states extra convention delegates if they hold their nomination contest after April 15 during the year of the election.[12] The Bush campaign objected to the proposal, however, on the grounds that it could extend the schedule, cost the candidates more money, reduce the influence of the large states, and lead to a divisive debate at the 2000 Republican National Convention, a debate which candidate George W. Bush did not desire. As a consequence, the Republican

Rules Committee has not supported the advisory commission's proposal, much less introduced it to the Republican convention for approval.

A Democratic Commission on Nomination Timing and Scheduling, approved by delegates at the 2004 Democratic Convention, also has attempted to spread out the caucuses and primaries by increasing the number of convention delegates for states that hold their primaries and caucuses later in the process.[13] In addition, the commission proposed—and the party accepted—a rules change that added one caucus and one primary to the early part of the Democratic nomination process. Following the Iowa caucus, Nevada, a state with a rapidly growing Hispanic population, also will hold a caucus. Following the New Hampshire primary, South Carolina, a state with a large African American population, will hold its primary. Following South Carolina, the Democratic window opens, allowing other states to schedule their presidential contests from the first Tuesday in February to the second Tuesday in June.

Should the Parties Institute a National Primary?

The hodgepodge of primaries, scheduling issues, low turnout, and dissatisfaction with the candidates who have won their party's nomination have led some to recommend a national primary in which both major parties would choose their nominees in a direct popular vote. The simplicity of this suggestion, the promise of bringing out more people to vote, and the expectation that the prospective nominees would have to address national issues like those they would encounter in office have generated support for such a proposal.[14]

Although proposals for a national primary vary, most would conduct the election in the early summer, preceding the national nominating conventions, which would continue to be held. Candidates who could demonstrate their popularity and electability, perhaps by obtaining a certain number of signatures on petitions or receiving a minimum percentage of support in the public opinion polls conducted in the months before the primary, could enter. Anyone who received a majority would automatically be the nominee. In some plans, a plurality would be sufficient, provided it was at least 40 percent. In the event that no one received 40 percent, a run-off election could be held several weeks later between the top two finishers, or the convention could choose the nominee from among the top vote getters.

Obviously, a national primary would be consistent with the democratic principle of one person–one vote. Moreover, the attention that such an election would receive from the press and the candidates should provide greater incentives for a higher voter turnout than currently exists, particularly in states that hold their nomination contests after the apparent winner has emerged. If more people participated, the electorate would probably be more representative than today's electorate that chooses the parties' nominees. And finally, the outcome of the vote should be clear; no longer could the press interpret winners and losers as it saw fit.

The flip side of a national primary, however, is that it would exacerbate the advantages that front-runners already have, particularly Washington-based insiders and large-state governors, people who can raise the money for an expensive and only partially subsidized national campaign. Lesser-known candidates, unless they were independently wealthy and willing to spend their own fortune on a national campaign, would have little chance of competing on an equal scale with better-funded candidates.

Another potential problem is that a national primary could increase divisiveness within the parties, contribute to the personification of politics, and weaken the organizational base of the parties. State leaders would have less influence on the presidential nomination process, and national party leaders might find themselves challenged by the national organization that helped elect the successful candidate. Moreover, a post-primary convention could not be expected to tie the nominee to the party, although it might tie the party to the nominee, at least through the general election.

The cumulative impact of a national primary, followed by national party conventions, followed by a national election might be too much campaign and election in too short a period of time. It might be more than the electorate is willing or able to absorb. Imagine the same themes and appeals, statements and advertisements, debates and more debates echoing across the land for a period of six months to a year. Voters might tune out; they might become even more cynical and distrustful of politicians, particularly if such a long national campaign produced a long list of promises that the winning candidate would be expected to fulfill and on which that candidate's presidency would be evaluated. Certainly, governing might prove to be more difficult if party leaders and members of Congress had little to do with the nominees' victory and thus lacked an incentive to follow the new president's lead.

Whether a national primary winner would be the party's strongest candidate is also open to question. With a large field of contenders, those with the most devoted or ideological supporters might do best. Candidates who don't arouse the passions of the die-hards, but who are more acceptable to the party's mainstream, might not do as well. Everybody's second choice might not even finish second unless a system of approval or of cumulative voting were used, each of which is likely to be very complex.[15] These potential negative consequences on the major parties have not inclined them to support such a plan, despite its general public appeal. And if there is little enthusiasm within the Democratic and Republican Parties for a national primary, then it is very unlikely that Congress would ever impose it on them.

NATIONAL NOMINATING CONVENTIONS: ANACHRONISM OR STILL RELEVANT?

At the presidential level, the changes in party rules have rendered national nominating conventions obsolete, at least as far as the selection of nominees is concerned. The identity of the likely candidate is known well in advance of the convention as a result of the caucuses and primaries. Even the vice presidential selection isn't the convention's to make. By tradition, the nominee chooses a running mate, and the convention ratifies the choice since a majority of the delegates are supporters of the presidential nominee.

So what's left for the convention to decide? Sometimes, national nominating conventions debate and resolve platform disputes, but most of the time, they don't. They ratify the document, which is a combination of principles and policies that a party committee, most likely controlled by the candidate, who has won the primaries and caucuses, has drafted.

If disputes do emerge, they often reveal real and deep-seated differences among rank-and-file partisans, but they come to light primarily because the mass media highlight them. In other words, news coverage is an incentive for minorities to publicize their disagreements, taking their fight to the convention floor even though the prospects for victory appear to be slight. Under the circumstances, what dissident groups gain is national visibility for their positions. Even the threat of embarrassing the nominee by taking an oppositional position to the floor may be enough for the leading candidate to concede some platform points in an effort to avoid the appearance of disunity.

Why hold conventions? If the delegates are chosen in accordance with party rules and are unlikely to change the pledges they have made to support particular candidates, if the convention rules are decided in advance, if the successful candidate for the presidential nomination is preordained by the primaries and caucuses, if that candidate can choose a running mate, if the platform is hammered out in advance, then why hold conventions at all? This is a question that the broadcast news media are asking with increasing frequency.

From the press's perspective, there's little news. In fact, correspondents and commentators often have to manufacture news by highlighting disagreements, no matter how small; by engaging in seemingly endless and often trivial commentary; and by suggesting potential conflicts, which may or may not come to pass.

Why cover political conventions if they aren't newsworthy? The major broadcast networks are doing less and less of it, leaving the proceedings to C-SPAN and continuous coverage to the twenty-four-hour cable news networks.

From the candidates', parties', and interest groups' perspectives, however, the conventions remain an important political tradition that they wish to continue. The assembled delegates constitute an anointing body that legitimizes the selection of the nominees and a responsive audience that demonstrates enthusiasm for what the party has to offer. The convention provides a national podium from which the candidates can launch their campaign and from which other leaders can gain recognition.

From the party's perspective, conventions provide a unifying mechanism, one that can help heal the divisions of the nomination process. They're a reward to the delegates for their past participation and an inducement for them to continue to work in the party's political campaigns, particularly the one that is just beginning. And, finally, they are publicity for the party, its positions, its candidates, and its supporters. But there is a problem.

Naturally, the party wishes to present itself in the best possible light: unified, enthusiastic, optimistic, with a clear sense of purpose, direction, and demonstrated governing abilities. Its leaders orchestrate the proceedings so that they will have this desired impact. The news media, in contrast, are interested in news (naturally, as they define it—new, unexpected, dramatic, and of human interest). They're also concerned with their public responsibility and their profitability, their bottom line measured in terms of audience, readers, subscribers, and ratings— the number who read, watch, or listen.

The objectives of the party and the news media are often in conflict. Parties need media coverage of their conventions far more than the news media need to report them, particularly if conventions are boring and predictable, as most of them in the last three decades have been. Presented with this dilemma, the parties stage their meetings to be as interesting and informative as possible. There are daily themes, scripts, films, celebrities, and politicians—all made available to live cameras and microphones. But the parties' elaborate public relations extravaganzas seem to reinforce the news media's contention that the conventions have become almost all pomp and ceremony, with little or no substance. Broadcast network coverage of the major party conventions, which has declined substantially, may soon be eliminated entirely with only cable news and public affairs networks covering parts of the proceedings.

Third-party conventions presently receive practically no live coverage on the major broadcast networks. H. Ross Perot's acceptance speech at his Reform Party convention in 1996 and Ralph Nader's at the Green Party convention in 2000 were aired only by cable networks, such as CNN and C-SPAN. Nader held a news conference in 2004 to announce his candidacy, which amounted to a sound bite on the evening news.

If the major networks no longer cover convention proceedings live, then are conventions still necessary? Will they survive? The parties hope so. Beginning in 2000, they launched interactive Web sites to provide information to and gain input from those who accessed their sites. The major networks also provided updated convention news on their Web pages. However, the number of "hits" these sites received during this period was substantially less than what they usually receive, suggesting a lower level of interest among the Internet-oriented electorate.[16]

If conventions are abolished, then how will parties unify themselves after a divisive nomination struggle? How will they decide on and approve a platform on the critical issues? How will they be able to engage and energize the public, particularly independent voters who tend to be less interested, less informed, and less involved? When will the general election campaign officially begin, or will it be an endless campaign from pre-candidacy to nomination to election and then to pre-candidacy again?

If regional primaries were to be established by voluntary agreements among states, by national rules mandated by the parties, or by an act of Congress, a national nominating convention could still serve as a potential decision maker in the event that the primaries were not decisive. It could act as a body that chose or ratified the vice presidential nominee and as a platform maker for the candidates in the general election. The cheerleader and launch-pad functions also would continue to be important for the convention.

Similarly, if a national primary were instituted and the leading candidate did not receive the required percentage of the vote, the convention could then choose the nominee from among the top candidates. It also could serve as the decisive body to approve a platform for the winning candidate.

THE INCUMBENCY ADVANTAGE

For all the hoopla about how open the nomination process has become, incumbents who run for reelection usually win. The deck is stacked even more against challengers in nominations than it is in general elections. Take Congress, for example. For the period from the end of World War II through the 2004 election, 202 House incumbents out of 11,931 were defeated in their quest for renomination (less than 2 percent), and 41 senators lost renomination out of 861 who sought it (less than 5 percent). Table 7.2 indicates incumbency success in renomination for Congress between 1946 and 2006.

Why do incumbents do so well? The system gives them important built-in benefits. These include greater name recognition, superior fund-raising skills, and more campaign experience, coupled with access to more experienced campaign aides. Incumbents frequently have grassroots organizations and the ability to give help to and get help from other party leaders. These benefits translate into great odds for most incumbents seeking renomination.

The incumbency advantage is enhanced by the absence of competition. For the obvious reason that it is so difficult to defeat them, incumbents face fewer challengers than do candidates who run for open seats (seats for which an incumbent isn't running), and when incumbents are challenged, it is often by candidates who cannot raise sufficient funds to mount an effective campaign against them.

Is the incumbency advantage good or bad for a democratic election process and for a democratic government? On the positive side, it provides the party with continuity in its candidacies. Because incumbents have an advantage in the general election, it enables the party to maintain its elective positions and constituents to keep their representative. The more senior a representative is, the greater that person's influence within the legislative body is likely to be and the more that representative is able to do for his or her constituents.

On the negative side, however, the incumbent's renomination advantage translates into more independence from the party. There's little a party's lead-

TABLE 7.2 Congressional Incumbents Seeking Renomination, 1946–2006

Year	Senate			House of Representatives		
	Total Seeking Renomination	Number Defeated	Percentage Defeated	Total Seeking Renomination	Number Defeated	Percentage Defeated
1946	30	6	20	398	18	5
1948	25	2	8	400	15	4
1950	32	5	16	400	6	2
1952	31	2	6	389	9	2
1954	32	2	6	407	6	1
1956	29	0	0	411	6	1
1958	28	0	0	396	3	1
1960	29	0	0	405	5	1
1962	35	1	3	402	12	3
1964	33	1	3	397	8	2
1966	32	3	9	411	8	2
1968	28	4	14	409	4	1
1970	31	1	3	401	10	2
1972	27	2	7	390	12	3
1974	27	2	7	391	8	2
1976	25	0	0	384	3	1
1978	25	3	12	382	5	1
1980	29	4	14	398	6	2
1982	30	0	0	393	10	3
1984	29	0	0	411	3	1
1986	28	0	0	394	3	1
1988	27	0	0	409	1	—
1990	32	0	0	406	1	—
1992	28	1	4	368	19	5
1994	26	0	0	387	4	1
1996	21	1*	5	384	2	1
1998	29	0	0	403	2	—
2000	29	0	0	403	3	1
2002	28	1	4	398	8	2
2004	26	0	0	404	2	—
2006	29	1	3	402	2	—

*Sheila Frahm, appointed to fill Robert Dole's term is counted as an incumbent seat.

Source: Harold W. Stanley and Richard G. Niemi, *Vital Statistics in American Politics, 2005–2006* (Washington, DC.: CQ Press, 2006), 51–52.

ership can do to a popular incumbent who chooses to deviate from the party's position on the issues.

SUMMARY: NOMINATION DILEMMAS IN A NUTSHELL

In theory, the movement to a nomination process in which more people have the opportunity to participate has opened the parties and theoretically expanded their base. From a democratic perspective, that's good. However, in practice, only a portion of the major parties' rank and file actually gets involved and votes. From a democratic perspective, that's bad. That the states that hold the early caucuses and primaries are not representative of the party as a whole, that the people who do participate in the caucuses and primaries tend to have the strongest ideological orientations, and that the candidates who benefit from the current system tend to be those with the greatest name recognition, the most money, and the most organizational support undercuts the democratic character of the nomination process. It also contributes to the cynicism and distrust of elected officials, political parties, and presidential candidates—certainly not a beneficial result for the parties, their candidates, their partisans, and the electorate as a whole.

Various proposals for reforming the nomination process at the presidential level have been advanced. The goal of these proposals—democratizing the presidential selection process even more by getting more of the party's rank and file to participate—is laudable. The end result, however, may be to advantage further front-runners (particularly incumbents), to create more division within the parties, and to make the parties more subject to the influence of those who win their nominations rather than the other way around. The parties are faced with a representational dilemma. Can they simultaneously reflect the wishes of their diverse base and also provide strong partisan, national leadership?

Now It's Your Turn

Discussion Questions

1. Why did the major political parties reform their nomination processes in the 1970s, and did the reforms achieve their desired goals?
2. From the perspectives of the parties, candidates, and partisan supporters, what are the main advantages and disadvantages of the current nomination processes for president and members of Congress?
3. How would you reform the parties' current nomination rules to mitigate the disadvantages to the parties, candidates, and partisan supporters? Do you support or oppose the changes in party rules that recent Republican and Democratic Party commissions have proposed? What effect, if any,

do you think these rule changes would have on the democratic character of the presidential nominating process?

4. Does the advantage that incumbents have in renomination undercut a democratic electoral system?

5. What impact, if any, does the process of nomination have on the structure of the parties and their ability to govern if elected?

Topics for Debate

Challenge or defend the following statements:

1. The changes in the major parties' presidential nominating processes have not worked and should be reversed.

2. Congress should enact a law that establishes a national primary for selecting the major parties' presidential nominees.

3. Because Iowa and New Hampshire are not representative of the entire country, they should be prevented from automatically holding the first caucus and primary election.

4. Aspirants for their party's presidential nomination should not be allowed to campaign before the year of the election.

5. National nominating conventions are irrelevant and should be abolished.

Exercises

1. You've been asked to head a committee to reform the way your party chooses its nominees. The primary goals that the party wants you to consider when you propose your reforms are, in order of importance, to:
   a. select the strongest and most qualified candidate to run in the general election,
   b. give all partisans an opportunity to participate in some way in the nominating process,
   c. increase the likelihood that the views of the winning candidate reflect the views of the rank and file, and
   d. have a nominating process that is open to all well-qualified candidates.

   In your plan, indicate:
   a. when and how the nominees for national office will be selected,
   b. the rules for determining who can run and who can vote,
   c. the penalties, if any, that you would impose on recalcitrant state parties,
   d. the method for approving or amending your reforms, and
   e. an explanation of how and why your proposed reforms will be an improvement on the present system.

2. Critique the following proposal, submitted by the author to the Democratic and Republican Committees, which were reexamining their presidential nominating processes in 2000.

A Proposal to Reform the Presidential Nomination Process

The clock cannot be turned back. Primaries and multistaged caucuses cannot be replaced by backroom politics. Nor can the parties impose specific dates or deals on the states. The regional primary proposal advanced by various secretaries of state is a good idea. If it receives state support, I think the party should back it.

I also would favor exceptions for a few states (perhaps Iowa and New Hampshire or others if the early few are to be rotated) to hold their contests earlier. Face-to-face interaction between candidates and voters brings the campaign to the average partisan in a way that mass media advertising, computerized mailings, and professional phone banks cannot.

But the parties need to regain control of *their* process. Here is what I recommend:

1. Hold a two-day convention in the early months of the election year. The purpose of the convention would be to present a set of party principles to which candidates for the nomination would have to agree before they could officially run for the party's nomination. This would not be a detailed platform but rather a set of basic values and positions to which each aspirant would have to subscribe. The national committee should choose the drafters of these principles. The principles would have to be accepted by the delegates as the first order of business of the convention.

2. The delegates to this convention would be selected by virtue of the positions they hold in government or in the party. All elected party officials at the national level (members of Congress and the president and vice president, if applicable), all state governors, big city mayors, and state legislative leaders, plus the members of the national committee, the chair and vice chair of the national party, all state party chairs, and past presidential candidates would make up the delegations.

3. Once the convention has accepted the party's principles, the convention would then choose the candidates who could run for the party's presidential nomination in the state caucuses and primaries. Potential candidates would need to obtain the signatures of 10 percent of the delegates to be placed in nomination by a delegate whose speech could not exceed fifteen minutes. After the nominations were completed, the convention would then vote on the list of candidates placed in nomination. Any candidate who received a certain percentage of the vote (somewhere between 20 and 25 percent) would be an official nominee of the party, eligible to run in its state's caucuses and primaries.

4. The second day of the convention would be a forum for the nominees. Each of the successful aspirants for the nomination would be invited to address the convention (and the American people via news media coverage) and explain why they want to be president, what they stand for in terms of policy, and what they would do in office.

5. After the nominees made their appeal at the convention, the nomination campaign would begin and would be conducted in much the same manner as it is today. The national parties could set up their own rules for allocating the vote to the delegates selected, as the Democrats currently do, or leave the rules up to the states, as the Republicans do. Scheduling would still be up to the states, except that no contest could be held until at least one month after the opening convention was completed. The only nominees who could run would be those chosen by the convention, although the party might want to consider a petition process by which a candidate could demonstrate sufficient public support to enter the contest at a later time.

6. Nominees would be expected to remit to the party some percentage of all money they have raised from the time they officially declared their candidacy and filed with the FEC. The purpose of such payment would be threefold: to help pay for the costs of the initial convention in which the candidates launched their nomination campaign, to give the party money for the generic advertising it would be expected to air after the nomination had been effectively settled but before the summer nominating convention, and to equalize fund-raising more than the current system does.

7. The party would hold its regular nominating convention during the summer but would compress the meeting into two or three days, during which the platform would be spelled out in accordance with the party's principles, the candidate would be officially designated as the party's presidential nominee, a vice presidential nominee would be chosen, and the acceptance speeches of the party's candidates would launch the presidential campaign.

INTERNET RESOURCES

- Congressional Quarterly: www.cq.com
  An excellent source of information on strategy and tactics. Publishes a variety of journals on politics and government, including *Campaigns and Elections,* which can be accessed through the general site or directly at www.camelect.com
- National Journal: www.nationaljournal.com
  Another excellent magazine for studying politics and government, with numerous links to its own and other publications.
- U.S. Department of Defense Federal Voting Assistance Program: www.fvap.gov
  Provides information on absentee voting.
- United States Electoral Assistance Commission: www.eac.gov
  The U.S. Election Assistance Commission (EAC) was established by the Help America Vote Act of 2002 (HAVA). Central to its role,

the commission serves as a national clearinghouse and resource for information and review of procedures with respect to the administration of federal elections.

- Yahoo! Presidential Election of 2008: http://headlines.yahoo.com Provides links to news sources, audio, video, magazine articles, and editorials on the ongoing campaigns.

SELECTED READINGS

Atkeson, Lonna Rae. "Divisive Primaries and General Election Outcomes: Another Look at Presidential Campaigns." *American Journal of Political Science* 42 (1998): 256–271.

Bartels, Larry M. *Presidential Primaries and the Dynamics of Public Choice.* Princeton: Princeton University Press, 1988.

Burden, Barry C. "The Nominations: Technology, Money, and Transferable Momentum," in Michael Nelson, ed. *The Elections of 2004.* Washington, D.C.: CQ Press, 2005.

Cook, Rhodes. *The Presidential Nominating Process: A Place for Us?* Lanham, Md.: Rowman and Littlefield, 2004.

Day, Christine L., Charles D. Hadley, and Harold W. Stanley, "The Inevitable Unanticipated Consequences of Political Reform: The 2004 Presidential Nomination Process," in William Crotty, ed. *A Defining Moment.* Armonk, N.Y.: M. E. Sharpe, 2005, 74–86.

Geer, John G. *Nominating Presidents: An Evaluation of Voters and Primaries.* Westport, Conn.: Greenwood Press, 1989.

Mayer, William G., and Andrew E. Busch, ed. *The Front-Loading Problem in Presidential Nominations.* Washington, D.C.: Brookings Institution, 2004.

Norrander, Barbara. "Ideological Representativeness of Presidential Primary Voters." *American Journal of Political Science* 33 (1989): 570–587.

Polsby, Nelson W. *The Consequences of Party Reform.* New York: Oxford University Press, 1983.

Shafer, Byron E. *Bifurcated Politics: Evolution and Reform in the National Party Convention.* Cambridge, Mass.: Harvard University Press, 1988.

Smith, Larry David, and Dan Nimmo. *Cordial Concurrence: Orchestrating National Party Conventions in the Telepolitical Age.* New York: Praeger, 1991.

Task Force on Campaign Reform. *Campaign Reform: Insights and Evidence* Princeton: Princeton University Press, 1998.

NOTES

1. The Supreme Court gave the parties this power in its 1975 landmark decision in *Cousins v. Wigoda* (419 U.S. 477). The Court held that political parties were private organizations with rights of association protected by the Constitution. Parties could compel state affiliates to abide by their rules of delegate selection for the national nominating convention unless there were compelling constitutional reasons for not doing so. The burden of proving these reasons was placed on the state that deviated from the party's rules.

   Although in theory the party has the power to enforce its national rules, in practice it is usually difficult to do so. State parties are subject to the election laws of the state. For the state party to conduct its own primary would be very difficult and costly and would force it to hold state caucuses and conventions, further contributing to the difficulty and expense.

2. Although Republicans profess the same broad goals, they mandated only one national rule for their state parties: that they not discriminate in the selection of delegates on the basis of race, creed, color, national origin, or gender. In other aspects of delegate selection, the GOP enforces whatever rules a state party observes.

3. The principal difference is that Republicans permit winner-take-all voting on a district or statewide basis, and the Democrats do not.

4. Paul Allen Beck and Frank J. Sorauf, *Party Politics in America,* 7th ed. (New York: HarperCollins, 1992), 234–235.

5. There are more challengers in a nomination contest to run against an incumbent of the opposition party in the general election than there are in the incumbent's party when that incumbent is seeking renomination. The more open system, however, keeps incumbents more attuned to their constituents' interests and needs, in part because of the threat of a challenger.

6. "2005 American Community Survey: Data Highlights," United States Census Bureau, 2006, http://factfinder.census.gov.

7. In addition to front-loading, there also has been a regionalization of the presidential nomination contests, with states in similar regions of the country agreeing to hold their primaries and caucuses around the same time, often on the same day. This movement, which began in 1988 with a southern regional primary, has continued and even expanded in each subsequent nomination cycle. It too gives advantage to candidates with established national and regional reputations—those who are well known, well funded, and well organized—and disadvantages those without such reputations and resources. Engaging in multistate campaigning and using extensive media require substantial resources, which front-runners usually have and outsiders usually lack.

8. David C. King, "The Polarization of American Political Parties and Mistrust of Government," in *Why Americans Mistrust Government,* Joseph S. Nye, Philip Zelikow, and David C. King, ed. (Cambridge, Mass.: Harvard University Press, 1997), 155–178, and David C. King, "Party Competition, Primaries, and Representation in the U.S. Congress," paper presented at MIT Conference on Parties and Congress, October 2, 1999.

9. This phenomenon was first identified by Herbert McCloskey, "Consensus and Ideology in American Politics," *American Political Science Review* 58 (1964): 361–382. See also Jeane S. Kirkpatrick, *The New Presidential Elite* (New York: Russell Sage, 1976). The phenomenon appears in the surveys of delegates since then.

10. In states in which there were both Republican and Democratic primaries in 2000, turnout averaged almost 18 percent, according to an analysis by the Committee for the Study of the American Electorate. Steven A. Holmes, "Many Stayed at Home," *New York Times,* September

1, 2000, A18. In 2004, estimated turnout was lower. It ranged from a high of 31 percent in California and 30 percent in New Hampshire to very low percentages in the states that held their contests after the nominee was effectively determined in early March. See the Web site of Professor Michael P. McDonald of George Mason University: http://elections.gmu.edu/voter_turnout.htm.

11. Divisive primaries, however, if they encourage turnout, can have the beneficial effect of mobilizing the party's electorate for the general election and subsequent contests. See Walter J. Stone, Lonna Rae Atkeson, and Ronald B. Rapoport, "Turning On or Turning Off? Mobilization and Demobilization Effects of Participation in Presidential Nomination Campaigns," *American Journal of Political Science* 36 (August 1992): 665–691.

12. The proposal would have grouped states according to population and forced them to hold their caucuses and primaries on the same day. Primaries for each of the population groups would be scheduled about a month apart, beginning in early March, with the least populous states going first.

13. The Democratic Party's commission recommended that the calendar be divided into four stages. The states that held their nomination contest during the first stage, the two-week period beginning with the first Tuesday in March, would receive additional delegates equal to 15 percent of their total number of pledged delegates. If they held their election during stage two, the three-week period beginning the third Tuesday in March, they would receive an additional 20 percent. If their selection date was in the third stage, the three-week period that begins the second Tuesday in April, they would be allocated an additional 30 percent, and if they held it after that and before the end of the Democratic nomination process on the second Tuesday in June, they would be entitled to an additional 40 percent of their total number of delegates.

14. Gallup Poll, "Electoral Reforms," April 10, 1988, as reported in *The Gallup Poll: Public Opinion 1988* (Wilmington, Del.: Scholarly Resources, 1989), 60–61.

15. Approval voting allows the electorate to vote to approve or disapprove each candidate who is running. The candidate with the most approval votes is elected. In a system of cumulative voting, candidates are rank-ordered, and the ranks may be averaged to determine the winner.

16. PC Date Online, a firm that monitors traffic on news sites, reported a 14 percent drop in the number of people who accessed these sites during the 2000 political conventions. Howard Kurtz, "Web Coverage Does Not Spark Convention Interest," *Washington Post*, August 14, 2001, C1.

chapter 8

Campaign Communications

How Much Do They Matter?

Did you know that. . .

- the Republican stereotype of Democrats as big-government, liberal do-gooders and the Democratic stereotype of Republicans as big business, mean-spirited conservatives have existed for more than seventy years?
- most people believe that personality issues are relevant and important even though they also believe that the news media places too much emphasis on them?
- political advertising in presidential elections began in 1952, and the first negative presidential ad was run in 1964?
- political consultants believe that they perform an essential role in the democratic electoral process, and more than 80 percent of them find negative advertising perfectly acceptable?
- recent checks into the content of political advertisements in presidential elections consistently find exaggeration, misleading statements, and factual errors?
- $1.6 billion was spent on advertising in the 2004 elections, and that more than $620 million of this amount was spent on the presidential election alone?
- the Internet now contains more campaign information that any other single media source?
- incumbents use the imagery of their public office to maximize their already large reelection advantages?
- the most influential negative ads in the 1988 and 2004 presidential election campaigns, the Willie Horton ad (1988) and the Swift Boat Veterans for Truth commercials (2004), were sponsored by outside groups and not by the official presidential and party campaign committees?

Is this any way to run a democratic election?

CAMPAIGN COMMUNICATIONS AND DEMOCRATIC ELECTIONS

Campaigns matter! They determine who wins. They highlight the principal issues with which the public is concerned and which newly elected officials must address. They influence the electorate: who votes, for whom, and why. They test the adequacy of the principal components of a democratic political system: free speech, public participation, group advocacy, meaningful choice, informed judgment, and ultimately, responsive and accountable government.

Although political campaigns are not the only factor that determines an election's outcome, its salient issues, turnout and voting behavior of the citizenry, and responsive government, they are a principal one that affects these aspects of electoral politics. That is why they are so important.

However, campaigns can and do fall short of achieving their democratic goals. Instead of clarifying the issues for the electorate, they can obscure them; instead of turning out voters, they can turn them off; and instead of providing a realistic agenda for the new government, they can create unrealistic public expectations that newly elected officials may not be able to meet. And as previously argued, they also can be an instrument by which the advantaged, those with superior resources,—money, organization, and leadership—maintain or extend their political influence. In short, campaigns can strengthen or weaken the democratic system, depending on how they are conducted and what impact they have.

The key question is not are campaigns necessary. Of course, they are. Rather the issue explored in this chapter is: How well do contemporary campaigns meet the goals of informing and motivating voters? To answer this question the chapter examines campaign communication from the candidates to the electorate. The discussion begins by exploring the kinds of information that should be most helpful to the electorate in making an informed voting decision. Then it turns to the type of information candidates usually convey in their basic appeals to voters and how their modes of communication can intentionally or unintentionally distort the message the electorate receives. Finally, the text looks at the impact of campaigning on voters and suggests ways in which communications could be improved.

The Need To Know

Campaigning is obviously an integral part of the electoral process. Candidates need campaigns to accomplish their principal objective of winning elective office. They also need them to learn about public concerns and to convince voters that they will address those concerns satisfactorily. The electorate needs the campaign for similar reasons, to voice their needs, espouse their interests, and gain the information necessary to decide which of the candidates (and parties) are more likely to benefit them in the years ahead.

What does the electorate need to know to make informed voting decisions? At the very least they need to be able to identify the candidates, make a judgment about what they will try to do if elected, and how successful they are likely to be in comparison to the others who are running. The promises candidates make, the positions they take, and priorities they enunciate should be reasonable guides to their performance in office. If they are not, then voters can hold incumbents, and to a lesser extent, their party, accountable in the next election. If they are, then voters can evaluate the performance of public officials who seek reelection on the basis of how their policies worked and what their consequences were for society.

Knowing what the candidates have to say, however, is only part of the information needed to make enlightened voting decisions. Voters need to know about the candidates themselves: their experience, their qualifications, and their personal strengths and weaknesses. This is where character fits in.

Elected officials may not be in a position to fulfill their promises even if they try to do so. New issues may arise; unexpected events can and probably will occur; and the economic, social, and political environment may change. Thus, it is important to anticipate how candidates will adapt to that change. Character provides an insight into work style, adaptability, and the capacity to handle new challenges.[1]

In addition to knowing about the candidates, their philosophy, policy positions, and character, the electorate also needs to know whether they stand a good, fair, or poor chance of winning. It would be nice to vote for a person who thinks as we do and in whom we have confidence, but it might prove to be meaningless if that individual has little or no chance of being elected. An intelligent voting decision may include the component of not wasting your vote.[2] For the vast majority of people, voting for someone who has little or no chance is not a smart vote, unless it is to prevent one of the other candidates from winning.

The Information Game

Given the importance of an issue debate to a democratic electoral process, how much information should candidates provide? Should they present a general map that indicates the policy directions they hope to pursue, and should they also fill in the details?

The Policy Perspective: Generalities v. Detail. If the amount of information most people have or are interested in knowing is any indication of what the public desires or is capable of learning, then candidates should be more general than specific. They should talk about their philosophies, their basic goals, and their priorities. But being too general also can be a disadvantage if a candidate is perceived as purposefully vague. That was the case when Republican Thomas E. Dewey ran for president in 1948. With a large lead in the polls, not wanting to alienate a predominantly Democratic electorate, Dewey spoke in platitudes and generalities that seemed empty and directionless when compared to President Harry S Truman's straight talk, specific promises, and Democratic imagery. Truman energized Democratic faithful sufficiently by the time of the election to win a surprising victory. The same criticism of being vague and talking in generalities was directed at George W. Bush by his Republican opponents at the beginning of the 2000 nomination campaign.

On the other hand, being too specific can turn off voters who do not care and alienate those who disagree. It can put the candidate, and if successful, the elected official in a position from which compromise on public policy is made more difficult, which is not a desirable outcome (except perhaps to true believers) in a governmental system that divides power and requires compromise most of the time.

The Republicans' Contract With America, the platform on which House Republicans ran in 1994, is a case in point. The Contract listed ten proposals that Republican candidates pledged to support if elected. The congressional party's refusal to compromise on these issues, particularly those that pertained to cuts in taxes and domestic spending was a major cause of the government shutdown in the winter of 1995–1996, a shutdown that reverberated to the congressional Republicans' political detriment. Similarly, Bill Clinton's promise to end discrimination against gays in the military is another illustration of a specific policy proposal that got the newly elected president into trouble at the very beginning of his administration.

The generality versus specificity dilemma often places candidates in a "dammed if you do, dammed if you don't" situation. To win their party's nomination and build their electoral coalitions, they need to make specific promises to specific groups. The members of these groups are frequently the most ideologically oriented party identifiers. Then in the general election, candidates usually have to broaden their appeal; most adopt a strategy of moving toward the center of the political spectrum in order to attract independent voters and supporters of the other party. These candidates face a difficult juggling act, made even harder by the fact that it has to be done in full public view. Promises are recorded by the news media, inconsistencies are highlighted, and contrasts in emphases are noted.

The alternate strategy of maintaining consistency in policy positions and priorities was the strategy George W. Bush pursued in 2004. This strategy energizes the base but does not necessarily broaden it. For candidates who adhere to this strategy, the key to success is maximizing partisan turnout by reinforcing the attitudes and opinions of people already inclined to support a particular party. Thus, the GOP mounted a turnout drive in 2004 that targeted "lazy Republicans," people likely to vote for Bush if they voted at all. In a highly polarized and equally divided electorate, "motivation becomes as important as persuasion," according to Matthew Dowd, chief strategist for the Bush-Cheney 2004 campaign.[3] In a diverse but nonpolarized environment, it may not be.

From the perspective of the electorate, information, needs, and desires vary. Within their own areas of interest and expertise people demand and digest much more information than they do in areas in which they have less knowledge and interest. Business executives may want detailed information on tax policy, investment incentives, and labor-management issues, but they may be much less interested in policy that does not have a discernible economic impact on them, perhaps a program to put one hundred thousand more teachers into classrooms or one that extends drug benefits to people on Medicare. On the other hand, homemakers with young children or older relatives living with them are probably more interested in these educational and health benefits and less in taxes and management issues.

Even if the public were not all that informed about a policy, there still is reason to demand that candidates discuss their proposals in some detail. Such a discussion tells the electorate a lot about the candidates themselves: their competence, their consistency, their communication skills, and to some extent, their candor. These traits have become increasingly important in candidate-oriented elections. Here is an example: in his 1972 presidential campaign George McGovern proposed a $1,000 grant to all poor Americans, those whose annual income was less than $12,000. But McGovern could not tell how much his plan would cost the taxpayers, which led many to question his understanding of these matters, much less the viability of the specific proposal he had made. Similarly, replying to criticism that he opposed supplementary appropriations for the military in Iraq, John Kerry said, "I actually did vote for the $87 billion dollars before I voted against it." Kerry's statement reinforced Republican criticism of him as a flip-flopper. In short, the promises candidates make and the arguments they use to support their positions indicate their knowledge, experience, and potential for making good policy judgments and governing successfully.

The Character Issue: Public v. Private Behavior. In recent elections, character issues have received much more attention, in some cases, even dominating coverage. In the 1996 presidential election, for example, only two policy issues, the economy and taxation, were mentioned more than Clinton's character on the evening news on the major television networks.[4] Ultimately, both types were the subject of considerable debate in the advertising, news coverage, and comments by the candidates.

Electing the right people and having confidence in them is nothing new, nor should it be. What is different today is the emphasis placed on personal behavior outside the public arena, which in the past was considered to be irrelevant and hence, was not reported as news. Are character in general and personal behavior in particular legitimate issues? Most observers think that they are, pointing to numerous contemporary examples in which character has affected performance. Richard Nixon's cover-up of the Watergate break-in and his disregard for the civil rights of others, Ronald Reagan's penchant for delegation and unwillingness or inability to supervise his aides closely, Jimmy Carter's reluctance to deal with the Washington political establishment or even to call members of Congress to ask them to support his programs, Bill Clinton's lack of integrity and candor when responding to allegations about his political dealings as governor of Arkansas and sexual improprieties, and George W. Bush's unwillingness to admit mistakes in the war and occupation of Iraq are all character-based problems that adversely affected these presidents' performances in office. It was no coincidence that much attention was devoted to George W. Bush's service in the Alabama National Guard and John Kerry's Vietnam War experience in the 2004 presidential election.

Assessing candidates' character is important for several reasons. It provides an indication of how they may react to unforeseen events and situations, how flexible they are, how they make decisions, and how they interact with their aides. It tells the electorate something about their work style, energy and confidence, empathy, honesty and candor, strength of character, and leadership skills.[5]

Overemphasizing character, however, can be harmful. It draws attention away from policy issues. It leads people to draw inferences about behavior that may have little or nothing to do with job performance. It attributes too much influence to personality as a driving force and not enough to other factors that can affect what people say and do—from the information they have to the goals they wish to attain to the procedures and precedents they are expected to follow in office. Character-based judgments also encourage flippant, often superficial assessments by those not trained in psychological analysis and even by those who are.[6]

A preoccupation with personality also can lead to unrealistic expectations, both good and bad, of what a single person can do in a political system that decentralizes power and responsibilities. Liberals feared Ronald Reagan's strong anticommunist views and George W. Bush's antiterrorism crusade combined with their "shoot-from-the-hip" speaking styles could plunge the country into more military encounters, whereas conservatives feared that Bill Clinton's penchant to please combined with his promises to end discrimination against homosexuals in the military, support affirmative action, provide a comprehensive healthcare program with universal coverage for all Americans, and stimulate the economy with more federal spending would result in an even bigger, more intrusive national government. The fears about Reagan and Clinton were not realized, in part because institutional and political checks within the system prevented these presidents from dominating the government so as to dictate public policy outcomes. However, the war in Iraq seemed to confirm the worst fears about Bush.

Spin: Positive v. Negative. Candidates obviously need to make their own case. They have to provide reasons for voting for them and against their opponents. To do so, they must state their positions and qualifications and somehow get their opponents' negatives onto the public record. They may do so by leaking them to the news media, mentioning them in their own campaign advertising, or referring to them in speeches, press conferences, and debates.

The electorate does need to know some of this information. People have to evaluate the strengths and shortcomings of a candidate in order to make an informed judgment about that candidate's suitability for the job. And as we know, the candidates themselves are not the best source for information about their own shortcomings. Most campaigns maintain an active opposition research operation on the belief that if they do not find the "dirt" on their opponents, no one may. They justify this research on the grounds that their opponents are engaging in it as well.

How much negativism is desirable? Too much can lead to public cynicism toward all of the candidates. It can lead to a perception that the voting choice is about the lesser of two (or more) evils. Too much negativism also can have a boomerang effect on those who resort to it too heavily. Steve Forbes and Robert Dole both saw their poll numbers decline as they began to air negative ads against their opponents in the 1996 campaign. Similarly, the adverse reaction to the Richard Gephardt–Howard Dean confrontation in Iowa in 2004 prompted Democrats John Kerry and John Edwards to stress their positive qualifications rather than their opponents' negative ones during their quest for their party's nomination; Kerry continued to air more positive than negative ads during the general election.[7] Finding the right balance that appropriately trumpets one's own strengths and an opponent's weaknesses should be the campaign objective, not an avalanche of criticism focusing on personality traits.

CAMPAIGN IMAGERY

Partisan Stereotyping

Campaign appeals can distort or clarify. In articulating their messages, candidates usually use partisan imagery. They do so to rouse the faithful, their core supporters. They also do so to stereotype their opponents negatively, particularly when they cannot find other policy or character issues that resonant with the electorate.

Sounding a partisan refrain conjures up familiar images about the parties, past and present, that are both positive and negative. For Democratic candidates, the positive images are economic; they stem from the roots of the Roosevelt realignment. This is why Democratic candidates tend to emphasize "bread-and-butter" economic issues, such as jobs, wages, education, and social benefits for the working and middle classes when they campaign for office. They contrast their empathy for the plight of the average American with Republican's ties to the rich and to the GOP's indifference, even hostility, toward the less fortunate.

From the Republicans' perspective, however, the economic images are very different. Republicans see themselves as defending the free enterprise, capitalist system against their liberal-leaning Democratic opponents who favor big government and its "give-away" programs, the so-called tax and spend liberals.

Social images are more complex. The Democrats stress equal opportunity, whereas the Republicans point to individual initiative. In the national security area the stereotypes are less distinctive, although Republicans have been associated with a more unilateral, neo-conservative ideology that emphasizes democracy, morality, and a strong military response to the continuing threat of terrorism at home and abroad; the Democrats have stressed diplomacy, multi-lateralism, and realism in their approach to national security issues.

Partisan stereotyping can be dangerous and misleading because it puts everyone in the same boxes. All Democrats become liberal, pacifist do-gooders and all Republicans turn into wealthy, law and order, mean-spirited conservatives. Such images cloud significant differences among candidates of both parties.

Stereotyping also is used to explain current positions and past actions. In 1988, Democratic presidential candidate, Michael Dukakis, was presented by his partisan opponents as a knee-jerk liberal who released hardened criminals from jail. To support this accusation, a group opposing Dukakis aired a commercial about a Massachusetts prisoner, Willie Horton, who raped and murdered his victims while on parole. The Bush campaign then reinforced the distinction between Bush's tough approach to criminals and Dukakis's leniency.[8]

To offset being stereotyped as a liberal in 1992, Bill Clinton called himself a "New Democrat" and took pains to differentiate his moderate policy orientation from the more liberal views of his Democratic predecessors. Similarly, George W. Bush emphasized his "compassionate" conservatism to distinguish himself from the colder Darwinian image of traditional, business-oriented Republicans intent on pursuing their economic goals.

In addition to partisan stereotyping, candidates may resort to "wedge issues," those issues that energize particular groups. Robert Dole attempted to use immigration as such an issue in the 1996 election campaign when appealing to Californians beset with problems stemming from the settlement of so many new immigrants in their state. In 2004, George W. Bush reiterated his support for a constitutional amendment that would have defined marriage as a heterosexual relationship.

If an issue is very controversial, and on some level socially unacceptable to raise directly in a campaign, "code words," such as right to life, family values, affirmative action, and same-sex marriage, may be used to alert those for whom these words have great and often emotional meaning and engender predictable reactions.

Partisan stereotyping can get in the way of meaningful debate. It can substitute for information, and it can unfairly typecast individuals in a manner that does not accurately reflect their values, priorities, positions, or what they would do if elected to office. It does not educate as much as it reinforces preconceptions, dispositions, and biases.

Experience and Incumbency

"Experience is the best teacher" is a maxim that incumbents would like voters to believe. They use their office imagery to compare their qualifications to those of their opponents, reminding voters what they have done for them and how they can use their influence to continue to work on their constituents' behalf.

As noted previously, being an incumbent is usually a great advantage, almost as great in the general elections as in the nominations. What incumbency imagery does is reinforce and extend the advantages that incumbents already have in running for reelection. The numbers speak for themselves. Table 8-1 notes the reelection rates for members of Congress since 1946.

Although incumbent presidents have not fared as well in reelections, because they are subjected to closer and more critical press scrutiny and a more competitive electoral environment, they still have won more than they have lost. Of the eighteen presidents who sought reelection in the twentieth century, only five (Taft in 1912, Hoover in 1932, Ford in 1976, Carter in 1980, and Bush in 1992) were defeated, but it also should be noted that several avoided possible defeat by choosing not to run again. The one incumbent so far in the twenty-first century, George W. Bush, was reelected.

Why are incumbents so advantaged? A lot has to do with their name recognition and the relatively low level of public knowledge about those who seek political office. Name recognition conveys a "known" quality. In general, people would rather vote for someone they have heard of than for someone about whom they know little or nothing.

Incumbents tend to be disadvantaged in only two types of situations: when bad times or multiple grievances hurt those in power, and when incumbents say or do something their constituents find very objectionable such as accept gifts from people who have an interest in certain public policy decisions.

The incumbency advantage unlevels the playing field. It puts the burden on the challengers to make the case for change. Unless they do so, they are unlikely to win. To defeat an incumbent requires resources. But as previously noted, unless challengers are independently wealthy or have considerable backing from their party, they usually are not able to raise nearly as much money as their incumbent opponents. This is why those who desire an elective office try to wait until a seat is open before seeking office, unless they calculate that the recognition they gain by running against an incumbent (and losing) will put them in real contention the next time around.

COMMUNICATION DISTORTIONS

Accentuating the Positive

Political advertising has become part and parcel of contemporary electoral campaigns. The ads are a big part of the distortion problem, in part because they are so effective. Candidates and their political consultants believe they need to advertise to reach voters. They may be right. If the grassroots organizations of political parties are not as strong as they once were; if the public is less interested, informed, and involved in electoral politics; and if most people spend a lot of time tuned into entertainment programming, then advertising in the mass media would seem appropriate.

Candidates for national office spend the bulk of their money on political advertising. At the presidential level, about two thirds of the public funds given to the principal nominees go into media spots, campaign biographies, and toward speeches or town meetings sponsored by the candidates' organizations. More than $620 million was spent on television advertising by or on behalf of the major party candidates in 2004, most of it in five major media markets.[9] For members of Congress the proportions and mediums vary, but the need for and use of political advertising does not.

Why do candidates and their consultants believe that advertising is so important and presumably so effective? The answer is that advertisements provide critical information that people need and may not get through their normal sources for news. They are repeated frequently, whereas news stories are not, or at least, not for as long.[10] Moreover, ads are dramatic; news reports may not be. Almost all advertising scripts have been pretested to find out which words and pictures best evoke the desired response. And ads target their audience more than broadcast journalists can. Most ads have a simple message. There is little subtlety, and the point is usually hammered home.[11]

The impact of advertising often is reinforced, because the advertising directs attention to items that already may be in the news. The ads themselves can become news if they are controversial enough, thereby repeating and reinforcing the message again and again.

Studies have shown that people actually obtain and recall more substantive information about the candidates and their policy stands from advertisements than they do from news reports.[12] All advertising is obviously not beneficial to a democratic electoral process. Ads often make their point by exaggeration and imbalance. Many tread lightly on truth. In its continuing study of the accuracy of political advertising, the Annenberg Public Policy Center at the University of Pennsylvania has operated a "fact check" in which it identifies misleading statements, inferences, and factual errors. The center has found that most campaign ads contain exaggeration, half-truths, and innuendos designed to create favorable or unfavorable impressions of candidates and their opponents.[13]

Advertising also costs a lot of money, which enlarges the campaign finance problem.

Excessive Negativity

One criticism of contemporary campaign commercials is that they have become increasingly personalized and negative, or at least that is what the public believes. (See Table 8.2.) The conventional wisdom, supported by empirical

TABLE 8.1 Congressional Reelection Rates, 1946–2006

Year	HOUSE OF REPRESENTATIVES			SENATE		
	Total Seeking Reelection Who Were Renominated	Defeated in General Election	Percentage Reelected	Total Seeking Reelection Who Were Renominated	Defeated in General Election	Percentage Reelected
1946	370	52	88.6	24	7	70.1
1948	385	68	82.3	23	8	65.2
1950	394	32	91.9	27	5	81.5
1952	380	26	93.2	29	9	69.0
1954	401	22	94.5	30	6	80.0
1956	405	16	96.0	29	4	86.2
1958	393	37	90.6	28	10	64.3
1960	400	25	93.8	29	1	96.6
1962	390	22	94.4	34	5	85.3
1964	389	45	88.4	32	4	87.5
1966	403	41	89.8	29	1	96.6
1968	405	9	97.8	24	4	83.3
1970	391	12	96.9	30	6	80.0
1972	382	13	95.5	25	5	80.0
1974	383	40	89.6	25	2	92.0
1976	381	13	96.6	25	9	64.0

1978	377	95.0	19	22	7	68.2
1980	392	92.1	31	25	9	64.0
1982	383	92.4	29	30	2	93.3
1984	408	96.1	16	29	3	89.7
1986	391	98.5	6	28	7	75.0
1988	408	98.5	6	27	4	85.2
1990	405	96.3	15	32	1	96.9
1992	349	93.1	24	27	4	85.2
1994	383	91.2	34	26	2	92.3
1996	382	94.5	21	20	1	95.0
1998	401	98.3	7	29	3	89.7
2000	400	98.5	6	29	6	79.3
2002	390	98.0	8	28	3	85.7
2004	402	98.3	7	26	1	96.2
2006	400	94.5	22	29*	6	79.3

*Includes Joseph Lieberman, who was not renominated by the Democrats but ran as an independent and won.

Source: Basic data from Norman J. Ornstein, Thomas E. Mann, and Michael J. Malbin, Vital Statistics on Congress, 1997–1998 (Washington, D.C.: CQ Press, 1998), 61–62; Updated with data from Harold W. Stanley and Richard G. Niemi, Vital Statistics on American Politics, 2005–2006 (Washington, D.C.: CQ Press, 2006), 51–52. Percentages determined by author.

TABLE 8.2	**Public Perceptions of Negativity in Presidential Elections**

Question: Compared to past presidential elections, would you say there was MORE mudslinging or negative campaigning in this campaign or LESS mudslinging or negative campaigning in this campaign?

	1992	1996	2000	2004
More	68	49	34	72
Less	16	36	46	14
Same (volunteered response)	14	12	16	12
Don't Know/Refused	2	3	4	2

Source: Pew Research Center for the People and the Press, "Voters Liked Campaign 2004, but Too Much 'Mud-Slinging'," November 11, 2004, http://people-press.org/reports/print.php3?PageID=912.

data, is that the proportion of negative advertising is increasing with each subsequent election.[14] From the perspective of media consultants, the people who design, market, and profit from the ads, there are more negative advertisements because they work. Political consultants generally subscribe to the proposition that the more negatives a candidates has, the less likely that candidate is to win.[15]

Negative advertising can have a boomerang effect, however. The George H. W. Bush campaign was reluctant to use negative advertising early in its 1992 campaign because it feared a "there-you-go-again response" from the press and public after its successful negative advertising campaign four years earlier. Campaign insiders were correct; voters were more leery of the negative ads in 1992.[16] When Robert Dole raised character issues about Clinton in his 1996 election advertising, Dole's poll ratings actually declined. The public reacted negatively to his negativism. However, President Clinton's negative ads in 1996 did not produce a similar reaction. The difference seemed to be that Clinton used contrast in his ads, mixing the positive with the negative. More importantly, his ads focused on policy positions, not personal failings.

What is the impact of negative advertising on voters? Studies based on experimental research indicate that negative messages can turn off voters, thereby decreasing turnout and increasing cynicism.[17] On the other hand, studies based on empirical research have reached a very different conclusion. These studies suggest that while negative ads may turn off some voters, they turn on others, specifically strong partisans energized by the criticism of an opponents' character.[18]

Not surprisingly, the public claims that advertising does not help them make their voting decisions.[19] Everyone seems to agree that false, inaccurate, and deceptive ads, positive or negative, are unfair and run counter to a democratic electoral process.[20] That so many of these negative spots have been sponsored by party and nonparty groups prompted the reformers who designed the BCRA in 2002 to include a "stand by your ad" provision that requires candidates to assert that they take responsibility for the ad. The framers of the law assumed that the provision would result in less negative advertising, but it did not do so in the 2004 presidential election. Table 8.3 lists the percentage of positive ads in the 2000 and 2004 presidential elections in the top seventy-five media markets.

Ad Monitors

If advertisements mislead the public, which many scholars claim that they do, should they be monitored, and if so, by whom? Some countries do not allow political advertising. Whether such a prohibition is good or bad is probably immaterial in the United States because the First Amendment to U.S. Constitution protects a candidate's right to advertise. But it does not necessarily follow that candidates should be free to say or claim anything they want under the banner of free speech. Just as obscenity is not protected by the First Amendment, neither is libel or slander. However, the Supreme Court has made it extremely difficult for public officials to demonstrate that they have been libeled or slandered by the news media. Falsehood alone is not sufficient evidence. Malice also has to be proven.[21]

Short of suing for libel and slander, what else can be done to promote and police "truth in advertising"? Perhaps the regulations for commercial advertising, which makes advertisers liable for the false claims of their products and gives an independent regulatory body, the Federal Trade Commission (FTC),

TABLE 8.3 **Positive Advertising in the 2000 and 2004 Presidential Elections (percentage positive)***

Sponsor	2000	2004
Candidate or Coordinated	64.8	43.6
Party	37.2	8.6
Interest Group	0.0	7.5
Overall	46.2	31.5

*According to another study by Lynda Lee Kaid, 42 percent of the verbal content of Bush ads were positive, compared to 66 percent for Kerry. Lynda Lee Kaid, "Videostyle in the 2004 Presidential Advertising," in Robert E. Denton Jr., ed., *The 2004 Presidential Campaign: A Communication Perspective* (Lanhan, Md.: Rowman and Littlefield, 2005), 287.

Source: Michael M. Franz, Joel Rivlin, and Kenneth Goldstein, "Much More of the Same: Television Advertising Pre- and Post-BCRA," in Michael J. Malbin, ed., *The Election after Reform: Money, Politics and the Bipartisan Campaign Reform Act* (Landam, Md.: Rowman and Littlefield, 2006), Table 7.1.

authority to prescribe penalties, could be applied to politics. However, it might be very difficult to prove an ad false if it only presents one aspect of a candidate's record or identifies only some of the positions that candidate has taken. Another problem would be which commission, the FEC or FTC, should oversee political advertising. The FEC's composition of three Democrats and three Republicans makes it extremely difficult to resolve a controversial, partisan issue.

What about the private sector? Should the news media monitor political advertising? They have already begun to do so. However, the amount of advertising in national campaigns greatly exceeds the attention and space the press has devoted to advertising scrutiny. Moreover, media monitors may not be the most expert or impartial judges.

Nonetheless, "ad watches," as they have been called, serve a useful purpose by calling attention to false claims and charges and helping to correct perceptions that the public may develop about the candidates and their issue positions. The knowledge that ads may be subject to close examination by the news media and public interest groups also encourages those who design them to be more careful about what they say and show.[22] On the other hand, ad watches often reinforce ads by making them into news items.

The first commercial that the Swift Boat Veterans for Truth produced and aired following John Kerry's speech at the Democratic National Convention is a case in point. Kerry spoke with pride about his military service in Vietnam and presented it as evidence that he was qualified to be president during a time of crisis. The Swift Boat ads contradicted Kerry's claims. Featuring men who said that they had served with Kerry in Vietnam, the vets disputed Kerry's acts of heroism; they also minimized the injuries he suffered, injuries that earned Kerry two Purple Hearts.

Almost immediately, the ad, which was only shown in small media markets in three states, became a news item on the 24-7 cable news channels and a hot topic on talk radio. The veterans who criticized Kerry were interviewed. The attention they received generated unsolicitated donations to the group sponsoring the ad. The money enabled the Swift Boat veterans to design and run additional commercials criticizing Kerry's conduct during and after the war. Despite challenges to the veracity of the ads and the veterans' contentions that they had served with Kerry, the ads effectively undermined Kerry's claim that his war record qualified him as a strong and courageous leader.

Checks on advertising also come from opposition candidates, public interest organizations, and even prominent people. Nancy Reagan strongly objected to footage from the assassination attempt on her husband that was included in a 1996 Clinton ad on gun control. After Mrs. Reagan's complaint, the Clinton campaign removed the objectionable footage, but not before the ad had been shown many times and had become a news item and point of controversy.

A similar controversy erupted in March 2004 when an ad for George W. Bush contained two seconds of footage from ground zero at New York City's

World Trade Center in which fire personnel were seen carrying a stretcher, presumably of human remains, draped in an American flag. Some families of the victims protested the "political exploitation" of the tragedy. Although subsequent Bush commercials omitted the scene, Bush's media consultants concluded that references to 9/11 evoked a very powerful and positive image of the president and continued to show ground zero and the president's actions after the terrorists attacks in their commercials.[23]

THE NEW TECHNOLOGY OF POLLING, TARGETING, AND MESSAGING: BETTER COMMUNICATION OR MORE EFFECTIVE MANIPULATION?

One of the major changes in political campaigns today is its professionalization. Run by experts at discerning public attitudes, designing public appeals, and directing them to the most receptive audience, these political consultants operating profit-making businesses have replaced the party pros and their precinct captains as the new handlers of contemporary political campaigns.

Today, every aspect of the campaign—from the public opinion polling to the focus group reactions to the pretested speech, from the orchestrated events to the guests invited to them, and from the cameras that record the action to the spin misters who echo the theme and fax the sound bite—has been planned, staged, and recorded by and for the mass media. Campaigns have become made-for-TV productions. It's a big show, with the candidates front and center and their aides working hard behind the scenes to make sure everything comes out all right, or if it doesn't, to fix it as soon as possible. Nothing is left to chance.

The bookends of the campaign are frequently public opinion polls. These surveys are used to find out what is on the public's mind; what the initial perceptions of the candidates, parties, and issues are; and what is concerning the groups within and outside the party's electoral coalition. Armed with this knowledge, organizers can develop the broad outlines of a campaign, including the strategic approach, the issue appeals, and the references to candidate traits both positive and negative.

The basic rule is to be careful. Winging it is viewed as dumb and dangerous. Spontaneity is out. Every major idea, promise, and most words are pretested in focus groups to gauge reactions and gain the most positive response. Once the message is designed and tested, it is then targeted to specific groups. There are four principal targeting mechanisms: telephone solicitation, direct mail, radio, and cable and local television. Broadcasting campaign appeals on the major networks or even on national cable networks is no longer viewed as the most cost-effective way to reach most voters. The rates are too high, the message is usually too broad, and the audience is too diffuse.

The targeting mechanism is used in conjunction with large databases that the parties and various political consultants have assembled over the years. Without knowing it, people become part of these mammoth datasets if they have ever made a contribution to a candidate running for office, to a group supporting a particular issue, or even if they subscribe to a particular publication.

Armed with the list and the special code words that turn on particular groups, the campaign targets its message toward those groups. In this way, people get their issues directed toward the candidate and receive the positions of the candidate that most closely accord with their views. What they do not get is the rest of that candidate's positions. The reason is that campaign handlers believe that the targeted group would not be interested in these positions, or worse yet, might be opposed to them. Besides, the greater the number of positions a candidate takes, the more likely voters will be confused about the candidate's policy priorities.

To make matters worse, people may not realize the limited scope and content of the information they do receive. The press does not cover the advertising campaigns with the same scrutiny that it reports on "real events."

Take the Clinton ads that appeared in major media markets beginning in the summer of 1995 and continuing through the nomination process. The ads purposely were not run in two of the largest media markets, New York and Washington, D.C., and only occasionally in a third, Los Angeles, the areas in which most of the national press corps live and work. This multimillion dollar campaign, which had much to do with improving Clinton's image and discrediting Dole's, received hardly any attention as news. In the words of Clinton's political adviser, Dick Morris, the person who designed the campaign:

> If the ads had run there [New York, Washington, and Los Angeles],
> the press would have grasped the magnitude of what we were doing.
> But if these cities remained "dark," the national press would not make
> an issue of our ads—of this we felt sure.
>   . . . As the ads were shaping voters; attitudes . . . few newspapers
> ran articles, much less front-page articles, on the ads. Television—the
> very medium we were using rarely mentioned the ads.[24]

Does this new campaign technology contribute to democratic dialogue? Is polling identical to having a conversation with a person or trying to persuade that person of the merits of certain policy proposals or one's qualifications for office? Who is talking and who is listening? Who is leading and who is following?

The new technology has turned the image of an informed electorate groping with the issues as presented by the candidates into one of almost inert objects of opportunity that candidates manipulate with their slick communications. Technology also has made candidates into composites of their consultants' professional imagery, and with their negative advertising has converted their opponents into caricatures of themselves. It has transformed a broad range of ideological and issue appeals into a narrow set of compartmentalized messages targeted to those who are most likely to approve and be energized by them.

Has the new communications technology undermined our democratic electoral process? Has it encouraged manipulation rather than persuasion? Does it create unrealistic expectations on the part of the electorate? If so, then technology has contributed to the rise in cynicism about politics and politicians that has been evident since the 1970s.

An overwhelming proportion of the population believe, "politicians will tell voters what they want to hear, not what they will actually try to do if elected." [25] Obviously, the new technology is not the sole cause and may not even be the principal cause of political cynicism and mistrust, but it is a contributor.

What can be done? The campaigns are unlikely to discard new technology, but media coverage could cover the impact of it more thoroughly. Moreover, this technology may change the electorate's appetite for information and the sources from which people acquire it. Campaigning on the Internet already has become the next phase of the communications revolution in American electoral politics.

CAMPAIGNING ON THE INTERNET

The use of the Internet as a communication vehicle began in the 1990s. The Clinton-Gore campaign communicated internally via e-mail. Once in office, the administration continued to use e-mails to keep its staff informed on policy and political matters. In 1993, the White House launched its own Web site, as did Congress. By 1994 some candidates running in the midterm elections and most major news outlets had sites on which they presented videos of the campaign and poll data, as well as news and informational items.

What followed was a rush to get online. In the ensuing years having a Web site evolved from occasional outreach efforts designed to gain attention and reach a relatively small number of voters into a necessity to get the message out, raise money, recruit volunteers, build crowds for campaign events, mobilize supporters, and get people out to vote.

The increase in campaign-related information available on the Web paralleled the growth of Internet users. Within a relatively short period of time, the number of users grew by leaps and bounds. In its 2005 report on Internet trends, the Pew Research Center for the People and the Press reported that 63 percent of the population eighteen years of age and older went online for news, entertainment, and communication. For those younger than eighteen years of age, the figure was even higher, 81 percent.[26]

Not only has usage increased, but users also are becoming more and more representative of the country as a whole. Table 8.4 list the demographic profile of Internet users in 2004.

Naturally, the increasing number of users has commanded the attention of candidates and their media advisers. Communicating with these users has

TABLE 8.4 Demographics of Internet Users (in percentages)

Gender	
Women	61
Men	66
Age	
18–29	78
30–49	74
50–64	60
65+	25
Race/Ethnicity	
White, non-Hispanic	67
Black, non-Hispanic	43
Hispanic	59
Community Type	
Urban	62
Suburban	68
Rural	56
Household Income	
Less than $30,000/yr.	44
$30,000–$50,000	69
$50,000–$75,000	81
More than $75,000	89
Educational Attainment	
Less than High School	32
High School	52
Some College	75
College+	88

Source: Trends 2005 (Washington, D.C.: Pew Research Center for the People and the Press, 2005), 63.

become an important function for the campaign organization. Speeches, ads, and schedules regularly are placed on candidates' Web sites. Increasingly, campaigns have opened blogs to engage their supporters and make them feel part of the campaign.

Soliciting contributions is another important opportunity provided by the Internet. In 2000, Republican John McCain raised $5 million on his Web site, most of it following his surprise victory over George W. Bush in the New Hampshire primary.[27] But McCain's effort paled in comparison to Howard Dean's during the 2003–2004 election cycle. Dean raised $51 million, much of it in small contributions from appeals on his Web site. In addition to money, Dean solicited volunteers to work in the states that had early primaries and caucuses.

That is not all. More than five hundred thousand people signed up on his site to receive campaign information. Thousands participated in a blog his campaign manager Joe Trippi established and on which Dean regularly made comments and responded to suggestions. The campaign kept in close touch with its supporters via e-mail and Web communications. The objective was to create a community in which those who accessed the Web site, followed campaign developments on it, debated strategy and issues on the blog, and felt a part of the campaign.

Dean's use of the Internet became newsworthy in itself. The press took notice. Other candidates followed suit. The result was a literal revolution in campaigning. The Internet provided a convenient and inexpensive way to inform the electorate and reach out to younger voters.

The new communications technology does not end here. Candidates also have begun sending text messages to the cell phones of their supporters. Their purpose is to keep them informed of latest events and challenges.[28]

From the perspective of the electoral process the reach of the new technology—the Internet and its interactive potential and text messaging—have contributed to the democratic character of elections. It informs and energizes the electorate. The Internet extends the political debate. It brings the campaign home. It has the potential to reverse some of the distortion of campaign communication. The accessibility and variety of news outlets allows the online public to be as knowledgeable as it desires, to check the veracity of claims from impartial as well as partisan sources, and to reduce candidates' dependence on nonparty groups for the money, mobilization, and material support.

There are, of course, potential hazards as well. Security can be breached, and campaign sites can be invaded. Rumors spread rapidly, as does misinformation. Moreover, people can put on their own blinders by accessing sites that conform to their partisan, candidate, and issue preferences. Nor are Web "hits" the same thing as attending a caucus meeting or voting in a primary election, as Howard Dean found out in Iowa and New Hampshire.

Nonetheless, if the Internet facilitates communication, if it better informs the electorate; if it brings more people into the campaign; and if it provides additional opportunities for candidates, parties, and nonparty groups to discuss the issues at greater depth, then the democracy is being well served and the election process is improved.

SUMMARY: CAMPAIGN COMMUNICATION DILEMMAS IN A NUTSHELL

Political campaigns are part and parcel of a democratic election process. They are important for several reasons. They enable candidates to interact with the electorate and hear the people's concerns. They also give candidates a podium from which to express their views, demonstrate their knowledge, respond to policy and personal inquires, and appeal for votes. For the voters, campaigns are equally important as a source of information and an opportunity to question the candidates or at least to evaluate their views and their qualifications for office.

The communication dilemma stems from conflicting candidate and voter needs and goals. The candidate's primary goal to win creates an incentive to shape the scope, content, and spin of the information provided to voters. Candidates stress their best issues, not necessarily the country's most important ones. They present a partial perspective, not a comprehensive one. The voters are left with an incomplete picture, and one in which the negatives often dominate. Is it any wonder that people are suspicious of politicians and disappointed with elected officials?

There are other information distortions in campaigns. Partisan appeals conjure up familiar stereotypes by which individuals and parties are categorized, sometimes unfairly and almost always too simplistically. Incumbency imagery is used to buttress the resources and recognition that already give those in office an immense advantage in being reelected. Symbols, code words, and sound bites have substituted for argument and debate. Messages are more effectively targeted with modern computer-based communications technology to rally the faithful, convince the undecided, and frequently inform less attentive and knowledgeable voters.

Personality issues are stressed, and character traits are highlighted. Whether these traits are relevant depends on varying conceptions of the job. For those who see election to high public office as a position of trust, respect, and great moral and ethical responsibility, having the proper virtues and leading the exemplary life are essential qualifications. For those who have a results-oriented view of public service, who are more interested in policymaking than personal modeling, for these individuals political skills, such as flexibility, persuasiveness, and pragmatism, communicative skills, and leadership abilities are the most relevant traits for the job.

All of the hype and hoopla, all of the promises and images, can create unrealistic expectations, which, if not met, can contribute to the mistrust of politicians, apathy in the elective process, and cynicism about government. Nonetheless, there have been some hopeful developments.

Campaign communications are being evaluated by partisan and nonpartisan public interest and news media groups. Candidates have to acknowledge that they approve ads that make claims on their behalf. There are more sources of information available to more people and more ways to get involved in campaigns. Candidates are using the Internet to reach a broader electorate, which may lessen their dependence on party and nonparty organizations. Voter turnout increased in 2004, to which the expanded channels of communication may have contributed. And people continue to believe that they have sufficient information to make an informed judgment on election day. If this belief accords with reality, then campaigns are serving some of their principal functions: to inform, to energize, to provide opportunities for public choice, and to guide government officials in the agendas they pursue and some of the decisions they make.

Now It's Your Turn

Discussion Queestions

1. Is information about personal behavior outside of office a relevant consideration for election to public office?
2. Does stereotyping add to or detract from an informed voting decision, particularly for voters who are less attentive to the candidates, their parties, and their policy positions?
3. Has the growth of issue advocacy contributed to a better informed electorate?
4. Should the federal government regulate truth in political advertising as it does in commercial advertising?
5. Is the incumbency advantage undemocratic? Does it facilitate or impede the operation of government?
6. Has the revolution in communications technology enhanced the democratic character of elections in the United States?

Topics for Debate

Challenge or defend the following statements:
- Candidates should be required to tell the truth in their political advertisements and be disqualified if they do not do so.
- The government should establish a nonpartisan, independent regulatory agency to monitor and regulate all political communications.
- Candidates who are the object of negative ads should be allowed to respond to them at the expense of the candidate, party, or groups that sponsored the negative ad.
- All candidates and parties should be required to establish interactive Web sites in which people can follow the campaign and communicate with the people running it.
- The country's "truth in advertising law" should be applied to political communications.

- The incumbent advantage is harmful to a democratic electoral process and should be modified in some way.

Exercises

1. A new federal agency has been established to monitor and regulate political advertising. You have been asked to develop the mission statement for this agency. In your statement indicate the principal goals of the agency, the methods you suggest for monitoring advertising, the kinds of activity that should be regulated, and the penalties that should be imposed on violators.
2. Assume that you have just been assigned by your local newspaper to be its ad monitor. Over the course of the election, monitor the advertising on local television and in the local newspaper for one week. In the story that you write for the paper indicate the scope and content of the ads, the relevancy and veracity of claims that were made in them, the groups to whom the advertisements were targeted, and your general evaluation of the effectiveness of this advertising on the electorate. Do you think that the advertising made a difference?
3. You have just been appointed Internet coordinator for your candidate's campaign. Write a memo to your candidate indicating the various ways in which the Internet could benefit his/her campaign. Also warn the candidate of any potential dangers.

INTERNET RESOURCES

Most of the sites for the previous chapter will be applicable for campaign communications as well. In addition the offices of incumbents running for reelections should be useful for monitoring their activities or linking to their campaign web site. For federal officials, begin with their institution:
- House of Representatives: www.house.gov
- Senate: www.senate.gov
- White House: www.whitehouse.gov
All candidates and their campaigns should be accessible through their parties.

Listed below are a few additional sites on the media:
- Accuracy in the Media: www.aim.org
  A conservative organization that monitors liberal bias in the press.
- Campaign Legal Center: www.campaignlegalcenter.org
  The Campaign Legal Center is a nonpartisan, nonprofit organization which works in the areas of campaign finance, communications and government ethics.
- Center for Media and Public Affairs: www.cmpa.com
  The best single source for evaluating the content and spin of news stories on the three major broadcast networks.

- Commission on Presidential Debates: www.debates.org
  The Commission on Presidential Debates (CPD) was established in
  1987 to sponsor and produce debates for the United States presidential and vice presidential candidates.
- The Pew Research Center for the People and the Press: http://
  people-press.org
  The Center is an independent opinion research group that surveys
  attitudes toward the press, politics, and public policy issues.

SELECTED READINGS

Cornfield, Michael. *Politics Moves Online: Campaigning and the Internet.* New
York: Century Foundation Press, 2004.

Dalager, Jon K. "Voters, Issues, and Elections: Are the Candidates' Messages
Getting Through?" *Journal of Politics* 58(1996): 486–515.

Denton, Robert E., ed. *The 2004 Presidential Campaign: A Communication
Perspective.* Lanham, Md.: Rowman and Littlefield, 2005.

————. ed. *The 2000 Presidential Campaign: A Communication Perspective.*
Westport, Conn.: Praeger, 2002.

Devlin, L. Patrick. "Contrasts in Presidential Campaign Commercials of
2004." *American Behavioral Scientist* 49 (2005): 279–313.

————. "Contrasts in Presidential Campaign Commercials of 2000."
American Behavioral Scientist 45 (2001): 2338–2369.

Geer, John G. *In Defense of Negativity: Attack Ads in Presidential Campaigns.*
Chicago: University of Chicago Press, 2006.

Jamieson, Kathleen Hall. *Packaging the Presidency: A History and Criticism of
Presidential Campaign Advertising.* New York: Oxford University Press,
1996.

————. *Dirty Politics: Deception, Distraction, and Democracy.* New York:
Oxford University Press, 1996.

Kaid, Lynda Lee. "Political Advertising," in Lynda Lee Kaid, ed. *Handbook of
Political Communication Research.* Mahwah, N.Y.: Lawrence Erlbaum
Associates, 2004: 155–202.

Kaid, Lynda Lee, and Anne Johnston. "Negative versus Positive Television
Advertising in U.S. Presidential Campaigns, 1960–1988." *Journal of
Communications* 41 (1991).

Kurtz, Howard. *Spin Cycle.* New York: Free Press, 1998.

Morris, Dick. *Behind the Oval Office.* New York: Random House, 1997.

Semiatin, Richard J. *Campaigns in the Twenty-First Century.* New York:
McGraw Hill, 2005.

Tedesco, John. "Changing the Channel: Use of the Internet for Communication about Politics," in Lynda Lee Kaid, ed. *Handbook of Political Communication Research*. Mahwah, N.Y.: Lawrence Erlbaum Associates, 2004: 507–532.

Trippi, Joe. *The Revolutuion Will Not be Televised: Democracy, the Internet, and the Overthrow of Everything*. New York: Harper Collins, 2004.

Troy, Gil. *See How They Ran: The Changing Role of the Presidential Candidate*. New York: Free Press, 1991.

West, Darrell M. *All Wars*, 4th ed. Washington D.C.: CQ Press, 2004.

NOTES

1. There is no one right way to adapt to change. From the perspective of those who hold certain policy positions paramount, the candidates' consistency and their determination to pursue their policy goals despite situational changes may be critical criteria in their evaluation. George W. Bush's conservative views and his antiterrorism policy, especially the war and subsequent occupation of Iraq, was seen by those of a similar persuasion as strength. Others less happy with Bush's policies and his unwillingness to change them despite the human and material costs of the war saw his actions as weakness, an inflexibility to adjust to changing times.

   In contrast, Bill Clinton's adaptability, his willingness to compromise in the light of opposition to many of his domestic policy proposals, was seen as a strength by those who wanted results, the half-a-loaf is better than no-loaf crowd, but a weakness by those who didn't know where he stood, what he believed, and what he would do next. These critics found him unprincipled, and they found that unnerving.

2. For others, candidate viability is less important than registering discontent by the act of voting itself or sometimes, by not voting. Some people wish to use their vote as a protest. Republicans in New Hampshire in 1992 were unhappy with President George H. W. Bush. About one third of them demonstrated their unhappiness by voting for Pat Buchanan in the Republican primary. Realistically, Buchanan had little chance of replacing the incumbent president, George Bush, for the Republican nomination, but angry New Hampshire voters did not care. They were more interested in registering their unhappiness with Bush and his policies. Similarly in 1996, 8.4 percent of those who voted cast ballots for H. Ross Perot, even though most of them must have known that it was very unlikely that Perot would win. In fact, some people may have voted for Perot because he had little or no chance of winning. Thus, there would be no danger in exercising this protest vote.

3. Matthew Dowd as quoted in *Campaign for President: The Managers Look at 2004* (Lanham, Md.: Rowman and Littlefield, 2006), 100.

4. "Campaign '96 Final: How TV News Covered the General Election," *Media Monitor* X (November/December 1996): 3.

5. Which of these traits is most relevant to the voting decision may vary, however. Some may be endemic to the job, whereas others are important because of the times or the frailties of the previous president.

6. Perhaps the most flagrant so-called personality analysis of a candidate occurred during the 1964 presidential election. *FACT* magazine sent a letter and survey to the more than twelve

thousand members of the American Psychiatry Association, asking them whether Republican Barry Goldwater was psychologically fit to serve as president. Approximately 19 percent of the psychiatrists responded, with two out of three saying "no." The magazine not only cited the psychiatrists' responses as evidence of Goldwater's unfitness for the presidency, but it also published comments, editing out some of the qualifying statements that the psychiatrists had included in their responses. Groups such as the American Medical Association and journals such as the *American Journal of Psychiatry* quickly criticized the study as bogus medicine that lacked scientific credibility and validity. Warren Boroson, "What Psychiatrists Say about Goldwater," *FACT* 4 (September/October 1964): 24–64.

7. L. Patrick Devlin, "Contrasts in Presidential Campaign Commercials of 2004," *American Behavioral Scientist* 49 (October 2005): 300.

8. The most potent of the Bush crime ads was titled, "Revolving Door." As prisoners were seen walking through a revolving door, an announcer said: "As governor, Michael Dukakis vetoed mandatory sentences for drug dealers. He vetoed the death penalty. His revolving-door policy gave weekend furloughs to first-degree murderers not eligible for parole. While out, many committed other crimes like kidnapping and rape. And many are still at large. Now Michael Dukakis says he wants to do for America what he's done for Massachusetts. America can't afford the risk." L. Patrick Devlin, "Contrasts in Presidential Campaign Commercials of 1988," *American Behavioral Scientist* 32 (March/April 1989): 389.

9. Devlin, "Contrasts in Presidential Campaign Commercials of 2004," 279. See also Michael M. Franz, Joel Rivlin, and Kenneth Goldstein, "Much More of the Same: Television Advertising Pre- and Post-BCRA," in Michael J. Malbin, ed., *The Election after Reform: Money, Politics and the Bipartisan Campaign Reform* (Lanham, Md.: Rowman and Littlefield, 2006), 142.

10. The principal exceptions are the twenty-four-hour news stations and channels that inevitably repeat their top stories.

11. There are exceptions, such as the "Wolves" ad produced by the Bush campaign in 2004, which showed a pack of wolves circling for the kill. With ominous music sounding in the background, an announcer talks about the cuts in intelligence and defense spending that Kerry and liberal Democrats supported prior to the terrorist attacks of September 11, 2001. The relationship between the wolves and the budget cuts is not made clear. Were the wolves the terrorists or just a general threat?

12. Thomas E. Patterson and Robert McClure, *The Unseeing Eye* (New York: Putnam, 1976), 58, and Craig Leonard Brians and Martin P. Wattenberg, "Comparing Issue Knowledge and Salience: Comparing Reception from TV Commercials, TV News, and Newspapers," *American Journal of Political Science* (February 1996): 172–193.

13. Annenberg Public Policy Center, University of Pennsylvania, www.factcheck.org. For empirical data on campaign negativity see Franz, Rivlin, and Goldstein, "Much More of the Same," 149.

14. The political consultants who design the negative ads place more of the blame of increased negativity and the cynicism that goes along with it on the news media coverage than they do on themselves. Although journalists admit to being too cynical, they do not think that they are too adversarial. Pew Research Center for the People and the Press, "Don't Blame Us: The Views of Political Consultants," June 17, 1998, www.people-press.org/reports/display.php3?ReportID=86.

15. The proposition that the greater the negatives about a candidate, the less likely he or she is to win was pioneered by Republican strategist, Lee Atwater, who directed the Bush campaign in 1988. See Thomas B. Edsall, "Why Bush Accentuates the Negative," *Washington Post,* October 2, 1988, p. C4.

16. Stephen J. Wayne, *The Road to The White House 1996: Post Election Edition* (New York: St. Martin's Press, 1997), 269.

17. Stephen Ansolabehere and Shanto Iyengar, *Going Negative: How Political Advertisements Shrink and Polarize the Electorate* (New York: Free Press, 1995), 141–142.

18. Craig Leonard Brians and Martin P. Wattenberg, "Comparing Issue Knowledge and Salience," *American Journal of Political Science* (February 1996): 172–193. See also Stephen Ansolabehere, Shanto Iyengar, and Adam Simon, "Replicating Experiments Using Aggregate and Survey Data: The Case of Negative Advertising and Turnout," *American Political Science Review* 93 (December 1999): 901–909.

19. Pew Research Center for the People and the Press surveys conducted after recent elections asked the following question: "How helpful were the candidates' commercials to you in deciding which candidate to vote for?" In each survey, a majority of voters found them not too helpful or not helpful at all. The Pew Research Center for the People and the Press, "Voters Liked Campaign 2004, but Too Much 'Mudslinging'," November 11, 2004, question 23, http://people-press.org/reports/print.php3?PageID=912.

20. Darrell M. West, L. Sandy Maisel, and Brett M. Clifton, "The Impact of Campaign Reform on Political Discourse, *Political Science Quarterly,* 120 (Winter 2005–2006): 642.

21. To demonstrate libel or slander, government officials and others deemed public figures must not only prove that the news item or advertising was false but also that it was published with malicious intent. The latter is very difficult to prove. See *New York Times Co. v. Sullivan,* 376 U.S. 254 (1964).

22. Fifty-six percent of the political consultants surveyed indicated that they believed ad watches have made campaigns more careful about the content of their ads. The Pew Research Center for the People and the Press, "Don't Blame Us," question 17.

23. Devlin, "Contrasts in Presidential Campaign Commercials," 282.

24. Dick Morris, *Behind the Oval Office* (New York; Random House, 1997), 139.

25. According to a national survey conducted by the *Washington Post,* the Kaiser Family Foundation, and Harvard University, "Why Don't American Trust The Government?" in 1996, 67 percent of respondents agreed strongly with the statement, "politicians will tell voters what they want to hear, not what they will actually do if elected," and 22 percent agreed somewhat. Only 10 percent disagreed.

26. Campaign news has become a major attraction for Internet users. Twenty-eight percent cited it in 2004 as a leading source for news. *Trends 2005* (Washington, D.C.: Pew Research Center for the People and the Press), 68.

27. Anthony Corrado, "Financing the 2000 Elections," in Gerald Pomper et. al., *The Election of 2000* (New York: Chatham House, 2001), 102.

28. Zachary A. Goldfarb, "Between Polar Opposites Is This Equator: Text Me," *Washington Post,* July 2, 2006, A4.

chapter 9

Elections and Government

A Tenuous Connection

Did you know that. . .

- divided partisan control of the national government has been the rule, not the exception, since 1968?
- in almost half of the states, the governor's party does not control both houses of the state legislature?
- in 2004 there was a total of 162 ballot issues in 34 states on which voters could register their preference and in 2006 there were 205 in 37 states?
- almost half of the policy measures on state ballots in the 1990s were approved by voters?
- by a two-to-one margin Americans in the 1990s indicated that they favored a smaller national government with fewer services than a larger one with more services? By a similarly large margin they also indicated that they opposed a decrease in government spending for Social Security, Medicare, education, the environment, health, and defense.
- Americans express more satisfaction with their democracy than do the citizens of most other democratic countries, despite the decline in the trust and confidence they have in their government?
- it is difficult to convert an electoral coalition into a governing coalition and keep that governing coalition together for an extended period of time?
- the distinctions between campaigning and governing have become blurred in recent years as elected officials engage in "constant campaigning" to maintain public support and position themselves for the next election?
- election mandates rarely occur, even when one party dominates the outcome, as in 1994 and 2006?
- according to the large 2004 exit poll, the issues that mattered most to voters in the election were moral values, the economy, terrorism, and the war in Iraq in that order?
- exit polls taken after the election explain more about the public opinion than do the actual returns themselves?

Is this any way to run a democratic election?

Who governs, and how prepared are they to do so? What priorities and policy positions should newly elected officials pursue, and which party and candidates are more likely to be successful in pursuing them? How can those in power be kept attuned to popular sentiment, responsible to public needs, and accountable for their actions in office simultaneously?

We hold elections to answer these questions. Elections determine the personnel for government and provide policy guidance for the new administration. They help forge and reinforce the coalitions that enable a government of shared powers and divided authority to make and implement public policy decisions. Finally, elections are the principal enforcement mechanism by which citizens keep those in power responsive to their needs and interests and accountable for their collective actions and individual behavior in office.

This chapter explores how well American elections serve these purposes. Do they make governing easier or harder? Do they provide direction and legitimacy for the public policies that ensue, or do they present mixed signals, undefined mandates, and conflicting claims upon those in positions of authority? Do they tie government decisions and actions more closely to the popular will, or do they more often reveal the absence of such a will? Do they encourage responsiveness in government or provide a nearly blank check for public officials?

The discussion begins by looking at the link between who wins, who governs, and how they govern. Then it moves to the policy mandate—what the election means and how it affects the policy decisions of newly elected officials. From the mandate and its impact the text turns to the tie between electoral and governing coalitions, the transference or maintenance of power by groups within the American polity. Finally, the chapter ends by completing the circle from public choice to government responsiveness, examining the extent to which elections hold public officials accountable for their decisions and behavior in office.

WHO GOVERNS?

The Compatibility of the Winners

The election determines the winners, but those winners are not always compatible with one another. They may not know one another, may disagree on the priorities and issues, and may have different perceptions of how to do their job in government. Yet they all come with an electoral mandate to represent their constituency and act in its interests. One issue that directly affects government's ability to function efficiently is how to enhance the compatibility of newly elected officials in an electoral system designed to mirror the diversity of the population and the character of the federal system more than reflect a national consensus or even mood.

The compatibility problem is largely systemic, the product of a constitutional framework designed to brake rather than promote the dominant opinions of the moment by creating differing but overlapping electoral constituencies and terms of office. It also is rooted in the contemporary political environment, in the self-selection process for running for office, in the unequal resources that the candidates possess, and in the decentralized party structure. Given the systemic problem, achieving compatibility in outlook, goals, and policy priorities requires stronger, more cohesive, national parties; an overriding national threat; or some issue that unifies the population and helps produce a consensus for action, such as the September 2001 attacks did for most of the American people.

A related issue pertains to the compatibility of those elected with those already in office—other elected officials, those who serve for fixed terms of office or at the pleasure of those in power, and civil servants. Rarely does the personnel of an entire governmental body change. And even though a complete turnover is theoretically possible in the House of Representatives and in many state legislatures, in practice, turnover tends to be very limited because of the incumbency advantages and the lack of competitive legislative districts. The fewer new people chosen for government in any one election, the less likely is the election to redirect what government does or how it does it. The absence of turnover limits the impact of those who wanted and voted for change.

From the perspective of a participatory democracy, muting the latest expression of the popular will is an unfortunate consequence of overlapping terms of office. The tradeoff is more experience, savvy, and continuity in government—all of which may produce better public policy over the long run and less legislative dependence on the executive branch for information and advice. With the limited knowledge that the public has on most issues, braking the emotion of the moment actually may result in a more considered judgment later on as "cooler heads" prevail and more information becomes available to more people who begin to understand the complexities of the issue better and the consequences of various policy options.

Obtaining a considered judgment in the public interest but not becoming prisoner to the public passion of the moment was part of the original rationale for dividing powers and for overlapping constituencies and terms of office. Leery of an aroused majority, particularly if that majority acted to deny minorities their rights, the framers of the U.S. Constitution wanted to place hurdles on the road to policymaking. Their system of internal checks and balances requires sustained support over time, across electoral constituencies, and within and among institutions of government to formulate new public policy.

That system, artfully designed in 1787, remains alive and well today. However, public expectations of the role of government have increased enormously. These expectations have been fueled in large part by the needs of an industrial and, later technological, society; by governmental responses to those needs, such as the New Deal and Great Society programs; and by politicians' promises made in their quest for elective office. How to overcome what the Constitution divides is *the* political challenge public officials face today, a challenge made more difficult by the autonomy of federal elections, divided partisan control of government, and competing policy agendas within and between the major parties and their elected officials.

Voting for the best person regardless of party reinforces the separation of powers. Add to this Americans' distrust of big and distant government and their more contemporary fear of ideologically driven party activists' imposing their policy priorities on the country, and one quickly arrives at a rationale for split-ticket voting. It's safer that way.

The point here is that the current electoral system, with its propensity to focus on the candidates and their policy positions, can result in a government of virtual strangers whose ties to their electoral constituency are stronger than their ties to one another.[1] To repeat this chapter's theme, contemporary elections mirror America's diversity more than they reflect a national consensus, a consensus that could serve as a guide for action as well as the foundation on which a governing coalition could be built.

The Qualifications of New Hires

Not only does an election determine those who will serve, it also influences those who will help them in office. Except for professional campaign consultants, who continue to provide elected officials with such for-profit services as polling and media consulting, the people most likely to accompany the newly elected into public service are those who worked long and hard on their campaigns. They are unified by their loyalty to the winning candidate, but may lack the analytical skills and substantive knowledge necessary for a staff job in government. Many of these aides lack governing experience, magnifying the initial adjustment problem for those elected to office, especially for the first time.

There are several reasons why newly elected officials turn to their campaign aides when choosing their advisory and support staffs. They owe them a lot, and undoubtedly some of these aides have ambitions of their own, which may include moving to the capital and working with the person they helped elect. Moreover, campaign workers have demonstrated their loyalty and industry, two important qualifications for good staffing. That they are not part of the previous team, which may have been rejected at the polls, also is seen as an asset by the winners. And finally, those who have just won election to a new office for the first time do not usually have the contacts and acquaintances that incumbents possess, but they are familiar with their campaign staff. They know what they can do. So why not hire them?

Actually, there are plenty of reasons for not doing so. The principal ones are that campaigning differs from governing, and the skills and attitudes required for each also differ, although there's some overlap between campaigning and the public relations' dimension of government.[2]

THE RELATIONSHIP BETWEEN CAMPAIGNING AND GOVERNING

Do contemporary campaigns facilitate or impede governing? Do they provide the skills necessary for elected officials to perform representative and policy-making functions, or do they divert their focus, harden their positions, and convert governing into constant campaigning? In truth, they do both.

Similarities: The Constant Campaign

Governing is becoming more campaign oriented than ever before. Increasingly it is conducted in the public arena and is poll driven. A principal motivation for elected officials making public policy decisions is how those decisions will affect their own reelection. Campaign skills may be useful for achieving these aspects of governing.

In campaigns, candidates and their entourages have to sell themselves and their policies to the electorate. They continue doing so once elected. Executive and legislative leaders in particular have to build support for their programs outside of government in order to enhance support for their enactment within government. They also must be concerned with their own popularity, because it is thought to contribute to their political influence and subsequent policy success.

Although both candidates and government officials appeal to the public, they do so in slightly different ways. In campaigns, the candidates try to lead the media, respond quickly to their opponents' charges and to press allegations, and continuously spin campaign-related issues. In government, elected officials announce policy, explain issues, and use the prestige of their office to enhance the credibility of their remarks. As public officials responsible for the formulation and execution of policy, they have to respond to critical media that tend to highlight the negative consequences of their decisions and actions. Moreover, they also have to contend with more investigative reporting than is possible within the limited time frame of a campaign. Candidates may be moving targets, but elected officials are sitting ducks, especially when term limits stop them from running for reelection.

In both campaigns and government, the press imputes the political motives of the subjects they cover. In the campaign having a political motive is expected; political motives are what campaigns are all about. Not so in government; there political motives may be viewed as petty, partisan, and personal. Government officials have to defend the reasons for and merits of their actions and do so in terms of the public interest. Thus, candidate Bill Clinton could criticize Bob Dole's policy positions even though his motive was political, but the congressional Republicans' focus on Clinton's behavior in office and the impeachment trial itself were seen by many as blatant partisan politics.

Once elected, incumbents keep their eyes on the next election and do their best to ready themselves for it by raising money and performing services. The representative role—servicing constituency needs, representing constituency views, and satisfying constituency interests in the short run—has become more important and less difficult. In contrast, legislating longer-term national policy has become less important but more difficult for individual legislators. Executive oversight has received more emphasis, particularly during periods of divided government. It contributes to partisan positioning for the next election and spotlights the watchdog activities of members of Congress.

That more and more governing functions are subject to media scrutiny and take place within the public arena has both positive and negative consequences for democratic government. It benefits democracy in that elected officials are motivated to stay closely tied to their electoral bases and more responsive to their constituency's needs. The cost of maintaining such ties, however, has been a growing public perception, fueled by the press, that elected officials follow, not lead, and do what is best for themselves (that is, get reelected), and not necessarily what is best for the country.

A second problem that stems from the campaign-oriented environment in government is the hardening of policy positions. If candidates for office are increasingly defined by and held accountable for the promises they made and the positions they took during the campaign, it will be more difficult for them as elected officials to make the compromises necessary to govern, particularly if those compromises have to be negotiated in full public view. Strong ideological beliefs today contribute to this problem as well.

The difficulties that a campaign-style atmosphere creates for government suggest that there are fundamental differences between campaigning and governing. Unless and until these differences are understood, the constant campaigning will continue to impede rather than facilitate the operation of democratic government.

Differences: Pace, Mentality, Orientation, and Experience

Pace—Hectic v. Deliberative. A campaign has to keep up with events and presumably stay ahead of them or face defeat on election day. It is frantic almost by definition. In a competitive electoral environment, a campaign exists in a state of perpetual motion; often, a crisis atmosphere prevails, and most have war rooms to deal with these perpetual crises. But all of this motion and activity ends on a certain day, the same day that most of the campaign's personnel are out of jobs and are jockeying for new positions, many of them in government.

Not so with government. It cannot operate in a perpetual crisis for extended periods without sacrificing the deliberation and cooperation needed to reach solutions to pending issues. Elected officials of the opposing parties still have to interact with one another after a major policy decision has been made. Whereas campaigns are a single battle with a definable end, government is a multiple set of political skirmishes fought before and after elections among many of the same combatants. The relationships within government and the problems with which it deals persist over time, across institutions, even over the course of several administrations.

Mentality—Win at All Costs v. Give and Take. A campaign is what political scientists like to call a "zero-sum game." If one candidate wins, the other loses and the game's over. The winners no longer have to consider the losers, who may fade quickly from the public spotlight. Government is not a zero-sum game. For one thing, the losers on a particular issue do not disappear once a battle has been lost. They stay to fight for another issue. The history of the clashes between environmental and economic interests between secular and sectarian groups, labor and management, and producers and consumers are good examples of continual conflicts that occur within the political arena.

Campaigns need to be run efficiently. Their organization and operation are geared to one goal: winning the election. In government, although efficiency is desirable, there are other equally important goals. A legislative body has to deliberate on issues of public policy. In doing so, it must conduct hearings to permit outside groups to be heard, forge compromise among the contending parties, and then oversee the executive branch's execution of the law. All of this takes time and involves different people with different constituencies in different parts of the government. The legislative process may not be efficient, but it must be representative and should be deliberative.

Similarly, there is also tension between efficiency and effectiveness within the executive branch. The Clinton administration tried to reduce the costs of government by downsizing the number of federal employees, whereas the administration of George W. Bush has focused on competition between public and private sectors, known as "competitive sourcing," to improve the operation of government and make it more efficient, a stimulant not a restraint on the capitalist system.

Orientation—Consistency v. Compromise. Candidates are judged by their potential for office. In demonstrating their qualifications, particularly if they aren't incumbents, they need to show that they have a grasp of the issues, have good ideas, and will keep their promises if elected. More often than not, keeping promises means adhering to the policy positions they articulated and highlighted during the campaign and trying to get them enacted into law.

Officeholders are judged by their performance as well as by conditions. They need to show results or at least be in a position to claim responsibility for some achievements. Adhering to policy positions and not compromising on them could jeopardize a record of achievement. Moreover, elected officials are subject to myriad pressures from within and outside of the government: the bureaucracy, the media, interest groups, and the legislature. Not only do these groups have different agendas, different constituencies, and different time frames, they also may have the clout to thwart new initiatives. These political forces cannot be ignored the way a minority group can during a campaign.

Not only are campaigning and governing different, so is the permanency of the coalitions on which candidates and public officials depend. Electoral coalitions usually stay together for the duration of the political campaign. Governing alliances shift more with the issues. Today's opponent may be tomorrow's ally and vice versa. Unlike those in campaigns, the losers and winners in government should not become permanent enemies.

Experience—Outsiders v. Insiders. The distinction between running and governing has been exacerbated of late by two developments: the changes within the electoral process that have provided greater opportunities for those with limited experience to run for office and the public's mistrust of those in power and its desire for new faces not connected to the current political establishment. In an increasing number of elections, lack of experience, in particular the absence of a connection to the "mess in government," is regarded as a virtue, not a liability. This was evident in 2006 when Democratic challengers defeated twenty-two Republican incumbents in the House and six in the Senate to gain control of Congress.

Not only are many challengers who win election neophytes to governing, but their campaign staffs most likely are neophytes as well. In the past, the political pros who ran the campaign had experience in electioneering and governing. Today, the political pros have been largely replaced by the professional campaign technocrats—pollsters, media consultants, political strategists, fund raisers, direct mailers, and grassroots organizers who sell their services to the highest bidders, some even without regard for partisanship.[3] These campaign technocrats usually have little if any governing experience and little desire to work *in* government; they do want to work *for* government, though, content to continue to sell their services to those in power, especially to incumbents getting ready to run again.

The others who work on campaigns are the trusted soldiers, the people who perform the day-to-day, nitty-gritty grunt work of staging events, writing speeches, doing research, dealing with the press, and setting up phone banks. They work long and hard for low salaries or for free; many are young, in or just out of college, with little government experience. They may be involved because they believe in the candidate, like the excitement of the campaign, or want a job once the campaign is over. They may even be doing it for social reasons, such as meeting like-minded people.[4] Whatever their motivation, they are not likely to have the inside information that a newly elected public official needs the most: knowing how things work and which people have the power to get things done.

The presidential transitions of Carter and Clinton suffered from many of these staffing inadequacies. The people they appointed to their White House staff came from their campaigns and had little or no experience in Washington politics or in dealing with the national press corps, the congressional leader-ship, and, in Clinton's case, the military establishment. Moreover, these newly appointed aides suffered from another malady that frequently afflicts the newly elected and their staffs: they came to power with chips on their shoulders. They assumed, probably correctly, that they had won because people had grievances against those in power. Because Carter and Clinton were outsiders even with-in their own party, they were suspicious of all those in the establishment, Democrats and Republicans alike. Initially, they tried to have as little to do with them as possible—with disastrous results.[5] Their legislative initiatives failed, their White Houses became embroiled in controversy, and they lacked a con-sistent policy message. By the time they got on their feet, they had lost much of the enthusiasm that accompanies a new administration into office.

George W. Bush ran against the strident partisan tone of Washington pol-itics, promising to return civility to political discourse and a bipartisan dimen-sion to governing. Although Bush lacked Washington experience, he was a close observer of his father's presidency and surrounded himself with experi-enced Washington hands as he began transition planning. As a consequence, the Bush administration got off to a much better start than did the administra-tions of Carter and Clinton. Running against the Washington establishment may be an effective campaign strategy, particularly if the public is unhappy with the way it perceives the government to be working, but it's not an effec-tive governing strategy, especially if the goal is to bridge institutional divide in order to make and implement new public policy.

The Impact of Campaigning on Governing

Contemporary campaigning has made contemporary governing more diffi-cult. Campaigns raise public expectations about public policy and public offi-cials at the same time that they feed into distrust of politicians and the politics in which they engage. They emphasize personal accomplishments in a system designed to curb the exercise of institutional and political power. They harden policy positions in a governmental structure that depends on compromise. They have increasingly brought partisan and ideological rhetoric into the pol-icymaking arena, where a pragmatic approach and quiet diplomacy is often needed to get things done. And the candidates have developed a public persona that they continue to project once in office, a persona that can get in the way of behind-the-scenes compromises on major issues with which they have been associated and on which they have articulated their policy positions, and thus in which they have a stake.

A second impact of campaigning on governing, especially since the 1970s, has been the increasing number of winning candidates who have not come up through the ranks and lack governing experience. These candidates may overes-timate their ability to make a difference and underestimate the views and legit-imacy of others who are part of the governing establishment. "Reinventing the wheel" wastes time and energy and increases the startup costs of government.

To make matters worse, candidates who are not incumbents usually do not have access to the information and expertise that government officials have on a regular basis. What they do have access to, however, are poll results that indicate political attitudes, salient issues, and public opinions on them. Armed with this information, it is relatively easy to craft a position popular with a specific group. Campaigning by public opinion polls is just a short step away from governing by public opinion polls. An increasing number of public officials seem to have taken this step.

Directions for Reforms

If contemporary campaigning has contributed to the difficulty of governing, what changes might reverse this pattern and make governing easier? More party control over the electoral process might reduce the number of free agents elected to government and impose more discipline on those who are elected. But how can this be accomplished in light of the reforms to the nomination process? Those who regularly participate in primaries and caucuses are not likely to voluntarily give up their right to vote on their party's nominees.

If terms of office were longer and if voters were more nationally focused and less interested in the short-term impact, then elected officials would have more opportunity to make decisions in what they believe are in the country's long-term interest, rather than their constituency's short-term interest. But then ties between government and the governed also would be looser, responsiveness might suffer, and incumbents might be even more advantaged than they are today. Term limits could reduce this advantage, forcing greater turnover in office, but they also would result in the election of less experienced and knowledgeable public officials who would need time to acquire expertise or would be more dependent on civil servants and professional legislative staff for support. Besides, term limits are undemocratic and unconstitutional for members of Congress.[6]

THE ELECTION AND PUBLIC POLICY

In addition to choosing who will govern—which candidates, parties, and staffs—elections should provide policy guidance for government: what issues to address, what approaches to take, and even what specific proposals to make. Except for policy initiatives, which are increasingly appearing on state ballots, elections refract rather than reflect public opinion on most issues. The reason they do so is because they are primarily designed to choose people, not policies.

The Movement toward Policy Initiatives

Voting on state constitutional amendments, policy initiatives, and other substantive measures has become an increasingly popular vehicle for individuals, and especially for organized groups, to pursue their policy agendas when they are unable to do so successfully through the legislative process. A majority of the states, primarily those in the West and Midwest, provide for voting on substantive policy issues. These votes illustrate direct democracy at work.[7]

But they usually also require substantial resources to be successful. Just to get on the ballot requires the signatures of a certain percentage of the state's eligible voters within a specified period of time. The higher the percentage of signatures required and the shorter the time frame, the more difficult and expensive ballot access will be. If an organization lacks enough of its own volunteers, including the foot soldiers who gather these signatures, it will have to engage an outside firm to collect them and pay as much as three dollars per name. The total cost can run into the millions, and that is just the first step.

A public relations campaign for the initiative also must be waged during the election period. If successful, it still may be challenged in the courts, as was California's Proposition 187, a ballot initiative approved by the voters that denied such state benefits as education and health care to illegal aliens and their families.[8] The legal charges can be substantial.

Interest groups have become adept at using the ballot initiative process to their own economic, ideological, or political advantage. The gambling industry, sports promoters, the Humane Society, and groups that want to impose legislative term limits, make English the official U.S. language, legalize the sale of marijuana for medical purposes, permit doctor-assisted suicides, issue school vouchers, increase taxes for education, and prevent same-sex marriage all have used the initiative process to circumvent or pressure recalcitrant state legislatures. Take the case of Governor Paul Cellucci of Massachusetts. Blocked by a Democratic legislature from lowering the state's tax rate, Cellucci threatened a ballot initiative to force the legislators to accede to his request.[9]

A few wealthy, public-interested individuals also have tried to use this process to achieve what they consider to be desirable public policy. Billionaire financier George Soros has spent millions in support of initiatives that would legalize the medical use of marijuana and provide for forfeiture of assets and rehabilitation rather than lengthy jail terms for convicted drug offenders. Paul Allen, the cofounder of Microsoft, contributed $3 million to a group that was supporting an initiative to establish charter schools in the state of Washington. Businessman Tim Draper spent $23 million of his own money on an initiative to provide school vouchers to children in California. The list goes on.[10]

Others have turned to initiatives to change policy, gain recognition, and even make money. Bill Sizemore has used the initiative process in Oregon probably more than any other state resident. He placed six initiatives on the 2000 ballot alone. He runs a business that collects signatures for ballot initiatives, so he makes money and tries to affect public policy at the same time. Sizemore also used his visibility in the state to run for governor in 1998, but he was defeated.[11]

The amount of money that it takes to mount a successful initiative drive and the fact that much of it may come from outside the state have led some states to try to limit the number of ballot initiatives and the influence of outside groups and people who do not live in that state. Colorado enacted legislation that permitted only its registered voters to circulate initiative petitions. It required that they wear badges identifying themselves and their affiliation and that the costs of initiative drives be made part of the public record. However, in 1999 the Supreme Court found that these restrictions violated the First Amendment by inhibiting communications with voters.[12]

In addition to the financial issue, there are other problems with the widespread use of these public referenda. Some are extremely complicated and difficult for the average person to understand, much less appreciate, all its implications and costs. Just reading them can take a considerable amount of time, which would hold up voting if everyone chose to do so. Moreover, initiatives circumvent the legislative process, thereby diminishing the role of those whose job it is to consider public policy issues, those who presumably have more qualifications to do so than the average person or voter.

According to political scientist Richard J. Ellis, an expert on the initiative process, there has been a steady increase in ballot initiatives since the 1970s. Whereas they averaged thirty-five per ballot in the 1970s and fifty in the 1980s, for the last two decades of the twentieth century the average number of state ballot initiatives was seventy-six per ballot, with the most (103) coming in 1996. Ellis reports that a little less than half of these initiatives have become law.[13] The numbers in the twenty-first century have been even higher. Table 9.1 lists the number of ballot measures in the twenty-first century.

Issue Voting in a Candidate-Oriented Environment

With the exception of voting on policy issues, most elections are imperfect mechanisms for determining public policy. People vote for a variety of candidates for a variety of reasons. Partisan affiliation, candidate qualifications, and issue positions are some of the factors that affect voting behavior. Of these, issues are least likely to be the primary focus for most voters.[14]

People also may be voting against candidates because they are unhappy with the job they have done, the conditions that occurred while they were in power, their personal behavior while in office, or even their traits or policy positions that have come out during the campaign. Such a negative vote, if discernible, may indicate what the electorate does *not* want but not what it *does* want, except perhaps by inference.

Another factor contributing to the difficulty of understanding the meaning of elections is that there are many candidates and many issues at many levels of government. People have different reasons for casting different votes. They may split their ballot, voting for candidates from different parties. This type of voting behavior produces mixed results from which a clear message is not always or easily discernible, despite political pundits' and exit pollsters' claims to the contrary.

If a voting pattern were to emerge, if one party were to win or maintain control of the legislative and executive branches, then there might be some rea-

TABLE 9.1 **State Ballot Measures, 2000–2006**

Year	Number of States	Number of Measures	Percentage Approved
2000	42	204	63
2001	—	—	—
2002	40	202	62
2003	8	22	64
2004	34	162	67
2005	12	45	49
2006	37	205	67

Source: Initiative and Referendum Institute, University of Southern California School of Law, www.iandrinstitute.org/ballotwatch.htm.

son for believing that voters were sending a message—although the substance of the message itself would not necessarily be clear. However, at the national level, such a pattern was the exception, not the rule, between 1968 and 2002. During this period, the same party controlled the White House and both houses of Congress for a total of only six years and four months. And even though there was one-party control at the beginning of George W. Bush's administration, the president could hardly claim an electoral mandate, having lost the popular vote. Under these circumstances, with mixed results in overlapping constituencies, what can the election returns tell us about the policy direction that newly elected officials should take? The answer is usually not very much.

The Absence of Policy Mandates
The national electoral system is not structured in a way that facilitates policy voting. It has encouraged partisan voting, but the declining use of the party-column ballot and the candidate orientation of many elections have made it more difficult to achieve partisan mandates today. Some do claim that the 1994 midterm elections produced such a mandate for the Republicans, as did the elections of 1932, 1964, 1974, and 2006 for the Democrats.

To have a mandate for governing, a party's candidates must take discernible and compatible policy positions that are distinguishable from the opposition's, and the electorate must vote for them because of those positions. Most elections do not meet these criteria. Candidates usually take a range of policy positions, often waffle on a few highly divisive and emotionally charged ones, and may differ from their party and its other candidates for national office in their priorities and their stands on other issues.

House Republican candidates did take consistent policy positions in 1994; all pledged to support the goals and proposals in their Contract With America.

Other Republican candidates, however, didn't take such a pledge. Nonetheless, the results of the 1994 election, in which every Republican incumbent for Congress and governor won and the Republicans gained seats in most state legislatures, were interpreted as a partisan victory. What did such a victory mean? What policy goals did it imply?

Newly elected Speaker of the House Newt Gingrich chose to interpret the vote as an affirmation of the ten basic goals and legislative proposals in the Contract With America. Such an interpretation provided Gingrich with a legislative agenda to pursue and promote in the House of Representatives. But his interpretation also created performance expectations that the Republicans were unable to meet outside of the House.

Moreover, it was probably an incorrect interpretation. The vote in 1994 was a repudiation of the Clinton administration and the Democratic-controlled Congress; it was also a rejection of big government, big deficits, and such big social programs as universal healthcare for all Americans. Indirectly, it could be interpreted as a vote for less government, lower taxes, and a smaller deficit. It was *not* a vote for the Republicans' Contract With America. How do we know? Exit polls indicated that only 25 percent of the voters and 20 percent of the population had ever heard of the Contract With America, much less knew what was in it. How, then, could the 1994 election be a mandate for the policy proposals in that contract if such a small proportion of the population were aware of those proposals?

The presidential elections of 1992, 1996, and 2004 also were seen as referendums on the administration in power; referendums which Presidents Clinton and George W. Bush won. The 2000 election was not, because Democratic candidate Al Gore chose to distance himself from President Clinton and emphasize his own policy views. Presidents who are reelected have received a vote of confidence for their past leadership; they have support to continue the policy actions that they initiated, but not necessarily to start something new. Beyond that, gleaning much meaning and guidance from an incumbent's reelection is problematic at best. Nonetheless, most presidents claim public support for their second-term goals, some of which they articulated during the reelection campaign.

Take George W. Bush following his 2004 election victory. Bush believed that his reelection ended Iraq as a political issue and gave him political capital to pursue his second-term domestic policy priorities: a national energy policy, the partial privatization of Social Security, tax reform, a new immigration policy, and an extension of his first-term tax cuts. Exit polls, however, offer little evidence that these priorities were on voters' minds on election day, much less were the primary reasons that Bush won reelection. (See Table 9.2.) Had the president not misread the meaning of the election, he might have saved himself the political embarrassment of failing to achieve most of these policy goals.

If officials are rarely given a clear mandate for governing, then how do they interpret the meaning of an election? How do they know what voters want and don't want them to do? Generally speaking, they assume that their constituency supports most of the policy positions they advocated, and they assume so because they won the election. That assumption, however, can get them into trouble.

Exit Polls and the Meaning of the Vote

The results of elections may not explain very much, other than who wins and who loses, but election-day surveys that probe voters' opinions and preferences to discern why they voted as they did do provide more information. Such surveys enable analysts to correlate the opinions and preferences with voting behavior and the demographic and attitudinal characteristics of voters. In this way, it is possible to interpret the meaning of the election.

Election day exit polls interview voters after they have cast ballots at randomly selected voting precincts across the country.[15] A large number of people are questioned: 16,627 in 1996, 10,017 in 1998, 13,130 in 2000, 13,660 in 2004, and 13,251 in 2006.[16] On the basis of their answers, analysts are able to discern the attitudes, opinions, and choices of groups of voters.

Exit polls are usually very accurate because of their large size (compared to about 1,000–1,200 for other national surveys) and because they are conducted at so many different voting precincts across the country over the course of election day. The principal limitation of this poll, however, is that it provides only a snapshot of the electorate on one particular day. It can't show how the campaign affected the public's attitudes and opinions or the impact of other factors over the course of the election. To discern such information, election analysts depend on the National Election Studies, a smaller survey conducted by the Survey Research Center at the University of Michigan and available to scholars through a consortium of universities. The Michigan survey interviews many of the same people before and after the election, thereby allowing researchers to discern opinion change over the course of the campaign and the factors that contributed to that change.

Although exit polls of the 2000 and 2004 elections were not necessary to show that the electorate was evenly divided in the presidential contests, the polls did reveal patterns that help explain why the elections were so close (see Table 9.2). The principal factor was partisanship. During these first two presidential election cycles of the twenty-first century, the major parties were at rough parity with one another, with partisans voting overwhelmingly for their party's nominees. Core groups within each party's traditional electoral coalition also voted along party lines: African Americans, Latinos, and organized labor for the Democratic candidates, and the Christian Coalition and other religious groups for the Republicans. The independent vote was also closely divided.

There were significant demographic, geographic, and attitudinal divisions within the electorate in addition to party and race. The gender gap, evident since the 1980s, got larger in 2000, but declined in 2004. Nevertheless, a major-

TABLE 9.2 Portrait of the American Electorate, 1996–2004

Percentage of 2004		1996			2000			2004		
		Clinton	Dole	Perot	Bush	Gore	Nader	Bush	Kerry	Nader
	Total Vote	49%	41%	8%	48%	48%	3%	50%	49%	1%
46	Men	43	44	10	53	42	3	54	45	1
54	Women	54	38	7	43	54	2	47	52	1
77	Whites	43	46	9	54	42	3	57	42	1
11	Blacks	84	12	4	9	90	1	11	89	0
9	Hispanics	72	21	6	35	62	2	42	55	2
2	Asians	43	48	8	41	55	3	41	59	—
63	Married	44	46	9	53	44	2	56	43	1
37	Unmarried	57	31	9	38	57	4	40	59	1
17	18–29 Years	53	34	10	46	48	5	44	54	1
28	30–44 Years	48	41	9	49	48	2	51	47	1
30	45–59 Years	48	41	9	49	48	2	50	49	1
25	60+ Years	48	44	7	47	51	2	53	46	0
4	Not H.S. Graduate	59	28	11	38	59	1	49	50	0
22	H.S. Graduate	51	35	13	49	48	1	51	48	1
31	Some College	48	40	10	51	45	3	53	46	0
26	College Graduate	44	46	8	51	45	3	51	47	1
17	Postgraduate	52	40	5	44	52	3	43	55	1
53	White Protestant†	36	53	10	56	42	2	58	41	0
27	Catholic	53	37	9	47	50	2	51	48	1
3	Jewish	78	16	3	19	79	1	24	76	—
22	White Born-Again Christian@	26	65	8	80	18	1	77	22	1

Union Household	24	59	30	9	37	59	3	39	60	1
Family Income	8									
Less than $15,000		59	28	11	37	57	4	36	63	1
$15,000–$29,999	15	53	36	9	41	54	3	41	58	0
$30,000–$49,999	22	48	40	10	48	49	2	48	51	0
$50,000–$74,999	23	44	48	7	51	46	2	55	44	1
$75,000–$99,999	14	41	51	7	52	45	2	53	46	0
$100,000+†	11	38	54	6	54	43	2	56	43	1
FAMILY'S FINANCIAL SITUATION IS										
Better Today	31	61	35	3	36	61	2	79	20	0
Same Today	39	46	45	8	60	35	3	48	50	1
Worse Today	28	27	57	13	63	33	4	19	80	1
Northeast	22	55	34	9	39	56	3	43	56	1
Midwest	25	48	41	10	49	48	2	51	48	1
South	31	46	46	7	55	43	1	58	41	0
West	21	48	40	8	46	48	4	45	53	2
Republicans	37	13	80	6	91	8	1	93	7	0
Independents	26	43	35	17	47	45	6	47	50	2
Democrats	37	84	10	5	11	86	2	10	89	0
Liberals	21	78	11	7	13	80	6	13	86	1
Moderates	45	57	33	9	44	52	2	44	55	0
Conservatives	33	20	71	8	81	17	1	83	16	1
Employed#	60	48	40	9	48	49	2	52	46	1
Unemployed#	40	49	42	8	48	47	3	49	50	1
First-Time Voters	11	54	34	11	43	52	4	45	54	1

(continued on next page)

TABLE 9.2 **Portrait of the American Electorate, 1996–2004** (continued)

Percentage of 2004		1996			2000			2004		
		Clinton	Dole	Perot	Bush	Gore	Nader	Bush	Kerry	Nader
52	Approve of Clinton's/Bush's Performance	20	77	2	90	9	1			
46	Disapprove of Clinton's/Bush's Performance	88	9	2	5	93	1			
MOST IMPORTANT ISSUE FOR VOTING										
5	Taxes							56	44	0
4	Education							25	75	—
15	Iraq							25	74	0
19	Terrorism							84	14	0
20	Economy/Jobs							18	80	1
22	Moral Values							79	18	2
8	Healthcare							22	78	—

† Includes all Protestants in 2000 and 2004.

@ Includes all people who identified themselves as part of the religious right in 2000 and 2004.

The 1996 question: Are you employed full time? In 2000 and 2004: Do you work full-time for pay? "Yes" answers were categorized as "employed," "no" answers as "unemployed."

Source: 1996 and 2000 general exit polls conducted by VNS for the National Election Pool, a consortium of the major news networks; 2004 general exit poll in 2004 conducted by Edison Media Research and Mitofsky International for the National Election Pool.

ity of women voted Democratic, and a majority of men Republican. Younger people were more likely to vote Democratic, especially younger, single women.

The geographic divide, red and blue states, remained significant and stable. The Democrats were strongest in the Northeast, the Mid-Atlantic states, and on the Pacific Coast; the Republicans' strength was in the South, the Rocky Mountain region, and much of the Midwest. The Republicans also won the rural vote, whereas the Democrats took the cities; suburbia was closely divided.

Ideology and religion reinforced the partisan, gender, and geographic divisions. Liberals continued their embrace of the Democratic Party, and conservatives were equally supportive of the Republican Party. Moderates sided more with the Democrats, particularly in 2000, counterbalancing the advantage that the larger number of people who identify themselves as conservatives give to the Republicans.

Traditional voting patterns continued among religious groups, with Protestants supporting Bush and the Republicans, Catholics divided, and Jews voting overwhelming for the Democratic presidential candidates. A sectarian-nonsectarian division was also evident. The more people regularly attended religious services, the more likely they were to have voted Republican.

In summary, the results of an election indicate who won, but not much else: not the reasons people voted as they did and not the mandate the winners usually claim. Elected officials who act as if they had a mandate usually are doing so to gain support within the government for the policy initiatives they wish to pursue. It is also important to understand that the more time that elapses after the election, the less important that election is a guide to policy and an influence on those who make it.

POLICY AND PERFORMANCE: RESPONSIVENESS AND ACCOUNTABILITY

Government is based on the consent of the governed. That's the reason why public officials are so concerned about the meaning of the election and why they may even claim it to be a mandate from the voters. That meaning or claim ties elections to government in three ways:

- Elections provide direction for public officials.
- Elections help generate popular support for achieving election-based goals and more specific campaign promises.
- Elections reaffirm the legitimacy of government and, to a large extent, what that government does.

Providing Direction

Campaigns are full of promises, both substantive and stylistic. They provide a broad blueprint for those in power. They also create a climate of performance expectations. These expectations are often hyped by the emphasis the candidates themselves place on certain character skills and traits they claim to possess and promise to use if elected—strong and decisive leadership skills, moral and ethical behavior, beliefs in an open and honest government, the desire for "a kinder and gentler America," a "never to tell a lie" upbringing, and a "compassionate conservatism" character. But candidates have to be careful not to promise too much. If they set too high a bar for themselves, they may not be able to clear it, with the result being that their popularity and probably the public's confidence in them will decline, and they will suffer as a consequence.

Normally, multiple campaign pledges and policy initiatives, low levels of information among voters, and most people's preoccupation with current conditions give public officials considerable leverage in designing policy, as long as they stay within the broad parameters of acceptability and have a beneficial short-term result. In this sense and on a collective level, the electoral process provides both opportunities and flexibility for those in government. What it often does not provide is the consensus required to make decisions on public policy happen. The task for legislative and executive leaders is to convert their election coalition into a governing coalition. And that task is not easy.

Getting Results

The public's focus shifts after the election. Some people become disappointed when their expectations go unmet. Constituencies clash within as well as between parties. Well-financed interest groups continue to exercise considerable power and spend millions lobbying for their policy goals. The end result may be that the election determines the policymakers. What it does not usually provide is the coalition across institutions of government that is necessary to get results. The principal task for elected leaders is to build that coalition and do so as quickly as possible by using their victory and the goodwill that ritually follows an election outcome to enhance their base of electoral support.

Having a partisan majority helps, but it does not guarantee success, as George W. Bush found out at the beginning of his second term. To get results, constant campaigning is necessary on a priority-by-priority basis. Pollsters are used to determine policy parameters and focus groups are employed to refine the language of messages and target each to the appropriate group or groups. Partisan and nonpartisan appeals are made, depending on the issue and the political configuration of public opinion. Interest group coalitions, organized by the White House or by the political parties, are used to promote the policy and mobilize support for it.

The absence of a stable governing coalition compounds the policymaking task within a constitutional framework that divides power and maintains that division by internal checks and balances. The U.S. Constitution was not designed to facilitate policymaking; it was designed to constrain it so that a dominant group could not be used easily or quickly to impose its particular policy perspective on others.

Ensuring Accountability: Individual and Collective

As a check on those in government, the electorate holds a trump card: rejection at the polls the next time around. The card isn't often played, however, for several reasons. The practical advantages of incumbency usually outweigh the theoretical option of voting someone out of office. With the exception of the president and other chief executives, it is difficult to assign individual responsibility for institutional action or inaction. It's even hard to assign individual responsibility for economic and social conditions, although executives do tend to receive more credit and blame than their influence over these conditions merits.

Another reason why it is difficult for the public to assess responsibility for what government does is that people generally are not well informed about the actions of government. They don't become well informed until the news media focus on a particular issue for a sustained period. The war in Iraq is a case in point. Initial coverage was shaped by the administration's claim that Iraq's possession of weapons of mass destruction (WMDs) posed a threat to the United States. Removing the government of Saddam Hussein was presented as the only acceptable option. During the military buildup and conduct of the war, American news coverage was favorable to the administration's objectives.[17] Subsequent news coverage was not. It emphasized the chaos, the resistance, the absence of WMDs, and the costs to the United States in terms of lives and money. Over time, the perceptions of reality presented in the news media turned the American people against the administration's policy and in favor of the pull-out of U.S. forces.

Assigning collective responsibility is even more difficult than holding individuals accountable for their own actions. When control of the government is divided, credit and blame are shared. Which institution and political party were to blame for the huge increase in the national debt that occurred during the Reagan years—the Republican president, the Republican Senate, or the Democratic House? And which institution should receive credit for the budget surpluses of the late 1990s—the Democratic president, the Republican Congress, or both? One of the most negative consequences of divided government is the inability to hold one party collectively accountable for public policy outcomes.

For individual behavior, however, responsibility can be pinpointed, even though it does not usually result in electoral defeat. There are some exceptions to the nonrejection rule by the voters. Outrageous personal behavior in office is one of them. Illegal acts, such as the theft of government property, acceptance of bribes, lying under oath, failure to pay income taxes or child support, even indulging on a regular basis in a prohibited substance like cocaine or marijuana, would probably produce sufficient negative media and public concern to force an official to resign from office or face the strong possibility of defeat in the next nomination or election. Similarly, immoral or unethical behavior, such as sexual improprieties, the flagrant misuse of public property, abusing the perquisites of office, or making serious false claims about one's military service or educational qualifications would also endanger an official's reelection prospects, if only to encourage a quality challenger.

Accountability in government is enhanced by the potential for election defeat, even if that potential is rarely achieved. In the increasingly public arena of government, under the eye of an investigative press, and with the public relations campaigns that one's partisan or ideological opponents can wage to highlight behavior and actions that might be viewed as objectionable by a sizable electoral constituency, public officials tend to behave as if they were in the spotlight most of the time. They probably perceive themselves as more visible to their constituency than they actually are. As a result, responsiveness and accountability are fostered by the electorate's holding a trump card even if it isn't played that often.

SUMMARY: ELECTIONS AND GOVERNMENT DILEMMAS IN A NUTSHELL

Elections provide a critical link between the people and their government. That link is the very reason for having elections: to choose the people who will make the major public policy decisions, to provide them with policy direction and political support, to give their decisions legitimacy, and to hold them accountable.

Elections satisfy these democratic goals, but they do so imperfectly. They determine the winners, but the winners are not always compatible with each other, much less with those already in power. Elections choose the most popular candidates (with the obvious exception of the 2000 presidential contest), but popularity and governing ability are not synonymous and in some cases may not even be closely related.

Elections for different offices at different levels of government over different time periods more often than not yield mixed verdicts. Governing becomes more difficult when the differences among elected officials outweigh their commonalities. Adding to the problem is the public's perception that successful candidates are and will continue to be primarily beholden to themselves, to their contributors, and to their constituents for election and reelection, but not necessarily to their parties, to their president, or to some larger public interest.

Doing what makes political sense for the folks back home becomes a primary guide to legislative decision making. As a consequence, the electoral process seems to mirror the country's diversity much more effectively than it reflects majority sentiment. This is a problem for governing at the national level, a problem that can be magnified by electing inexperienced candidates who in turn select inexperienced staff for advisory and administrative positions in government. To some extent, however, public opinion polls that reflect national popular sentiment counter the constituency orientation of legislative bodies.

The differences between campaigning and governing remain significant. Campaigns have definite winners and losers; government does not. Campaigns are replete with political and ideological rhetoric. Such rhetoric is an impediment to compromise in policymaking. Campaigns generate a crisis atmosphere; such an atmosphere is not conducive to the deliberation and adjustments that must accompany sound policymaking.

However, to the extent that governing is being conducted more and more in the public arena, the campaigning skills of going public, that is, of tailoring and targeting messages to special groups to build support and achieve a favorable impression, are becoming an increasingly important component of governing.

Elections are supposed to guide public officials in what they do and in when and how they do it, but their outcomes often present mixed verdicts and messages. Unless the electorate is voting directly on a policy initiative, it is difficult to cull the meaning of an election, much less translate that meaning into a policy agenda for government. Exit polls and other national surveys provide some guidance about voters' attitudes, opinions, and the most salient issues, but they aren't exact measures, and certainly not blueprints, for governing. As a consequence, public officials usually have considerable discretion when making policy judgments, as long as they do so within the broad parameters of mainstream politics.

The potential for election defeat, combined with negative publicity and a "thin skin" for criticism, keeps elected officials responsive to their constituency, more so on an individual than on a collective basis. Accountability is enhanced by the increasingly public arena in which decision making occurs, by an attentive media, and by an opposition that wishes to gain political advantage from the decisions and actions of their partisan opponents. It is made more difficult by divided partisan control of government.

Elections are also important for converting promises into performance. The key here is not only the composition of the majority, but also the ability of its elected leadership to convert their winning electoral coalition into a winning governing coalition. To be effective, that coalition has to cross constituency, institutional, and sometimes even partisan lines, which is why its composition may shift on an issue-by-issue basis.

Do elections serve government? Yes, they do. They renew and reinforce the link between the elected and the electorate. They contribute to policy direction, coalition building, and legitimacy for and accountability in government. But they do so imperfectly and often indirectly, and they sometimes impede rather than enhance governing.

Now It's Your Turn

Discussion Questions

1. Is the election of public officials who are more ideologically and politically compatible with one another a good or bad development for American democracy? Explain why or why not.

2. How would federal elections have to be changed if the electorate were given the opportunity to vote on the issues rather than just on the candidates running for office? Would the meaning of elections be clearer and governing made easier by issue voting?
3. Can the representative character of government and collective responsibility in government be enhanced at the same time?
4. How do elections affect the permanent government, what the bureaucracy does, and how it does it?
5. Now that you have completed this book, how would you answer the question posed by its title: "Is this any way to run a democratic election?" What are the principal strengths and weaknesses of the U.S. electoral system from a democratic perspective?

Topics for Debate

Challenge or defend the following statements:

1. To enhance responsiveness and accountability in government, all elected public officials should stand for reelection at the same time every four years.
2. The electorate should be given the opportunity to express its opinion on the ten most salient national issues when voting on election day.
3. No congressional impeachment and conviction of the president should take place unless approved in a special election by American voters.
4. All candidates for the presidency should be required to announce their cabinet choices at least one month before the election.
5. All new public officials should be required to take a course on the structure and operations of the institution to which they were elected or appointed.

Exercises

1. Upset by the gap between democratic theory and practice, a presidential commission has been studying ways to make American elections more compatible with the goals of a democratic political system. The commission has identified three objectives that it hopes any new electoral process will meet:
   a. Public preferences for individual candidates and the priorities they should pursue should be clearly identified.
   b. Public opinion on the most salient and controversial policy issues should be determined.
   c. The public's evaluation of how well those in power have performed in office should be indicated.

   With those objectives in mind, suggest changes to make American elections more compatible with democratic goals. Also tell the commission how you would implement the changes you are suggesting and their likely impact on government.

2. List the campaign promises that George W. Bush made in his 2004 presidential campaign. You can find these promises on the Web site of a major news organization that provided extensive coverage of the 2004 election, such as CNN, MSNBC, Fox News, the *New York Times,* and the *Washington Post.* Determine, if you can,
   a. how Bush prioritized these promises,
   b. which of them he has tried to achieve and which of them he actually has achieved, and
   c. which of his promises he has ignored, modified, or reversed.

   On the basis of your analysis, how would you rate Bush's success in converting his campaign agenda into a governing agenda and then into public policy in his second term?

INTERNET RESOURCES

Most major media sources report the large election exit poll in detail. The Gallup Organization (www.gallup.com), as well as the Pew Research Center for the People and the Press (www.people-press.org) conduct pre- and post-election surveys and make the results available on their Web sites. For a longitudinal analysis, the pre- and post-National Election Surveys conducted by the Center for Political Studies at the University of Michigan (www.umich.edu /nes) are the source of data that most political scientists use when analyzing elections. However, these data usually are not available until about six months after the election. The Election Assistance Commission issues the official results of the national election on its Web site (www.eac.gov); however, the fastest listing of unofficial results is on the wire services, such as the Associated Press (www.ap.org).

SELECTED READINGS

Abramson, Paul R., John H. Aldrich, and David W. Rohde. "The 2004 Presidential Election: The Emergence of a Permanent Majority?" *Political Science Quarterly* 120 (2005): 33–57.

————. *Change and Continuity in the 2004 Elections.* Washington, D.C.: CQ Press, 2006.

Campbell, James E. "Why Bush Won the Presidential Election of 2004: Incumbency, Ideology, Terrorism, and Turnout." *Political Science Quarterly* 120 (2005): 219–241.

Conley, Patricia Heidotting. *Presidential Mandates: How Elections Shape the National Agenda.* Chicago: University of Chicago Press, 2001.

Dahl, Robert A. "Myth of the Presidential Mandate." *Political Science Quarterly* 105 (1990): 355–372.

Fishel, Jeff. *Presidents and Promises*. Washington, D.C.: Congressional Quarterly Books, 1985.

Gaddie, Ronald Keith, and Charles S. Bullock III. *Elections to Open Seats in the U.S. House: Where the Action Is*. Lanham, Md.: Rowman and Littlefield, 2000.

Ginsberg, Benjamin, and Alan Stone, eds. *Do Elections Matter?* Armonk, N.Y.: M. E. Sharpe, 1996.

Jacobson, Gary C. "Polarized Politics and the 2004 Congressional and Presidential Elections." *The Political Science Quarterly* 120 (2005): 199–218.

Miller, Arthur H., and Martin P. Wattenberg. "Throwing the Rascals Out: Policy and Performance Evaluations of Presidential Candidates: 1952–1980." *American Political Science Review* 79 (1985): 359–372.

Popkin, Samuel L. *The Reasoning Voter*. Chicago: University of Chicago Press, 1991.

Wattenberg, Martin, ed. "2004 Presidential Election." *Presidential Studies Quarterly* 36 (2006): 141–296.

NOTES

1. The term "a government of strangers" was first suggested by Hugh Heclo in his book *A Government of Strangers* (Washington, D.C.: Brookings Institution, 1977).
2. For an excellent discussion of the differences between campaigning for and governing in the presidency, see Charles O. Jones, *Passages to the Presidency* (Washington, D.C.: Brookings Institution, 1998).
3. A good example of the latter is Dick Morris, who came to President Clinton's aid after the Democrats' defeat in the 1994 midterm elections. Morris, who engineered Clinton's reelection victory, had previously worked as a political consultant for Clinton in his third campaign for the Arkansas governorship, as well as for such conservative Republicans as Trent Lott, the Senate Republican leader, and Jesse Helms, a senator from North Carolina.
4. Like the candidate they supported, they also may have little executive experience and be unfamiliar with the formal and informal procedures of the institution to which their candidate has been elected and with the people who work there.
5. Although senior members of the Reagan administration did not fall into this morass with the political establishment, they did do so with civil servants who staffed the federal bureaucracy. Reagan and his supporters distrusted the national government, particularly the bureaucracy, and they tried to circumvent the permanent government when putting their priority proposals in place. The problem was that Reagan's newly appointed department heads and their aides lacked the expertise to get things done. Over time, most of Reagan's political appointees grew to depend on and respect the civil servants who worked for them.
6. *U.S. Term Limits, Inc. v. Thornton*, 514 u.s. 779 (1995).

7. In addition to policy initiatives, some states also have a procedure known as a *referendum,* which allows a state legislature to place items directly before the voters on an election ballot.

8. A federal district court in San Francisco found that many of these restrictions were unconstitutional.

9. Richard J. Ellis, "The States: Direct Democracy," in *The Elections of 2000,* Michael Nelson, ed. (Washington, D.C.: CQ Press, 2001), 141.

10. Ibid., 143–145.

11. Ibid., 137.

12. *Buckley v. American Constitutional Law Foundation,* 97 u.s. 930 (1999).

13. Ellis, "The States," 134.

14. For issues to be the most important influence on voting behavior, voters must have an opinion about them, perceive differences in the candidates' positions, and then vote on the basis of these differences and in the direction of their own policy positions.

15. The random selection is made within states in such a way that principal geographic units (cities, suburbs, and rural areas) and a precinct's size and past voting record are taken into account. Approximately 1,200 representatives of the polling organization administer the poll to voters who are chosen in a systematic way (for example, every fourth or fifth person) as they leave the voting booths. Voters are asked to complete a short questionnaire (thirty to forty items) designed to elicit information on voting choices, political attitudes, candidate evaluations and feelings, and the demographic characteristics of those who voted. Several times over the course of the day, the questionnaires are collected and tabulated, and the results are sent to a central computer bank. After most or all of the election polls in a state have been completed, the findings of the exit poll are made public. Over the course of the evening they are adjusted to reflect the actual results as they are tabulated.

16. No exit poll was released in 2002 because of a computer failure and other technical problems.

17. "TV News Turned Sour on Bush after Iraq War Ended," Center for Media and Public Affairs, Press Release, December 17, 2003, www.cmpa.com/pressReleases/TVNewsTurnedSour.htm.